Lesbian and Gay Marriage

Lesbian and Gay Marriage

Private Commitments,
Public Ceremonies

Edited by Suzanne Sherman

TEMPLE UNIVERSITY PRESS

Philadelphia

Temple University Press, Philadelphia 19122
Copyright © 1992 by Suzanne Sherman. All rights reserved
Published 1992
Printed in the United States of America

The paper used in this publication meets the minimum
requirements of American National Standard for Information
Sciences — Permanence of Paper for Printed Library Materials,
ANSI Z39.48–1984 ⊗

Library of Congress Cataloging-in-Publication Data
Lesbian and gay marriage : private commitments, public ceremonies /
  edited by Suzanne Sherman.
        p.   cm.
  Includes bibliographical references.
  ISBN 0-87722-974-0 (cloth). — ISBN 0-87722-975-9 (paperback)
  1. Gay couples — United States.   2. Homosexuality — Religious
aspects.   I. Sherman, Suzanne.
HQ76.3.U5L47   1993
306.73'8 — dc20   92-9299

Photo credits: pp. 30, 50, 86, 110, 148 (top photo), 175 (top photo), 212, 268 —
Sabrina; p. 36 — Sofia Lee Morán; p. 43 — Tom Wachs; p. 66 — Bruce Hunt; p.
73 — © Demian, 1991; p. 100 (bottom photo) — Shirley Eland-Gach; p. 121 — Day
Garson/Pat Lopez; p. 133 — Joanne Brey; p. 158 — Mary Whitlock; p. 182 — Carl
Avery Blount; p. 190 — Patti Brunelle; pp. 203–4 — Andi Faryl Schreiber; p. 220 —
Angela Coppola; p. 228 — Ross Atkinson

In memory of my mother,
who taught me the importance of fairness,
and taught me to care

Contents

PART THREE
Public Ceremonies

PART FOUR
Ceremony Officiators

Acknowledgments

I deeply appreciate and am touched by the many women and men who opened their hearts and shared their stories with me for this book. Some are represented and some are not; all deserve thanks. I am also grateful to the many people who took time to flip through their address books and give me lists of potential interviewees, and to the photographers who allowed me to use their photographs.

I thank my editor, Michael Ames, for his skillful work and careful attention, and Temple University Press director David Bartlett for his belief in the importance of this book.

Friends sustained me through the months when tapes that needed transcribing were stacked beside a calendar filled with interview appointments, which sat on top of lengthy transcriptions I would edit many times before final form. Jennifer helped me brainstorm and walked with me every step along this journey. Dear, more-word-wise-than-she-thinks Sabrina offered hours of time and insightful comments as a manuscript reader, in addition to her help as a photographer. Kathryn took time out of her busy schedule to read through drafts. And my brother, Steve, was an invaluable help not only as a manuscript reader but as a consultant and a constant support. My dad and Sally, my grandfather, and my sister also lovingly supported me in this project at every point. And I must mention another one whose attention and warmth kept me going through the months of work — my tabby cat, Buddy, who napped on my wrists in front of the keyboard, always my quiet company.

Lesbian and Gay Marriage

Introduction

In the summer of 1988, I received a wedding invitation printed in lovely purple ink on lavender paper from two lesbian friends I had not seen in some time. It was an invitation to the celebration of the relationship of Jeanne and Sandra Sinclair. I was asked to respond using the delicately inscribed card.

I had to sit down. Jeanne and Sandy Sinclair? What had happened to Sandy Silver? I read the invitation again. The ceremony would be held in a Unitarian Universalist church. Would they stand before a minister wearing lace gowns and trailing veils in a mimicry of a patriarchal heterosexual tradition? Did they think people wouldn't take their commitment seriously without this? They still wouldn't get income-tax breaks or legal protections for hospital visitation or survivorship. They still wouldn't be accepted as "spouses" when it came to family discounts, employer-provided medical benefits, and other family-member-only privileges, even with a shared last name. I was fascinated. And a little envious, too.

I have always had conflicting feelings about marriage. I like the idea of having the attention, gifts, and emotional and financial rewards that heterosexuals get when they choose their life partner. Yet I abhor the tradition of ownership, of woman as property, and I loathe the tradition of name changing, with its attendant absorption and loss of identity.

Though I don't believe that tax breaks and other benefits should be attached to marital status, I acknowledge that society understands marriage to mean a greater level of commitment, and a greater level of love, between two people. If lesbians and gays cannot marry, then the myth that our relationships are not as meaningful as those of heterosexuals will persist. It occured to me for the first time that marrying — even without benefits attached — could be a political act. How brave to go forward with one's desire, whether or not it is driven by cultural conditioning, and demand the fairest possible treatment at every step along the way.

But was it also an act of selling out? Was marrying an admission that the nuclear-family form is superior to new forms? I was very curious to know what motivated this couple — and all lesbian and gay couples who marry. Had they explored their reasons and the meaning of their actions? Or, as it is with so many heterosexual couples, was it an act taken without great forethought because of cultural conditioning and because many lesbians and gays want to be accepted in the mainstream of society?

I called friends and asked if anyone had been to such a ceremony. Everyone I spoke to on the West and East coasts had been to at least one wedding, or had heard of them happening more and more often. But "marriage?" they asked. "Do you have to call it that?" They had heard it called "bonding ceremony," "celebration of commitment," or maybe "union ceremony." They warned me to be careful not to call it "marriage" because some lesbians and gay men could be offended by that word. Their admonition only made me more curious.

It was true that the invitation I had received said "a celebration of the relationship." But Jeanne and Sandy were going to hold the ceremony in a church with a minister, say their vows, exchange rings, and have a hotel-room reception with dancing and a three-tier cake. (There would be no garter throwing or bouquet tossing, they promised; after all, they were feminist and not into those patriarchal traditions.) Following the reception, they would go directly to the airport to catch their flight to Hawaii for a week-long honeymoon they were buying with their "ceremony" gift money.

And so this book began. I wanted to hear from couples who had "married" and from those who had resisted the institution. I sought to discover whether a wedding makes for differences in relationships, if couples who marry tend to have religious affiliations, if married couples are more likely to be monogamous, how feminists come to terms with their desire for marriage, and how those who do not exchange public vows maintain their commitment.

The chapters by Thomas Stoddard and Paula Ettelbrick that make up Part One, "The Marriage Debate," present some of the pros and cons of same-sex marriage. Following these essays are pieces adapted from interviews with twenty-four lesbian and gay couples, some married, some resolutely unmarried. I have edited their transcripts and, at times, arranged their words for logic and cadence. The couples and the people featured in "Ceremony Officiators" have reviewed my versions of their interviews.

I contacted couples nationwide through gay/lesbian journals and newspapers, religious organizations, specialized social groups, and by word of mouth. There are nonreligious couples as well as Protestants, Catholics, Jews, Quakers, and Wiccen spiritualists. There are voices of African Americans, Latinos, a Filipino, a Lebanese-Syrian, a Native American, and people from every region of the United States. The couples have been together anywhere from three to thirty-eight years. The possibilities for including couples that could further round out the book were endless, but eventually I had to draw the line and accept the diversity of this collection.

Part Two, "Private Commitments," is a collection of interviews with long-term couples who intend to be together for the rest of their lives but who do not believe in the need for a wedding or other public ceremony to solidify or announce their commitment. Part Three, "Public Ceremonies," is a collection of interviews with long-term couples who have had a public wedding ceremony.

The stories of the weddings go beyond describing outfits and procedures, as couples explain why it was important to them to make a public commitment. They talk about how their families responded to the wedding invitation, among other things. Some of these tales are very painful: rejection at the bakery when a couple ordered a wedding cake with two grooms on top, family members who refused to come to weddings well attended by loving friends, the young couple who have already bought side-by-side gravesites they will occupy after living together for decades, never legally recognized as anything more than friends or roommates. And next to these are the stories like that of a father rushing to the window of the exiting limousine to hand his son a bottle of champagne and offer a kiss, or of a mother, who did not want to hear that her son was gay, ending up by following the example of her "in-laws" and attending a PFLAG (Parents and Friends of Lesbians and Gays) meeting where she became the contact point for kids whose parents reject them.

Though the weddings share practices with heterosexual traditions, there emerged through the interviews some characteristics that are unique to lesbians and gays. Unlike heterosexual couples, it seems common for lesbians and gay men to celebrate their original anniversary — whether the date of first meeting, their first kiss, or moving in together — *instead* of the wedding anniversary. Couples who celebrate both dates tend to consider the original anniversary the real one. A lesbian or gay wedding is rarely a celebration of a beginning; it is most often a celebration of an existing commitment.

According to the ministers, priests, and rabbis I interviewed, the same-sex couples tend to have been together for a much longer time than the straight couples they marry. Because of that, and because there is not the traditional social pressure on the lesbian or gay couple to marry, the clergy feel that same-sex weddings are more often true celebrations of the love in relationships. I felt it was important that some viewpoints of people who officiate lesbian and gay holy-union ceremonies, or weddings, be heard alongside the personal stories of couples.

Part Four, "Ceremony Officiators," features a Catholic priest who is forbidden to hold blessings of same-sex relationships in church buildings, a Presbyterian minister who is allowed by the governing body to perform the ceremonies as long as she does not consider them marriages, a rabbi of a large lesbian and gay congregation who holds traditional Jewish ceremonies in temple, a Southern Baptist minister whose congregation was booted out of the denomination because he publicly stated he believed that lesbians and gays should have the same access to marriage as do heterosexuals, a high priestess who marries lesbians in ritualized tryst ceremonies, and a minister of a Metropolitan Community Church (MCC) in Louisville, Kentucky.

✳ Until the late 1960s, it was nearly impossible for same-sex couples to find a minister or rabbi to preside at a union ceremony. The MCC, founded in 1968 in Los Angeles by the Reverend Troy Perry, was the first religious group to include union ceremonies for gays and lesbians in its bylaws. Since then, a great shift toward including gays and lesbians in a variety of religions has taken place. Congregations that publicly welcome lesbians and gays have formed (though not all allow holy unions to be held in the churches). The Unitarian Universalists' policy is inclusive of lesbians and gays, and their policy statement sanctions holy unions. Presbyterians (2.9 million members) have the More Light, Presbyterians for Lesbian and Gay Concerns, program; Episcopalians (2.5 million members) have Integrity, a lesbian- and gay-affirming community; and United Methodists (8.9 million members) have close to fifty "reconciling" (lesbian- and gay-inclusive) congregations.[1]

The Reform movement in Judaism has five gay and lesbian congregations affiliated with it (in San Francisco, Philadelphia, Miami, Chicago, and Los Angeles).[2] There is no official policy on same-sex weddings; choices are left to individual rabbis and congregations. Although the Lutheran church (5.2 million members) believes that homosexuality runs counter to God's original plan, it allows open gays and lesbians to join. American Baptist and Southern Baptist churches have autonomy in their policies toward lesbians and gays. Their practices, however, may not be accepted by the parent associations, and some congregations are expelled because of their stands. The Mormon church (7 million members) is far from sanctioning same-sex unions and still excommunicates openly gay or lesbian members.[3]

Presbyterians experienced a small step forward in 1991. At the legislative assembly gathering in Baltimore, after review of a lengthy task-force report on sexuality, the governing body ruled that same-sex union ceremonies could be performed in the denomination's churches by Presbyterian pastors so long as sessions (congregations' ruling bodies) and pastors did not consider the ceremonies a marriage.

The Roman Catholic church (55 million U.S. members) now lets open gays and lesbians join and will ordain open gays — if they are celibate. Dignity, the 5,000-member nationwide affiliation of lesbian and gay Catholics who worship together, is rarely allowed to hold its meetings in Catholic church buildings. Moreover, Catholic priests do not often officiate holy unions. In Part Four, two gay Catholic priests present their viewpoints. Father Robert Arpin works within the church and is open about being gay and about having AIDS; Father James Mallon is active with the Philadelphia Dignity chapter.

That churches are considering these matters is a change from the early 1950s, when marriage was a topic on the agenda of the first political "homophile" organization in the United States, the Mattachine Society.[4] The gay marriage the Mattachines discussed was "marriage-like" — gay relationships in which couples formed cohabiting relationships and behaved as married women and men do. At that time, this was revolutionary. In Part Two, a founder of that early political group, Harry Hay, and his partner, John Burnside, discuss their views on the subject and talk about their twenty-nine-year relationship.

Marriage was not a hot topic for the first lesbian social group, the Daughters of Bilitis, in the mid-1950s. Lesbians were then only just beginning to consider coming out.[5] Daughters of Bilitis cofounders Phyllis Lyon and Del Martin also talk about their early days together and their views on marriage in Part Two.

Gay and lesbian marriage became more common after the gay liberation/visibility movement took off following the 1969 Stonewall riot and after the founding of the Metropolitan Community Church. The gay marriages that took place in the early 1970s were often drag; at that time, straights were the only role models for marriage, and butch/femme role playing was more in fashion than it has been since. In Part Three, San Franciscans Terry Tibbetts and Don

Wright describe their drag wedding (with five hundred guests), held during a period the August 5, 1970, issue of the *Advocate* (then subtitled *Newspaper of America's Homophile Community*) called "a gay marriage boom." A decade and a half later, two thousand couples and thousands of spectators stood in front of the Internal Revenue Service building to participate in an ecumenical, spiritual, and very political wedding ceremony. The 1987 March on Washington Wedding raised consciousness in both the gay community and the heterosexual mainstream.

When I interviewed the unmarried couples for Part Two, I discovered that many of them share my feelings about the legal advantages of marriage.[6] While they would not have a ceremony if same-sex marriage were made legal, most of the couples I interviewed would marry if the option were available in order to simplify some of the legal protections that they have established and to gain some of the benefits that might apply to them. At the same time, they feel that the system of offering benefits to married people is unfair and exclusionary.

On the federal level, for example, heterosexual married couples can receive annuity and pension plans where a spouse or family member is included as a beneficiary; they have protections in housing rights, renewal leases, and survivorship; they receive automatic inheritance and Social Security and veterans' benefits, including medical and educational services; and they can make use of immigration and tax laws. On the state level, married couples can enjoy advantages in the areas of adoption and foster care; custody and visitation rights for nonbiological parents; divorce protections that include community property and child support; donor insemination, including termination of parental rights; wrongful-death benefits to the surviving partner and biological children; and judicial safeguards that include domestic-violence protection orders and crime victims' recovery benefits.[7]

Employment benefits are another area where lesbian and gay couples suffer discrimination because of marriage laws. Employment benefits for married persons today comprise up to 40 percent of an employer's average personnel costs. A same-sex couple may live together for one year or for thirty years — share finances, jointly own property, raise children together — and yet earn 40 percent less than their married colleagues receive through such fringe benefits as spousal medical insurance and pension plans.

There have been some gains at the municipal level in recent years. In growing number, cities are passing legislation to offer benefits to domestic partners of city employees. A few cities allow couples to register as domestic partners to establish evidence of interdependence, which theoretically can offer protection where inheritance, visitation rights, and other family-only rules apply.[8] However, lesbians and gays are not unanimously in favor of registration. As the interviews in this book reveal, some people regard domestic-partnership registration as a distraction from the need to gain rights to marry with full access to benefits and protections; others believe that registration is superior to marriage because it recognizes alternative family structures.

In 1989, following a forty-year campaign by gay-rights activists, Denmark became the first country to effectively legalize marriage for same-sex couples.[9] The campaign in this country has begun on the state level in a few instances, but it is largely being fought by a handful of individuals rather than by statewide coalitions because of divided opinion within the lesbian and gay community.

The couples I interviewed for this book have offered their stories with such openness and with so much loving tenderness toward one another that during the transcribing I sometimes paused and replayed the transcription tapes just to listen to their voices again. It is my hope that among the readers there is the person who gains courage by hearing these voices speak out about love and marriage. The more we hear our voices breaking silence, the easier it is to speak again, and to speak boldly and honestly — whether to say "I do," or to define our families our own ways.

Suzanne Sherman

Notes

1. Membership figures for the various denominations are from Don Lattin, "Churches Re-examining Sex Teaching," *San Francisco Chronicle* [date unknown], 1991, A-1.

2. Reform Judaism, the oldest branch of contemporary Judaism (the others are the Conservative, Orthodox, and Reconstructionist), began in the United States in the mid-1800s. A large, mainstream movement, it upholds the fundamentals of Judaism in modified form. It is the branch that is most welcoming of gays and lesbians, though Reconstructionists and Conservatives also tend to be accepting.

3. A gay and lesbian Mormon social and support group, "Affirmation," meets in several locations in California, Arizona, and the Great Lakes region. There are also Affirmation groups in Salt Lake City, Utah, and in Seattle and Spokane, Washington.

4. For a detailed account of the Mattachine Society's founding by activist Harry Hay (and for more on the formation of the men's spiritual movement he and John Burnside began, the Radical Faeries), see the biography by Stuart Timmons, *The Trouble with Harry* (Boston: Alyson Press, 1990).

5. For more on the history of gays and lesbians in the first half of the twentieth century, see Andrea Weiss and Greta Schiller, *Before Stonewall: The Making of a Gay and Lesbian Community* (Tallahassee, Fla.: Naiad Press, 1988).

6. The June 6, 1989, *San Francisco Examiner* "Gay in America" series nationwide poll found 86 percent of lesbians and gays in favor of legalized same-sex marriage.

7. Derived from Lambda Legal Defense and Education Fund, *Domestic Partnership: Issues and Legislation*. (See the Resource Directory for ordering information.)

8. As of 1992, more than one hundred public and private employers recognize domestic partners and extend to them some of the rights accorded married couples. Cities that offer domestic partnership registration for all citizens are Ann Arbor, Mich.; Berkeley, Calif.; Ithaca, N.Y.; Madison, Wis.; Minneapolis, Minn.; San Francisco, Calif.; Washington, D.C.; and West Hollywood, Calif. Cities and counties that offer benefits for domestic partners of employees are Alameda County, Calif.; Berkeley, Calif.; East Lansing, Mich.; Laguna Beach, Calif.; San Francisco, Calif.; San Mateo County, Calif.; Santa Cruz County and City, Calif.; Seattle,

Wash.; Takoma Park, Md.; and West Hollywood, Calif. Some cities have instituted bereavement and/or family illness leave plans for domestic partners but do not offer any other domestic-partner-related benefits: Ann Arbor, Mich.; Cambridge, Mass.; Dane County, Wis.; Delaware; Hennepin County, Minn.; Los Angeles, Calif.; Madison, Wis.; Minneapolis, Minn.; New York, N.Y.; Travis County, Tex.; West Palm Beach, Fla.

In March 1992 the District of Columbia passed a law that allows unmarried adult couples living together to register as domestic partners. The registration will entitle partners of city employees to be covered by city health insurance and give private employers tax incentives to cover domestic partners in their health insurance.

9. Termed "registered partnership," the status approximates marriage and confers some legal protections and benefits but does not allow couples to adopt children or be married in state churches. At least one partner must be a Danish citizen, and the couple's status is not recognized outside Denmark. There are no countries yet where lesbians and gay men enjoy the full rights of marriage. The best way to "legalize" a union is with legal documents such as wills, powers of attorney, and a written relationship agreement.

Part One

The Marriage Debate

1

Why Gay People Should Seek the Right to Marry

Thomas B. Stoddard

Even though, these days, lesbians and gay men cannot enter into marriages recognized by law, absolutely every gay person has an opinion on marriage as an "institution." (The word "institution" brings to mind, perhaps appropriately, museums.) After all, we all know quite a bit about the subject. Most of us grew up in marital households. Virtually all of us, regardless of race, creed, gender, and culture, have received lectures on the propriety, if not the sanctity, of marriage — which usually suggests that those who choose not to marry are both unhappy and unhealthy. We all have been witnesses, willing or not, to a lifelong parade of other people's marriages, from Uncle Harry and Aunt Bernice to the Prince and Princess of Wales. And at one point or another, some nosy relative has inevitably inquired of every gay person when he or she will finally "tie the knot" (an intriguing and probably apt cliché).

I must confess at the outset that I am no fan of the "institution" of marriage as currently constructed and practiced. I may simply be unlucky, but I have seen preciously few marriages over the course

Thomas B. Stoddard, a lawyer and writer, lives in New York City. He is on the adjunct faculty of New York University School of Law. Between 1986 and 1992 he served as executive director of Lambda Legal Defense and Education Fund. This chapter is reprinted, with some changes, from *OUT/LOOK National Gay and Lesbian Quarterly*, no. 6 (Fall 1989) by permission of the author and the publisher.

of my forty years that invite admiration and emulation. All too often, marriage appears to petrify rather than satisfy and enrich, even for couples in their twenties and thirties who have had a chance to learn the lessons of feminism. Almost inevitably, the partners seem to fall into a "husband" role and a "wife" role, with such latter-day modifications as the wife who works in addition to raising the children and managing the household.

Let me be blunt: in its traditional form, marriage has been oppressive, especially (although not entirely) to women. Until the middle of the last century, marriage was, at its legal and social essence, an extension of the husband and his paternal family. Under the English common law, wives were among the husband's "chattel" — personal property — and could not, among other things, hold property in their own names. The common-law crime of adultery demonstrates the unequal treatment accorded to husbands and wives: while a woman who slept with a man who was not her husband committed adultery, a man who slept with a woman not his wife committed fornication. A man was legally incapable of committing adultery, except as an accomplice to an errant wife. The underlying offense of adultery was not the sexual betrayal of one partner by the other, but the wife's engaging in conduct capable of tainting the husband's bloodlines. (I swear on my *Black's Law Dictionary* that I have not made this up!)

Nevertheless, despite the oppressive nature of marriage historically, and in spite of the general absence of edifying examples of modern heterosexual marriage, I believe very strongly that every lesbian and gay man should have the right to marry the same-sex partner of his or her choice, and that the gay-rights movement should aggressively seek full legal recognition for same-sex marriages. To those who might not agree, I respectfully offer three explanations, one practical, one political, and one philosophical.

The Practical Explanation

The legal status of marriage rewards the two individuals who travel to the altar (or its secular equivalent) with substantial economic

and practical advantages. Married couples may reduce their tax liability by filing a joint return. They are entitled to special government benefits, such as those given surviving spouses and depend-
ents through the Social Security program. They can inherit from
one another even when there is no will. They are immune from
subpoenas requiring testimony against the other spouse. And marriage to an American citizen gives a foreigner a right to residency in
the United States.

Other advantages have arisen not by law but by custom. Most
employers offer health insurance to their employees, and many will
include an employee's spouse in the benefits package, usually at the
employer's expense. Virtually no employer will include a partner
who is not married to an employee, whether of the same sex or not.
Indeed, very few insurance companies even offer the possibility of a
group health plan covering "domestic partners" who are not married to one another. Two years ago, I tried to find such a policy for
Lambda, and discovered that not one insurance company author-
ized to do business in New York — the second-largest state in the
country, with more than seventeen million residents — would ac-
commodate us. (Lambda has tried to make do by paying for individual insurance policies for the same-sex partners of its employees
who otherwise would go uninsured, but these individual policies
are usually narrower in scope than group policies, often require
applicants to furnish individual medical information not required
under most group plans, and are typically much more expensive per
person.)

In short, the law generally presumes in favor of every marital
relationship, and acts to preserve and foster it, and to enhance the
rights of the individuals who enter into it. It is usually possible,
with enough money and the right advice, to replicate some of the
benefits conferred by the legal status of marriage through the use of
documents like wills and power-of-attorney forms, but that protection will inevitably, under current circumstances, be incomplete.

The law still looks upon lesbians and gay men with suspicion,
and this suspicion casts a shadow over the documents they execute
in recognition of a same-sex relationship. If a lesbian leaves prop-

erty to her lover, her will may be invalidated on the grounds that it was executed under the "undue influence" of the would-be beneficiary. A property agreement may be denied validity because the underlying relationship is "meretricious" — akin to prostitution. (Astonishingly, until the mid-1970s, the law throughout the United States deemed "meretricious" virtually any formal economic arrangement between two people not married to one another, on the theory that an exchange of property between them was probably payment for sexual services; the Supreme Court of California helped unravel this quaint legal fantasy in its 1976 ruling in the first famous "palimony" case, *Marvin v. Marvin*.) The law has progressed considerably beyond the uniformly oppressive state of affairs before 1969, but it is still far from enthusiastic about gay people and their relationships — to put it mildly.

Moreover, there are some barriers one simply cannot transcend outside of a formal marriage. When the Internal Revenue Code or the Immigration and Naturalization Act say "married," they mean "married" by definition of state statute. When the employer's group health plan says "spouse," it means "spouse" in the eyes of the law, not the eyes of the loving couple.

But there is another drawback. Couples seeking to protect their relationship through wills and other documents need knowledge, determination, and — most important — money. No money, no lawyer. And no lawyer, no protection. Those who lack the wherewithal to retain a lawyer are simply stuck in most circumstances. Extending the right to marry to gay couples would assure that those at the bottom of the economic ladder have a chance to secure their relationship rights, too.

The Political Explanation

The claim that gay couples ought to be able to marry is not a new one. In the 1970s, same-sex couples in three states — Minnesota, Kentucky, and Washington — brought constitutional challenges to the marriage statutes, and in all three instances they failed. In each of the three, the court offered two basic justifications for limiting marriage to male-female couples: history and procreation. Witness this passage from the Supreme Court of Minnesota's 1971 opinion in *Baker v. Nelson:* "The institution of marriage as a union of man and woman, uniquely involving the procreation and rearing of children within a family, is as old as the book of Genesis. . . . This historic institution manifestly is more deeply founded than the asserted contemporary concept of marriage and societal interests for which petitioners contend."

Today, no American jurisdiction recognizes the right of two women or two men to marry one another, although several nations in northern Europe do. Even more telling, until recently, there was little discussion within the gay-rights movement about whether such a right should exist. As far as I can tell, no gay organization of any size, local or national, has yet declared the right to marry as one of its goals.

With all due respect to my colleagues and friends who take a different view, I believe it is time to renew the effort to overturn the existing marriage laws, and to do so in earnest, with a commitment of money and energy, through both the courts and the state legislatures. I am not naive about the likelihood of imminent victory. There is none. Nonetheless — and here I will not mince words — I would like to see the issue rise to the top of the agenda of every gay organization, including my own.

Why give it such prominence? Why devote resources to such a distant goal? Because marriage is the political issue that most fully tests the dedication of people who are not gay to full equality for gay people, and it is also the issue most likely to lead ultimately to a world free from discrimination against lesbians and gay men.

Marriage is much more than a relationship sanctioned by law. It is the centerpiece of our entire social structure, the core of the traditional notion of "family." Even in its present tarnished state, the marital relationship inspires sentiments suggesting that it is something almost suprahuman. The Supreme Court, in striking down an anticontraception statute in 1965, called marriage "noble" and "intimate to the degree of being sacred." The Roman Catholic church and the Moral Majority would go — and have gone — considerably further.

Lesbians and gay men are now denied entry to this "noble" and "sacred" institution. The implicit message is this: two men or two women are incapable of achieving such an exalted domestic state. Gay relationships are somehow less significant, less valuable. Such relationships may, from time to time and from couple to couple, give the appearance of a marriage, but they can never be of the same quality or importance.

I resent — indeed, I loathe — that conception of same-sex relationships. And I am convinced that ultimately the only way to overturn it is to remove the barrier to marriage that now limits the freedom of every gay man and lesbian.

That is not to deny the value of domestic-partnership ordinances, statutes that prohibit discrimination based on marital status, and other legal advances that can enhance the rights (as well as the dignity) of gay couples. Without question, such advances move us further along the path to equality. But their value can only be partial. Measures of this kind can never assure full equality. Gay relationships will continue to be accorded a subsidiary status until the day that gay couples have exactly the same rights as their heterosexual counterparts. To my mind, that means either that the right to marry be extended to us, or that marriage be abolished in its present form for all couples, presumably to be replaced by some new legal entity — an unlikely alternative.

The Philosophical Explanation

I confessed at the outset that I personally found marriage in its present state rather unattractive. Nonetheless, even from a philosophical perspective, I believe the right to marry should become a goal of the gay-rights movement.

First, and most basically, the issue is not the desirability of marriage, but rather the desirability of the right to marry. That I think two lesbians or two gay men should be entitled to a marriage license does not mean that I think all gay people should find appropriate partners and exercise the right, should it eventually exist. I actually rather doubt that I, myself, would want to marry, even though I share a household with another man who is exceedingly dear to me. There are others who feel differently, for economic, symbolic, or romantic reasons. They should, to my mind, unquestionably have the opportunity to marry if they wish and otherwise meet the requirements of the state (like being old enough).

Furthermore, marriage may be unattractive and even oppressive as it is currently structured and practiced, but enlarging the concept to embrace same-sex couples would necessarily transform it into something new. If two women can marry, or two men, marriage — even for heterosexuals — need not be a union of a "husband" and a "wife." Extending the right to marry to gay people — that is, abolishing the traditional gender requirements of marriage — can be one of the means, perhaps the principal one, through which the institution divests itself of the sexist trappings of the past.

Some of my colleagues disagree with me. I welcome their thoughts and the debates and discussions our different perspectives will trigger. The movement for equality for lesbians and gay men can only be enriched through this collective exploration of the question of marriage. But I do believe many thousands of gay people want the right to marry. And I think they will earn that right for themselves sooner than most of us imagine.

2

Since When Is Marriage a Path to Liberation?

Paula L. Ettelbrick

"Marriage is a great institution . . . if you like living in institutions," according to a bit of T-shirt philosophy I saw recently. Certainly, marriage is an institution. It is one of the most
venerable, impenetrable institutions in modern society. Marriage
provides the ultimate form of acceptance for personal, intimate relationships in our society, and gives those who marry an insider status of the most powerful kind.

Steeped in a patriarchal system that looks to ownership, property, and dominance of men over women as its basis, the institution
of marriage has long been the focus of radical-feminist revulsion.
Marriage defines certain relationships as more valid than all others.
Lesbian and gay relationships, being neither legally sanctioned nor
commingled by blood, are always at the bottom of the heap of social acceptance and importance.

Given the imprimatur of social and personal approval that marriage provides, it is not surprising that some lesbians and gay men
among us would look to legal marriage for self-affirmation. After all,

Paula L. Ettelbrick is legal director of the Lambda Legal Defense and Education
Fund and adjunct professor of law at New York Law School. This chapter is reprinted, with some changes, from *OUT/LOOK National Gay and Lesbian Quarterly*, No.
6 (Fall 1989) by permission of the author and the publisher.

those who marry can be instantaneously transformed from "outsiders" to "insiders," and we have a desperate need to become insiders.

It could make us feel okay about ourselves, perhaps even relieve some of the internalized homophobia that we all know so well. Society will then celebrate the birth of our children and mourn the death of our spouses. It would be easier to get health insurance for our spouses, family memberships to the local museum, and a right to inherit our spouse's cherished collection of lesbian mystery novels even if she failed to draft a will. Never again would we have to go to a family reunion and debate about the correct term for introducing our lover/partner/significant other to Aunt Flora. Everything would be quite easy and very nice.

So why does this unlikely event so deeply disturb me? For two major reasons. First, marriage will not liberate us as lesbians and gay men. In fact, it will constrain us, make us more invisible, force our assimilation into the mainstream, and undermine the goals of gay liberation. Second, attaining the right to marry will not transform our society from one that makes narrow, but dramatic, distinctions between those who are married and those who are not married to one that respects and encourages choice of relationships and family diversity. Marriage runs contrary to two of the primary goals of the lesbian and gay movement: the affirmation of gay identity and culture and the validation of many forms of relationships.

When analyzed from the standpoint of civil rights, certainly lesbians and gay men should have a right to marry. But obtaining a right does not always result in justice. White male firefighters in Birmingham, Alabama, have been fighting for their "rights" to retain their jobs by overturning the city's affirmative-action guidelines. If their "rights" prevail, the courts will have failed in rendering justice. The "right" fought for by the white male firefighters, as well as those who advocate strongly for the "rights" to legal marriage for gay people, will result, at best, in limited or narrowed "justice" for those closest to power at the expense of those who have been historically marginalized.

The fight for justice has as its goal the realignment of power imbalances among individuals and classes of people in society. A

pure "rights" analysis often fails to incorporate a broader understanding of the underlying inequities that operate to deny justice to
a fuller range of people and groups. In setting our priorities as a
community, we must combine the concept of both rights and justice. At this point in time, making legal marriage for lesbian and
gay couples a priority would set an agenda of gaining rights for a
few, but would do nothing to correct the power imbalances between those who are married (whether gay or straight) and those
who are not. Thus, justice would not be gained.

conclusion Justice for gay men and lesbians will be achieved only when we
are accepted and supported in this society despite our differences
from the dominant culture and the choices we make regarding our
relationships. Being queer is more than setting up house, sleeping
with a person of the same gender, and seeking state approval for
doing so. It is an identity, a culture with many variations. It is a
way of dealing with the world by diminishing the constraints of
gender roles that have for so long kept women and gay people oppressed and invisible. Being queer means pushing the parameters of
sex, sexuality, and family, and in the process transforming the very
fabric of society. Gay liberation is inexorably linked to women's
liberation. Each is essential to the other.

The moment we argue, as some among us insist on doing, that
we should be treated as equals because we are really just like married couples and hold the same values to be true, we undermine the
very purpose of our movement and begin the dangerous process of
silencing our different voices. As a lesbian, I am fundamentally different from nonlesbian women. That's the point. Marriage, as it
exists today, is antithetical to my liberation as a lesbian and as a
woman because it mainstreams my life and voice. I do not want to
be known as "Mrs. Attached-To-Somebody-Else." Nor do I want to
give the state the power to regulate my primary relationship.

Yet, the concept of equality in our legal system does not support
differences, it only supports sameness. The very standard for equal
protection is that people who are similarly situated must be treated
equally. To make an argument for equal protection, we will be required to claim that gay and lesbian relationships are the same as

straight relationships. To gain the right, we must compare ourselves to married couples. The law looks to the insiders as the norm, regardless of how flawed or unjust their institutions, and requires that those seeking the law's equal protection situate themselves in a similar posture to those who are already protected. In arguing for the right to legal marriage, lesbians and gay men would be forced to claim that we are just like heterosexual couples, have the same goals and purposes, and vow to structure our lives similarly. The law provides no room to argue that we are different but are nonetheless entitled to equal protection.

The thought of emphasizing our sameness to married heterosexuals in order to obtain this "right" terrifies me. It rips away the very heart and soul of what I believe it is to be a lesbian in this world. It robs me of the opportunity to make a difference. We end up mimicking all that is bad about the institution of marriage in our effort to appear to be the same as straight couples.

By looking to our sameness and de-emphasizing our differences, we do not even place ourselves in a position of power that would allow us to transform marriage from an institution that emphasizes property and state regulation of relationships to an institution that recognizes one of many types of valid and respected relationships. Until the Constitution is interpreted to respect and encourage differences, pursuing the legalization of same-sex marriage would be leading our movement into a trap; we would be demanding access to the very institution that, in its current form, would undermine our movement to recognize many different kinds of relationships. We would be perpetuating the elevation of married relationships and of "couples" in general, and further eclipsing other relationships of choice.

Ironically, gay marriage, instead of liberating gay sex and sexuality, would further outlaw all gay and lesbian sex that is not performed in a marital context. Just as sexually active nonmarried women face stigma and double standards around sex and sexual activity, so too would nonmarried gay people. The only legitimate gay sex would be that which is cloaked in and regulated by marriage. Its legitimacy would stem not from an acceptance of gay sexuality, but because the Supreme Court and society in general fiercely protect the privacy of marital relationships. Lesbians and gay men who do not seek the state's stamp of approval would clearly face increased sexual oppression.

Undoubtedly, whether we admit it or not, we all need to be accepted by the broader society. That motivation fuels our work to eliminate discrimination in the workplace and elsewhere, fight for custody of our children, create our own families, and so on. The growing discussion about the right to marry may be explained in part by this need for acceptance. Those closer to the norm or to power in this country are more likely to see marriage as a principle of freedom and equality. Those who are acceptable to the mainstream because of race, gender, and economic status are more likely to want the right to marry. It is the final acceptance, the ultimate affirmation of identity.

On the other hand, more marginal members of the lesbian and gay community (women, people of color, working class, and poor) are less likely to see marriage as having relevance to our struggles for survival. After all, what good is the affirmation of our relationships (that is, marital relationships) if we are rejected as women, people of color, or working class?

The path to acceptance is much more complicated for many of us. For instance, if we choose legal marriage, we may enjoy the right to add our spouse to our health insurance policy at work, since most employment policies are defined by one's marital status, not family relationship. However, that choice assumes that we have a job and that our employer provides us with health benefits. For women, particularly women of color who tend to occupy the low-paying jobs that do not provide health-care benefits at all, it will not matter one bit if they are able to marry their woman partners. The opportunity to marry will neither get them the health benefits nor transform them from outsider to insider.

Of course, a white man who marries another white man who has a full-time job with benefits will certainly be able to share in those benefits and overcome the only obstacle left to full societal assimilation — the goal of many in his class. In other words, gay marriage will not topple the system that allows only the privileged few to obtain decent health care. Nor will it close the privilege gap between those who are married and those who are not.

Marriage creates a two-tier system that allows the state to regulate relationships. It has become a facile mechanism for employers to dole out benefits, for businesses to provide special deals and incentives, and for the law to make distinctions in distributing meager public funds. None of these entities bothers to consider the relationship among people; the love, respect, and need to protect that exists among all kinds of family members. Rather, a simple certificate of the state, regardless of whether the spouses love, respect, or even see each other on a regular basis, dominates and is supported. None of this dynamic will change if gay men and lesbians are given the option of marriage.

Gay marriage will not help us address the systemic abuses inherent in a society that does not provide decent health care to all of its citizens, a right that should not depend on whether the individual (1) has sufficient resources to afford health care or health insurance, (2) is working and receives health insurance as part of compensation, or (3) is married to a partner who is working and has health coverage that is extended to spouses. It will not address the underlying unfairness that allows businesses to provide discounted services or goods to families and couples — who are defined to include straight, married people and their children, but not domestic partners.

Nor will it address the pain and anguish of the unmarried lesbian who receives word of her partner's accident, rushes to the hospital, and is prohibited from entering the intensive-care unit or obtaining information about her condition solely because she is not a spouse or family member. Likewise, marriage will not help the gay victim of domestic violence who, because he chose not to marry, finds no protection under the law to keep his violent lover away.

If the laws changed tomorrow and lesbians and gay men were allowed to marry, where would we find the incentive to continue the progressive movement we have started that is pushing for societal and legal recognition of all kinds of family relationships? To create other options and alternatives? To find a place in the law for the elderly couple who, for companionship and economic reasons, live together but do not marry? To recognize the right of a long-time, but unmarried, gay partner to stay in his rent-controlled apartment after the death of his lover, the only named tenant on the lease? To recognize the family relationship of the lesbian couple and the two gay men who are jointly sharing child-raising responsibilities? To get the law to acknowledge that we may have more than one relationship worthy of legal protection?

The lesbian and gay community has laid the groundwork for revolutionizing society's views of family. The domestic-partnership movement has been an important part of this progress insofar as it validates nonmarital relationships. Because it is not limited to sexual or romantic relationships, domestic partnership provides an important opportunity for many who are not related by blood or marriage to claim certain minimal protections.

It is crucial, though, that we avoid the pitfall of framing the push for legal recognition of domestic partners (those who share a primary residence and financial responsibilities for each other) as a stepping-stone to marriage. We must keep our eyes on the goals of providing true alternatives to marriage and of radically reordering society's view of family.

The goals of lesbian and gay liberation must simply be broader than the right to marry. Gay and lesbian marriages may minimally transform the institution of marriage by diluting its traditional patriarchal dynamic, but they will not transform society. They will not demolish the two-tier system of the "haves" and the "have nots." We must not fool ourselves into believing that marriage will make it acceptable to be gay or lesbian. We will be liberated only when we are respected and accepted for our differences and the diversity we provide to this society. Marriage is not a path to that liberation.

Part Two

Private Commitments

3

Patt Denning and Kathie Cinnater

Oakland, California

People are attempting to squeeze themselves into what I consider an abhorrent ritual, where one person is basically made the property of the other. They ought to throw parties instead of saying "I do."

Patt, forty-two, and Kathie, fifty, have been together for seventeen years and have lived together for fifteen. Kathie is a painter and teaches at San Francisco Art Institute. She describes herself as having a green thumb and takes all the credit for the aesthetics of their life together. Patt is a psychologist who describes herself as currently overworking for the Department of Mental Health in San Francisco, working in private practice, and teaching at "whatever university will tolerate my rude mouth." As they put it, "We've lived in the San Francisco Bay Area since 1978 in various houses with various dogs, cats, and flowers. We have yet to say the 'F' word (forever)."

❧

Kathie: We celebrate our anniversary on the 13th of March, the first day my name appears in Patt's datebook. We don't know whether it's the first time we heard of each other or went out together, but after we'd been together a year Patt went into her book and dug up this date, with my name misspelled, and we've always celebrated it.

Patt and Kathie

Our friends threw a big party for us for our tenth anniversary, which we had nothing to do with except for providing a guest list. I don't remember if there was a cake, but I know they charted our biorhythms for the day we met — we were both at our intellectual lows and physical highs, which was really funny. They made us dance under a spotlight. Someone actually held the spotlight over us while we danced. It really was a lot of fun. In 1990 we also had a big party because it was our fifteenth anniversary and it coincided with our first year in our house. We always celebrate somehow.

Patt: We've never had a private commitment ceremony, never exchanged rings — we give presents and we borrow, but we don't pledge.

Kathie: Union ceremonies remind me too much of heterosexual marriages. They seem to be about kinds of relationships we don't want to imitate.

Patt: People are attempting to squeeze themselves into what I consider an abhorrent ritual, where one person is basically made the property of the other. As much as you try to pull that ritual apart and make it equal, it really doesn't seem equal. I personally hate rituals of all kinds.

Marriage has never been a goal for me. When I was a kid — and I was heterosexual as far as I knew — I assumed that I would never marry. It seemed like such a silly or horrible idea. So I don't feel like I've given up anything by being queer. And I think that is part of the struggle of some lesbians in wanting to have a marriage. They grew up with that wish, that hope, that fantasy, or that pressure from their family, and when they came out, something was destroyed or left behind that they want to recapture.

I also can't separate marriage from religion. I'm a staunch atheist. I don't like feminist spirituality any more than I like Christian or Jewish spirituality. I believe strongly in the separation of church and state.

Before Kathie, I was somewhere between promiscuity and serial monogamy for about five years, and then I wasn't monogamous our first year. But we were both lesbian feminists. If someone had mentioned marriage to me at the time, I would have said, Feminists don't do those kinds of things. We're trying to break tradition, we don't want to use old rituals.

Kathie: Marriage was never a goal for me, either, although this relationship has turned out to be a more traditional marriage-like relationship than I anticipated mine would be when I came out. But that's kind of incidental. We're monogamous, we've been together seventeen years, our goal is to stay together as long as we possibly can. We own the house together, we've owned another house together. We have some joint investments, we have wills that give each other everything unless we die within thirty days of each other, we have a durable power of attorney for health matters. We keep our everyday finances mostly separate. We both contribute to our joint account for household expenses, both pay half of the mortgage.

Still, I couldn't get up in front of people and say vows, because life doesn't seem to work out that way. When I was growing up, I had a traditional fantasy of getting married and having a middle-class family life. But when I came out, which was mostly because of the influence of feminism and because I had rethought a lot of the values I'd grown up with, it was too exhilarating and refreshing to want to perform that tradition in a slightly different form. I thought the whole social structure was changing. I thought marriage was over for everyone; I had hoped it was.

Patt: I discovered feminism in probably 1972. Stonewall and gay politics had been going on, but I didn't hear about it. I heard about radical leftist politics and then radical feminist politics. What I was involved in and what feminists at that time were involved in was a radical restructuring of society that would benefit all groups of people. What I see with the gay-liberation movement is that it's primarily a political movement aimed at getting the benefits of society for us queers. Not that I have turned down any of the benefits of this society, but it's not my purpose to try to get a piece of the heterosexual pie. I'd rather see relationships and priorities for society change radically. And I don't think that gay liberation is really about changing that; I think it's about including queers in whatever already exists.

Kathie: I never used to identify as gay. I identified as lesbian feminist because I felt that being gay was not nearly as radical a position in life. But now I really do think it is, especially because gay politics has become so feminist in a way, because gay men are more politicized. They have a more feminist analysis about their position in the world.

Wedding ceremonies are something that I associated with gay men for many years. I thought it was because gay men were in a position to become more socially acceptable. I thought of them as middle-class people, many of whom had power in their community. They were more focused on being accepted by the mainstream community. I think that's part of what's going on in the lesbian community now. Lesbians have more money, more visibility, more power; many are successful professionals. They're doing what gay men did fifteen years ago.

I'd feel better about marriage if it weren't taking place in an environment of reactionary traditional values. The whole thing that's happening politically and socially in this country — a new focus on family, revitalized Christian values — the whole culture's gone so far to the right on emphasizing family values (whatever they are) that the gay and lesbian community is forced to go to the right, too, because we're part of it. From that point of view, I don't think highly of it; I think it's a reflection of the fact that we're all living in a much more rigid society.

Patt: Our relationship is based on commitment. Breaking up is the last option we would ever think of. That's what we've said, and that's what we've lived. People who get married seem to be celebrating their love rather than having a commitment ceremony. It seems it's about their excitement and the wonder of being in love and all the hope that goes along with that, and I think that's wonderful. But I think they ought to throw parties instead of saying "I do."

Kathie: I see marriage as a legal contract. One of the reasons ceremonies don't do much for me is that they're a ritualized contractual act. If the contract were going to benefit me in some way, I'd really have to think about it a lot.

I wish there was a lot more variety, that there weren't just two exclusive choices: married or single. On forms, I check the box "single," but neither category really fits me or is descriptive of the way I live. What I like about domestic-partnership legislation is that it includes people who live in households and don't necessarily have a traditional, sexual relationship. I like to think that there are great varieties of ways to live with people and relationships you can call families or partnerships. That is one reason I don't go for ceremonies. But I can see where for other people it could be a political — and a radical political — act.

Patt: Domestic-partnership legislation is exciting to me. Domestic-partners legislation is about single people, it's not just about gays and lesbians. I'd do anything — get blessed, walk past crucifixes — if it was what I had to do to register, if it would have an impact. It's not a conflict of values for me. Domestic-partnership legislation is a psychological recognition, it's economic, it's political.

If there were clear benefits to legalized gay marriages, I'd certainly sign the papers, but I can't imagine that we'd walk up the aisle together. I think these ceremonies are going to be our downfall.

4

Dennis W. Weber and Kelvin Ray Beliele

Albuquerque, New Mexico

Our ideal was to live a different life than the traditional.

Dennis, forty-four, and Kelvin, forty-one, have been to-gether for twenty-two years. They met through a mutual friend December 31, 1969, in Kelvin's hometown in Oklahoma. They began living together in June 1970 and, except for a few months in 1975, have lived together since. They moved to attend the University of Oklahoma together in 1971. Along with a handful of others, they were responsible for starting the gay-liberation movement in Oklahoma in the early 1970s. They have lived in Albuquerque since 1977, where Dennis works in the hotel industry and Kelvin is a civil servant and free-lance writer. For four years, Dennis and Kelvin lived with a third man in a triadic relationship.

Kelvin: We celebrate our anniversary every year, the year we started being lovers — 1970. For the lack of a better term for it, we call it our union anniversary.

Dennis: At our twenty-year anniversary, we had a big party. We invited old friends from college, both gay and straight friends we've stayed in contact with. People treated it a little like a wedding. They brought presents, even though we'd said in the invitations that people didn't need to bring presents.

Dennis and Kelvin

When we met, I was twenty-one and Kelvin was eighteen. I think some people feel happy to see a younger gay couple that's been together such a long time. There just aren't as many long-term gay couples around as there are long-term lesbian couples.

We were just coming out when we first met. Many of the people in our social group held very traditional values, they wanted to be like the straights. We didn't want to be like the straights. Plus, we were very political and tired of being on the front page of the paper. We wanted to get away from politics for a while. So we left Oklahoma and came to New Mexico.

Kelvin: We've never been monogamous, sexually. There have been times when we've only had sex with each other, sometimes for months at a time, but it was never a conscious decision. I don't know whether being nonmonogamous has made us stay together longer, because nonmonogamy has always been in our relationship. It's not as if we entered into the relationship one way and then changed it.

I think for men of our generation (coming out in the late 1960s, early 1970s), monogamy really wasn't fashionable. Gay men who came of age at the time we did tended to view sexual activity as a statement of the movement. Having lots of partners was part of that liberation.

I think most men I enter into sex with now view it as recreational, that we're just playing. And there are men that Dennis and I, either together or individually, have had long-term sexual relationships with, and those men are friends. There are many definitions of what kind of commitment you can take away from a sexual experience.

Dennis: I understand that just because somebody's good-looking and sexually attractive doesn't mean Kelvin wants to leave me and go live with that person, or vice versa. We were lovers when we met. We're still lovers. I'm very attracted to Kelvin. We know couples who live together and regard themselves as a couple, and they don't have sex. We've always said, Why live with somebody if you're not going to screw?

Kelvin: We lived with another man as our lover for four years. We'd been together ten years at the time.

Dennis: It began by Kelvin inviting him to stay at our house as a roommate because he needed a place to live. This was after Kelvin had been having sex with him. But we lived as roommates only a few weeks. Then he moved into our bedroom.

Kelvin: To some extent there was love and commitment, and trust. But it just didn't work out, as so many relationships don't. I think we all brought too much baggage to that relationship and we were unable to sort through it during that time. The other man and I both became sober during that relationship, which certainly changed our perceptions of each other and of reality.

Dennis: That was where we had problems, trying to balance affection, love and sexuality, trust and emotional support. It got imbalanced pretty quickly.

Our ideal was to live a different life than the traditional. I've known some other male couples who've had a third partner, sometimes a woman. The sexual part is always the easiest since that's the part you can enter into with less emotion. But it's very difficult to maintain a triangle relationship.

Men can have a sexual relationship without necessarily having emotional ties to it, in my opinion, because women are programmed differently than men. I shouldn't speak for lesbians, but I think women are encouraged to feel differently about being in love than men are, that men have always been told it's okay to have sex without feelings for the person.

Kelvin: I think women are taught to love and men are taught to screw, that's it.

Dennis: What happened in our relationship, I think, was that I was living with two people who were trying to get sober. I had to deal with how I was always getting involved with people who needed help. We went to a family therapist at an alcoholic treatment center, a straight therapist. He said that the other man wanted the trust and intimacy he saw in Kelvin's and my relationship, but he was jealous of it because we had something between us he couldn't have. We have little things we've shared as a couple that are very hard for others to understand. For someone coming in and trying to be part of the couple relationship, it's very unfair, and they get frustrated by it.

Kelvin: A major problem was that he didn't want us dealing with anyone we knew before we knew him. He didn't want us talking at all about our life before him.

Part of me is very traditional, into the world of couples and lace curtains, picket fences and happy-ever-after. I'm very emotional, very romantic, very sentimental. I'm not so sure you can have that kind of life in a threesome. For the longest time I thought that couples weren't a necessary way of being, but now I believe that if you're not coupled, if you don't have that love or that marriage, you're missing something.

Dennis: Some triads have been successful, but I think to be the most successful, the trio has to start together. I don't know any triads that last very long.

We talked about living in a communal situation with the spiritual group we were in. The intellectual stimulation, the sense of family, the support appealed to us. But like the other people in the group, we don't feel ready to sacrifice the privacy we're used to. For now, the idea of moving into a communal situation with that group is on the back burner.

We share ownership of just about everything. We don't have joint accounts, but if Kelvin pays for lunch one day, I don't owe him money, for example. I pay the house and car, and Kelvin pays the bills.

Kelvin: Everything has always been both of ours. Maybe that's partly what keeps us together, wondering who would get what if we were to break up.

Dennis: We're going to grow old together. I can see it — Kelvin will be outside gardening, I'll be inside clipping coupons.

Kelvin: We're very different and very much the same in some ways. We're very much alike in our political views. We both come from small towns in rural Oklahoma. We both have Fundamentalist

Protestant backgrounds, with the church a focal point of our
lives. That's part of the reason we're against the Christian Church;
we saw so much bigotry and hostility in it.

Dennis: We both like to read and like a lot of the same writers.
Whether it's because we live together or not, I don't know.

Kelvin: That was part of the problem with the man we lived with;
he didn't have the literary or artistic interests we have.

Dennis: The way we handle problems is by first getting to the point
where we can acknowledge we have one. Coming from dysfunc-
tional families, we find we sometimes have to confront the other
and really work to get it out. I had a very difficult time expressing
my feelings in therapy because I was raised where you *never* express feelings.

Kelvin: For whatever reason, considering our background, Dennis
and I have always been able to talk. We've been able to share
feelings, even if we bumble through. It's that sense of trust that
we can be fools with each other, that we can make really big
mistakes in our lives and know that the other will be there.

Dennis: For example, I was recently passed over for a promotion at
work and was having a very difficult time with it. I was bringing
it home a lot of the time.

Kelvin: He kept saying "I'm just fine," even though he was sitting in
a dark room. It took some shouting to get it to the surface, and
then we were able to talk about it and deal with it the best we
could. I said to him, "If you're not going to come home and tell
me what's wrong, how am I going to know it's not about us?"

Dennis: We're in a new time now. We feel it is very important to be
out. That's one reason I'm interested in the legalization of marriage. I think it would really help people at work understand our
relationship.

Kelvin: It would also help some people come out.

Dennis: We've thought about having a ceremony, but we have some
fundamental disagreements with the institution, with the Christian sense of it. It's very heterosexual, and we're not heterosexual.
And it's a real man/wife thing, which usually gets into role play-

ing where there's the dominant person and the one who's submissive to the other's will.

Kelvin: It's silly and needless in our situation.

Dennis: But we would get married if it was legal. Insurance would be much fairer for both of us. It would uncomplicate my leaving things to Kelvin. We're writing our wills because we both feel very strongly that our families might not be willing to respect our wishes otherwise.

Kelvin: I have no problem with others getting married, and we do know a number of gay people who have had weddings. I think it's personal preference. For us, it would just be a symbolic ritual, and we don't need that kind of symbolism.

5

Phyllis Lyon and Del Martin

San Francisco, California

Although we've been together almost forty years and own our home jointly, we've been told that legally, we are strangers.

Phyllis and Del celebrated their thirty-ninth anniversary on Valentine's Day, 1992. They met in Seattle in 1949, eventually became lovers, and, in 1953, moved in together in San Francisco's Castro district. Both have been active in human rights, gay/lesbian concerns, and women's issues since the 1950s. In 1955, they were founders of the Daughters of Bilitis, the first lesbian organization in the United States. In 1972, they wrote *Lesbian/Woman*.[1]

❧

Phyllis: We met when we were both working for a Seattle trade publication. I was assistant editor of the weekly and monthly magazines, and Del was hired from San Francisco to edit the daily construction-reports paper. The publisher had characterized his new editor as a "gay divorcee" — no one knew then just how "gay."

Some months after Del arrived, we went with a coworker to the Press Club for cocktails. During the conversation, the subject of homosexuality came up and Del said, "I am one." To my knowledge, Del was the first lesbian I'd ever met. I was very

Del and Phyllis

excited — so excited, in fact, that when I got home I called all my friends from work to tell them the news!

Del: That was way before "outing" became popular.

Phyllis: Fortunately, only one person was bothered by the news, and it didn't impair Del's relationship with her boss or her job.

Del: We were good friends for the next three years, until Phyllis decided to leave Seattle to go on a motor trip across the country with her sister. At that point, I made a pass, which she completed, and we became lovers. The trip with her sister ended in disaster. After a few months, her sister contracted polio in New Orleans. Phyllis called me frequently on the trip.

Phyllis: And during the month I spent with my sister in the hospital in New Orleans, I called even more often, and always collect! Del ran up quite a phone bill.

With Del in Seattle and me back with my family in San Francisco, the phone bills continued until we decided to move in together. Del arrived in San Francisco the evening of Valentine's Day 1953. We set up house in an apartment on Castro Street. We felt like a couple of aliens in this neighborhood that didn't tolerate queers. We had no idea that we would be forerunners of a movement that would liberate the Castro area.

Del: Our parents lived in San Francisco, which proved to be somewhat of a problem. Especially during holidays. Phyllis's sister finally suggested that we move out of town. We decided to go to New York. But our problems with the parents relaxed after that decision. We bought a new car and found a little house on a hill overlooking the city, which we just couldn't resist buying. So we stayed in San Francisco. The year was 1955.

Phyllis: It was fortunate for us that we didn't leave, because that year we got a phone call from a friend asking us to join a group forming a social club for lesbians. That was how the Daughters of Bilitis began. It was also the beginning of our active involvement in the struggle for civil and human rights for lesbians and gays, women, and ethnic minorities.

We didn't have much when we moved into this house. I had a bunch of books and records and she had a bunch of books and records. I had a car, I had a radio phonograph. We had a couch that pulled out into a three-quarter bed, the refrigerator, the stove, and the cabinets in the kitchen. We had absolutely no money left after buying the house. But, it worked out. And it just kept on working out. It seems that if you're going to plan to stay together, it really makes some sense to act as if that's what you mean to do.

Del: Neither of us thought about having a wedding ceremony. We did, however, consider that we were making a lifetime commitment.

Phyllis: We were madly in love, mad, passionate love.

Del: We gave each other jade rings after we moved in together. I guess the rings were part of our commitment. We've been wearing them for years. And — I can't get mine off!

Phyllis: It's true. She's bound to me forever!

Del: We merged our finances after we moved in together.

Phyllis: We never thought of this as mine or that as Del's. Everything was ours.

Del: The first year was the most difficult. Even though we'd been good friends for three years, getting adjusted to living with each other was hard. But we kept working it out.

Phyllis: When people ask us the secret of how we've stayed together so long, we say we do it one day at a time.

Del: We've always celebrated our anniversary from the time we began to live together. February 14th is easy to remember!

Phyllis: We celebrated our thirty-eighth anniversary by going on Olivia's Valentine Cruise to the Bahamas. Being aboard ship with six hundred dykes is an exhilarating experience. And there were commitment ceremonies performed by the ship's captain, which we witnessed.

Del: We had a big anniversary party once, for our twenty-fifth anniversary, in 1978.

Phyllis: We decided the twenty-fifth called for a special celebration. We made it a two-day weekend open house because our house is so small. We sent out two hundred invitations. About four hundred people came. What was to have been a private party with friends turned into a public event! Many of our guests were strangers.

It became public because San Francisco Supervisor Carol Ruth Silver, as a surprise, had requested that the board of supervisors issue us a certificate of honor "in appreciative public recognition of distinction and merit" on the occasion of our twenty-fifth anniversary and for our years of devoted service to the city. Ordinarily, such certificates are routinely approved by the board without comment. This request — an honor for a lesbian couple — led to a fifty-minute debate.

Del: "Twenty years of what?" shouted Supervisor Quentin Kopp. Supervisor Lee Dolson said some citizens had moral reservations about such relationships, and the board "shouldn't rub their noses in it." Others expressed outrage at these comments. Kopp replied, "Toleration, yes; glorification, no!"

The vote was eight to two in favor of awarding the certificate. It was presented to us at our home by Supervisors Silver, Ella Hill Hutch, and Harvey Milk (the city's first elected gay official).

Because of the controversy, reporters at the board meeting made the Lyon-Martin anniversary a media event. We were interviewed for both daily newspapers and for radio and television, which gave us the opportunity to let the public know that many lesbian and gay relationships are long-lasting.

Phyllis: Back in the 1960s, there were "covenant" services conducted by clergy involved in the Council on Religion and the Homosexual for some lesbian and gay couples. Ministers of the Metropolitan Community Church routinely performed holy union ceremonies. The *San Francisco Chronicle* ran a series of articles on the subject in 1970, then printed an editorial calling for legalization of homosexual marriage. But the issue was not a priority of the emerging gay-liberation movement.

Del: During the Anita Bryant–led religious crusades of the late 1970s, the California legislature decided not to take any chances and made the marriage law gender specific.

Phyllis: But now, in the 1990s, there is strong support to change the law back again, making marriage a contract between two persons instead of between a man and a woman.

Del: It's time our institutions and decision makers take a reality check. As alternative families, we are among the majority.[2]

Phyllis: To us, social change is creating options, recognizing diversity, and giving individuals or groups room to make differing choices. Everyone should be able to exercise the right to make commitments by civil or religious marriage, as certified domestic partners, or some other alternative.

Del: Although we've been together almost forty years and own our home jointly, we've been told that legally, we are strangers. In order to protect each other, lesbian and gay couples have to draw up all sorts of legal documents — property wills, living wills, powers of attorney for health and financial decisions in case of incapacity.

Phyllis: We spend a lot of money to get almost the same kind of coverage you get automatically if you're a married person.

We don't want a religious ceremony ourselves, but we uphold the right of other couples to celebrate their relationships in any way that fits for them. We support and are active in pushing for the legitimacy of lesbian and gay marriage and domestic-partnership legislation.

Del: A lot of people have asked why we weren't out demonstrating and demanding our rights in the 1950s. It was a scary time. We were considered to be perverts, illegal, immoral, and sick. Gay bars were raided by police, known homosexuals lost their jobs, parents disowned gay sons or lesbian daughters. Minors were sent to shrinks or institutionalized until they denied their homosexuality. And the U.S. government was conducting purges of lesbians and gays in civil service and in the military.

In the 1950s, lesbians didn't know they had rights as citizens. Those of us who were somewhat "out" were very careful not to compromise those who were "in." Almost everyone used pseudonyms in the 1950s. Drawings were more apt to be used in our publications than photographs. Cameras were barred from our public meetings and conventions. The term "lesbian" was rarely used. "Gay" was a secret code word we used to identify each other and meet others like ourselves.

Phyllis: Through peer counseling, rap groups, and meetings with professionals (doctors, lawyers, and psychologists), as a group we began to feel validated and many of our fears were alleviated. We couldn't start a movement until we had established self-esteem.

Del: Society is changing. Despite the religious right's crusades against us, we have made consistent gains in the past three decades. The time will surely come when same-sex relationships will no longer be a big deal — except to the individuals involved.

Notes

1. Phyllis Lyon and Del Martin, *Lesbian/Woman* (San Francisco: Glide Publications, 1972); Volcano Press published an update of the book in 1992.

2. Analysis of the 1990 figures from the Census Bureau shows that 53 percent of San Francisco's households are defined as nontraditional, about the same as in 1980. The national figure for such households is 30 percent (of 92 million households), according to a report in the *San Francisco Examiner*, July 5, 1991. Seattle was second in the percentage of nontraditional households, followed by Washington, D.C., and Minneapolis.

6

Tede Matthews and Chuck Barragan

San Francisco, California

---

*It's strange that people celebrate a wedding like that's a big
accomplishment when the real accomplishment is staying
together with somebody and having your lives weave
together. People should celebrate longevity.*

Tede (pronounced "Teddy"), forty-one, and Chuck, thirty-
four, have been together since spring 1984. Tede is a writer,
political activist, and member of the Modern Times Bookstore collective in San Francisco. Chuck works in personnel for a law firm
and is a writer and contributor to the anthology on bisexuality *Bi
Any Other Name* (Boston: Alyson Press, 1990).

❧

Chuck: We've been together since the day we met. We didn't live
together until December of that year, but we were basically
hooked on each other from the start. That's the anniversary we
celebrate, the day we met in March. We give little gifts to each
other, go out to dinner, talk about it. On our fifth anniversary we
actually had a public celebration.

Tede: We had a big party at El Rio, the bar where we met.

Chuck: I wanted to throw a little party for Tede, but then he decided why not have a real party, and it started growing. We
agreed to have it at our bar, El Rio, and have it catered, just
make it a fun affair and celebrate our five years together, which I

49

Chuck and Tede

saw as being a real milestone considering how different we are from each other.

Tede: Our friends came together to celebrate our relationship. It was a real mixed crowd — from Chuck's very straight coworkers to my wild Latina lesbian artist friends. That was all the validation I wanted. In our everyday life I feel that we get a lot of respect for our relationship.

I call our relationship "being married," but to me, it means being committed to somebody. I'd never been five years with another person. I think it's strange that people celebrate a wedding like that's a big accomplishment when the real accomplishment is staying with somebody and having your lives weave together. So many people spend thousands of dollars on a wedding and then divorce in a few years. I think people should celebrate longevity.

Chuck: Our commitment has never been anything really spoken. We just understand that we're in this for the long haul. We're crazy about each other and we don't expect things to change. It's a given that it's Chuck and Tede, we've been together, and we're going to stay together. Nothing's going to come between us.

Tede: It's the first time I've felt that if bad things do happen, I don't have to worry about the relationship breaking up. Occasionally we look at each other and find it hard to believe we've been with somebody for over seven years. We think about growing old together. We've already got our rocking chairs.

Chuck: We don't have written agreements about what goes on, or financial agreements, it just works without our having to spell it out. We have separate bank accounts but everything is shared pretty much fifty-fifty. I pay a little bit more for rent, because I earn a bit more than Tede, and I feel it's only fair for me to do that. But it's right down the middle for utilities.

Tede: We write down the groceries on a little list. When we go out to eat or to a movie, we trade off on treating each other. It's never really verbalized much because it just works out.

Chuck: I went to law school and I believe in having wills and powers of attorney. I've already filled out a will naming Tede. I've also had a power of attorney drafted for health care. My sister knows about both of these and has copies, so parts of my family know that I have a relationship with this man and if anything should happen, there are steps outlined that should hopefully give him the authority to take care of me.

Tede: I didn't go to law school, I'm an anarchist, and I hate the state having anything to do with my life. So I've put it off. But I do intend to do it. I really should because my mother, who is cool and hip, is very old, and my father died, which leaves my sister, who is a right-wing Fundamentalist homophobe, and I would not want her to step into my life and do anything. So I know I have to do something, especially in light of the Sharon Kowalski case.[1]

My father and mother have known since the early 1970s that I'm gay. They pretty much accept Chuck as a son-in-law. My mother sends a little check for Christmas, and she says, This is for you and Chuck. Last August, after my father died, my mother came out and stayed with us. It was the first time she'd met Chuck. We got to hang out in the kitchen and be with Mom. My mother's a wonderful person. My sister — I don't throw it in her face, or anything — but I always talk about Chuck, and maybe she'll mention his name after I've said it six times in a row.

Chuck: My parents and two sisters and all my relatives live in Los Angeles. One sister and her husband moved up to San Jose recently. I told her about me and Tede a couple years ago. She accepts us totally. In fact, we got joint Christmas presents and we get joint cards and letters. We're into bears (teddy bears, of course!), and she sends us appropriate bear things. She's the only person I've told in my family. Another sister sort of guessed it, and my San Jose sister confirmed it.

When my parents come up to visit, Tede and I take them out. They basically know, but it's unspoken. It's sort of traditional in Latin families — they understand what the relationship is, but they don't want to discuss it. When they stay with us, we sleep together and they sleep in my room. Last year, Tede and I went down for a wedding, and I just introduced him by name. I'm sure people speculate and know it, but I'm not going to go out and tell them.

Tede: I was at all the wedding rehearsals, I took pictures for the family, I was at all the parties at the house. A Latino family is used to being an extended family, and I think anyone's welcome in the family as long as you don't talk about stuff. On one hand, it's better than Anglo families that want to send you to a shrink, or convert you, or whatever, but on the other hand you're invisible as a couple, you're not validated as a couple. But I'm there as a member of the family. Last time his parents were here, his mother insisted that we have our picture taken and that I be in it for the family album.

Chuck: I realize that's probably breaking the rules of the politically correct approach of coming out and dealing with it, but I'm not into that. I want to do things my way, let my parents know what I want them to know, and let them assume otherwise. I don't like this whole idea about, "Hi, I'm Chuck, I'm bisexual. This is my lover, Tede. Respect me." I can't be that way even if I may want to be; it's just not my style.

Tede: The concept of coming out was developed by white middle-class gays. People wonder why what's seen as the gay movement is so white and middle class. The modes of being and communicating were developed by a certain class and race of people. So of course it's going to speak more to those people. I would love to relate to Chuck's mother more as a mother-in-law, but I prefer to be there with the family — they don't act uncomfortable around me.

Chuck: As far as being bisexual in regard to my relationship, it doesn't mean anything different from being homosexual or heterosexual in terms of my lifetime commitment. It just means that the person I'm with is my life partner, and I love him and expect him to be there. It's a relationship. I don't see that being bisexual makes any difference. If I was going to fool around, I'd fool around with men or women. That's it. People assume that because you're bisexual you're a "swinger," as if you can't be responsible to one person because they're just one gender. I don't have to have the other gender in my life, but it's an option.

Tede: I was definitely prejudiced against bisexuals before I met Chuck. I'm more open-minded about bisexuality than I used to be. I've had two bisexual lovers who I felt were using bisexuality as a cop-out and not being openly gay, or just not dealing in a healthy way with their sexuality, so they used women as a weapon against me. That hasn't happened with Chuck.

Chuck: He was hoping I'd convert.

Tede: I was never prejudiced against bisexual women. As a feminist, I could see that bisexuality was a healthy thing. But I saw bisexuality in men as another form of male supremacy, of men taking anything they wanted in life, again, in a sexual way. That was a certain form of sexism on my part, that a man couldn't do it as a healthy expression of his sexuality.

Chuck: I consider our relationship fairly monogamous. There have been times when one of us has been away on travel. Tede's a writer, and he goes away to Central America. The first time he left me for three months, it was very hard for me to stay monogamous. We didn't have an agreement on monogamy, and we fooled around without having one. I think we came to the realization that we were kidding ourselves that we could be totally monogamous when we were away from each other. We came to an understanding that when we're away from each other for an extended period, it's okay to be intimate as long as we're safe and we realize that it's just an experience, and it's kept out of the house. We are life partners and we let the other people know it. The few times we've had an "extended" relationship, it's for pleasure and that's it.

Tede: Except for the hideous rug.

Chuck: I have to explain that. Tede was gone and I had an affair with a woman I met. I was totally honest about my relationship with Tede, and I thought she understood. We got together a few times, and it was very nice, but I think she fell in love with me. And she brought me back a rug from a trip to Mexico. She really wanted to keep it going, even though she knew about me and about my partner. Basically, she finally got the message, and I got rid of the rug.

Tede: That was after he said he was going to hang it over his bed. I said, No way, José. Hideous, tacky thing!

Chuck: Anyway, Tede has also received gifts from friends down in Nicaragua. I didn't say anything about his gifts, so I assumed he wouldn't say anything about mine.

Tede: Oh, a card maybe. He did find a card I received from Nicaragua once and went and had it translated by a friend of his.

Chuck: I would say that "mostly monogamous" describes us.

Tede: There's a swinging gate on the cage. It works for me. I don't think 100 percent sexual monogamy is that healthy. I haven't felt that way since my first relationship, which was heavily battering. I almost got killed by my lover over jealousy. After that, I really combated being a jealous person. I feel that it's a very harmful emotion — not that I don't have it when there are hideous rugs! Monogamy among men . . . there isn't much place for it in the gay community, even though there are probably thousands of gay male couples in the city here that are committed to each other. But I think gay men have trouble recognizing relationships and giving validity and place in the gay community to other men having long-term relationships, though it's more of a premium now with AIDS.

Chuck: I think marriage is a relic from the past. It's basically slavery to another person. I just don't like the whole idea of marriage; I think it's totally wrong. It's unrealistic to say to people we're going to be together the rest of our lives, we're going to be legally bound by this, and all these rights and obligations flow from this ceremony. If you look at the divorce rate, people cannot realistically expect to plan their life around one person. Everybody is so different, not everybody can meet those standards.

Tede: Marriage puts a concept as more important and more central to the structure of this patriarchal society than the actual happiness and growth of the people within it. The old vows were for the woman to love and obey the man — a marriage of man and wife. This thing called "marriage" becomes almost like a third person in the relationship, and that's not the kind of relationship I want. I want our relationship to be a refuge for us and a place for growth and commitment.

I call Chuck my lover. I think that "life partner" sounds like you're in business, and "significant other" is not an endearing term. To me, "lover" means commitment. If I was just going out with somebody, I'd call them "boyfriend."

Chuck: I say "lover," or "significant other," since people know what that means.

We don't wear relationship rings. Tede wants to exchange rings, but I refuse to. I've offered to give him one if he wants it, but I'm not going to wear one. It's like a symbolic ring through the nose. It's like you're trying to say to the world, You should know what that means, and watch out. If people want to know if you're single or not, they should ask you.

Tede: I don't see it as something I'd be doing for anyone else. I see it as something between us.

Chuck: I know you feel that way, but I don't need that kind of symbolism in my life.

I would only get married if I was going to get something very substantial out of it. I don't have quite the same attitude as Tede about the state, though I respect his opinion. To be honest, since I've got the power of attorney and his name on all these insurance forms, the state already knows about his being my partner, or someone will, if they get access to this information. Our relationship is already a matter of legal record.

As far as the domestic-partnership registration goes, I don't plan to do it. I've done my share of enforcing our relationship based on the will and the power of attorney and the fact that everybody I deal with at work regarding my finances and insurance knows about Tede because his name is on my beneficiary cards. I think I've done all I can at this point to preserve any rights.

Tede: I don't believe in registering just to be part of the numbers. If there was a practical reason — if it would give us lower taxes, or as far as insurance goes — then maybe I could see more reason to do it. The way this world is going, I really don't want the government to have any more information on me than it already has. I don't trust that this country has the ability to take care of gay people's lives. Passing the domestic-partners bill in San Francisco didn't stop this city from being the main capital of hate crimes against gays in the nation in 1990. What it does in some ways is create a complacent atmosphere where gay people may feel every-thing's better here. I remember in the old days when a gay person got killed by a homophobe, the community would be in an up-roar. Now it's just like, Oh, we let the police deal with that. I don't feel that in the long run these new laws are going to liber-ate us.

I don't think couples should have privileges single people don't have, whether you're heterosexual, gay, or lesbian. I resent the fact that married people get lower taxes. But as long as there is this institution of marriage and heterosexuals are getting that privilege, then gay people should be able to do it too.

I think this is the first time in the history of the world that a lesbian or gay life-style is really considered or seen as an option. For many, it's seen as a sick option, but they can no longer deny that homosexuality exists, especially since the days of Anita Bryant, when gay groups started popping up in every town in the United States. There's a gay movement coming up in Asia, Africa, Latin America, eastern Europe — I think there's hardly a place in the world where people don't know that there are people living a homosexual life. Kids grow up knowing that homosexuals do live as lovers — no matter what the concept of that is, they know about it. I was so repressed, I didn't even think of having a male lover until I was twenty. I didn't grow up with fantasies of having a hus-band.

When we were coming out in the Gay Liberation Front in the early 1970s, we were angry, we didn't want to have anything to do with the patriarchy and we were totally against monogamy. The couple was seen as a patriarchal institution. Now, you can see young people in Queer Nation with the same anger but a different focus. Because of the groundwork set by gay militants and feminists where alternative sexual life-styles could come out, a lot of people who never felt the need to be militant, never felt the need to question or even understand what gay liberation was, are coming out. Gay liberation is more of a political way of think-ing where you really question patriarchal, heterosexist institutions, ways of relationships within a culture. Gay rights is wanting to have the same rights as heterosexuals and not wanting to have the legal hassles. Those intersect a lot, but I think there's a real difference. The movement today is a gay-rights movement.

Chuck: I have a feeling we've had good effects on each other. Tede is becoming less self-righteous in his activism, he's toned down his rhetoric. And I'm being less of a middle-class, structured person. We're definitely having an effect on each other.

Tede is my first male lover. He's my first in many ways. I'd never dealt before with somebody who is so progressive and radical, who's really been out there and done it all. When we first met, he was telling me all these things he'd been involved with — movies, plays, living in communes. I sat there thinking, Good lines, might impress somebody, but hey, it's a one-night stand, so what the heck. He still does it all, but our relationship has really brought some stability to his life and opened some windows and doors in mine. He's shown me things I never would have realized before.

Tede: I feel very grounded with Chuck. He is very supportive about my writing. And he's not just mushy, "Everything you write is wonderful, dear." He's got a good critical eye and can give good feedback. There are times when I'm home alone and have time to write — even if he's tired when he gets home, he'll give me an ear and read over my stuff. That's really helpful. My search for that person is over. In place of that searching and hunger I've got satisfaction and support, which has really enriched my life and given me a whole lot more power for what I want to do.

Note

1. Karen Thompson was denied hospital access to her lover, Sharon Kowalski, after Sharon was severely disabled in a car accident in Minnesota in 1983. After an eight-year battle in the courts, in 1992 Thompson won guardianship. For more information, see Karen Thompson and Julie Andrzjewski, *Why Can't Sharon Kowalski Come Home?* (San Francisco: Spinsters/Aunt Lute, 1988).

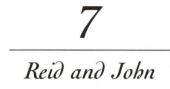

7

Reid and John

Georgia

I felt that God had sent John to me to be my life mate;
therefore it was already sanctioned and ordained by God.

Reid, fifty-eight, and John, forty, have been together for seventeen years. Reid is pastor of a Metropolitan Community Church (MCC) and in that role officiates many holy unions. John has studied education and nursing, and has a doctorate in health education, the field in which he now works.

❦

John: We've talked about having a holy union to the extent of saying that we don't want one. It naturally comes up in conversation since Reid does so many.

Reid: It hardly seemed necessary to us. We certainly weren't going to jump into that when we first got together. I had gone through years of being single and had decided I'd quit looking and I'd turn my life over to whatever God could do with it. It was at that point I got into the ministry and started the church.

I had prayed for years that I'd have a life mate that would share my faith. A few weeks after the church started, John showed up. I felt that God had sent John to me to be my life mate; therefore it was already sanctioned and ordained by God.

We met at the annual New Year's Eve watchnight service at the MCC in Quincy, Illinois. We end and start the year in communion with God. Every year, we spend the eve of our anniversary in church together.

John: We both have New Year's Day off work—which is great. We usually give each other gifts and go out somewhere nice for supper.

Reid: We've never exchanged rings. Neither of us are very much into jewelry.

John: We definitely have a lifetime commitment. When we first got together, we talked a great deal about life goals and how we felt about relationships. I was fairly young, only twenty-three, when we first got together. I was still going through school, becoming who I wanted to be professionally and realizing that it might take me to different parts of the country.

We decided early on that we wouldn't allow anything to come between us. We've really worked at that. We've made sacrifices about where we wanted to live and what we did professionally to help the other out at different points.

Reid: I don't know how many times the primary breadwinner has reversed. But John's got his Ph.D. now and I'm in the ministry, so I'll never catch up anymore! That doesn't seem to be a problem for John.

We both sense the importance of being individuals and helping the other toward self-actualization. Before we left Quincy, I asked John if he would consider staying in school there another two years and, in return, I would go with him wherever he needed to go to get his Ph.D. and for his first job. If he'd stay those next two years, then I'd follow him the next two moves. It's worked wonderfully. There is some give and take all the time.

We get along quite well. I can't even recall the last time we had a serious argument. We've said that we'll never be physically violent. If either of us was ever violent, we'd probably run into each other getting out the door, because neither of us believes in it. I also feel that one needs to be calm. When you get pushed, the natural reaction is to push back. We're both conscious of that and we just don't allow it to happen. Sometimes you just need to stop and wait until the adrenalin stops pumping.

John: It's real important to talk about things. And it's easy not to talk and imagine the worst. As difficult as it sometimes is to bring things out in the open, things aren't usually as bad as you imagine them.

Reid: Around the house, we share cleaning in a kind of laid-back way. John usually takes care of the lawn, because I have bad allergies. He does most of the cleaning in the house, for the same reason. I'm supposed to do the laundry, and yet if I'm at church, he'll do a load. I'll apologize for not getting it done because it's my job, and he says, "But you were busy." We don't keep track. It's not that I owe him one.

John: If the house gets a little messy, nobody gets upset. If it doesn't happen, it doesn't happen, and it'll probably get done the next day.

Reid: I think we're both very sensitive to each other having a bad day and just not wanting to do anything except watch the boob tube and have a yogurt before going to bed, and just let it go at that. We're not so rigid that we say, well, hey, this is Thursday, so we have to clean the bathroom, or whatever.

I rarely get a night off. Saturdays are the only day I have off, but I'm not really off, because Saturdays I have holy unions or church outings, or something. Of course, we're together at the church outings, but it's different. If my Saturday is going to get chopped up, we make sure we spend Friday night together.

John: We handle our finances jointly. We have joint bank accounts, we buy houses and cars and everything jointly. I just have my check deposited and Reid balances the checkbook.

Reid: I overheard John once saying to someone, "One of the nicest things about meeting Reid is I no longer have to balance my checkbook!"

We present each other as "spouse," and we call each other "spouse." I'm used to being open, even when we lived in southern Illinois. When we first moved here, I said right in front of a waterbed salesman, "Let's get a queen size for the guest room, but let's get the king size for our room." If the guy was shocked, well, he didn't say anything about it. When we bought the house, we went to a realtor who, the second time we met with him, said, "How long have you fellas been together?"

John: My family treats us as a couple now, but they didn't for the first ten years we were together. They came down for my graduation when I got my doctorate. Immediately after that, they invited us both home, and from then on treated us like a couple in the family. It was very hard to get used to that after ten years of them not even talking about Reid.

Reid's family accepted me immediately as a member of the family. In fact, the first time I met most of them was at a family reunion, and they included me in the decision making for the next family reunion. We'd only been together a year or two at that time.

Reid: Before that reunion, which was held mostly so people could spend time with my dad, I wrote to him and said I wanted John to come (he had already met John). He fired back, "If John's not coming, I'm not going!" So that settled it. The whole family had to accept John or there'd be no party.

I first told my dad about my sexuality because he was visiting me and I had to go to church and had to tell him what I was doing, that I was giving up my newspaper career to go into the ministry. He didn't sleep much that night, he told me later. The next morning he said he was concerned. He said, "Son, but can you make a living at that?" And I said, "I'll make it; God will provide." He wanted to go down and see the church that Saturday. He built the communion table, the pulpit, and the kneeling rail, and all of those things are still in the Quincy church. He later took communion for the first time in his life, from me, at age sixty-nine. It was a real touching moment for me.

John: We don't send many cards, but the ones we get from our families are sent to both of us. And my family sends Reid birthday cards.

Reid: And Christmas gifts! I get gifts from the whole family!

John: We occasionally talk about adopting children. We would both really like to have children, but I don't think we ever will. We certainly understand the intense responsibility of raising a child, and we would be more than willing to take on that responsibility.

Reid: But adoption rights are just not going to happen in this state.

John: If marriage was made legal and if we had the legal benefits that came with it, we would do it, without a doubt. I'm not sure we would have a ceremony. I'm not too big on ceremonies or rituals. I go to holy unions a lot, but I could easily never go to one. I have a hard time understanding all the hoopla that goes on with it. At the same time, I do see that they mean a lot to the people, so I go and participate in them. I've been a witness a few times, and I actually sang for one or two.

Reid: I did twenty-one holy unions in the last calendar year, a little less than the pastor before me, but then he did only an hour of counseling and I require four hours, which is enough to discourage some people. And that's fine with me. Because if they don't think it's worth spending that amount of time to talk about the relationship, then I'm not so sure I want to spend time talking about it either. I don't want a holy union to be a Band-Aid on a relationship.

In the four hours of preunion counseling, I'm determining whether they're serious and whether they've looked at the problems that we know can crop up in lesbian and gay relationships. I'm usually quite satisfied at the end of these meetings, and where I'm not, I tell them. If they want to proceed at that point, I don't think I should withhold my services. My attitude is only to be a servant of God for what is important to people; my judgment doesn't need to enter into it at all.

I counsel couples that, should the relationship break, they are under a commitment to get in touch with me and file a dissolutionment paper. At that point, I would insist on talking to both parties, at least by telephone, to try to determine whether there were irreconcilable differences. If it seemed that was the case, then I send them the three–part dissolutionment form we order from the fellowship for their signature and my files. That's part of the denominational work. I keep a file of all the holy unions I've ever done.

One of the first questions I ask if someone wants a holy union is if they've been previously married or have had a holy union. If they have, I want to see the divorce papers or dissolutionment form before we proceed.

If marriage was made legal for same-sex couples I think it would relieve a lot of anxiety. We've all heard horror stories where the spouse is denied hospital visitation rights by the family of origin. It would also solve a lot of problems our community has with legal matters concerning estates, and wills and living wills. And financial implications — we're strapped with individual income taxes although we live in the same household.

John: Legalized marriage would also lend some social support for same-sex relationships to stay together. That support is almost nonexistent now. And we all deserve it.

8

Gil Mangaoang and Juan Lombard

Los Angeles, California

----

*There is a certain status attached now to long-term
relationships. It wasn't much more than ten years ago that
the mood was one of how many boyfriends do you have, how
could you be with just one person for so long?*

Gil, forty-five, and Juan, forty-six, have been together for
sixteen years. Gil is assistant registrar of a law school and a
student in urban studies. Juan is studying for a second degree, in
nursing. The couple met in the mid-1970s and have lived together
most of the time since, except for a two-year break when they had a
temporary separation and Gil lived in Hawaii.

❧

Gil: We have a formal anniversary celebration — the Gay Freedom
Day parade! We met on Gay Freedom Day, 1976, in San Francisco. We started living together in January 1978.

Juan: When Gil first raised the question of living together, I was
tentative. I'm a product of the sixties, a time when the whole
concept of marriage was different. It was seen as oppressive to
women, it was a forced commitment. When I came to San Francisco, I worked at thinking it was better to have a series of boyfriends; gay oppression was linked to marriage.

I've changed a great deal. I think marriage is a vital institution
in terms of bonding. And in terms of the gay community taking

Juan and Gil

the steps necessary to sustain itself. We do need a sense of commitment.

Gil: I come from that same period of time, but I went through serial monogamy before I met Juan. I was in a three-year relationship with a woman and in another relationship before that, which lasted a year or so. Marriage is something I've always subconsciously wanted. I think the social atmosphere is now more accepting of that idea, so it's much more appealing for me.

Juan: Up until a few years ago, having a commitment ceremony wasn't a major issue for either of us. Seeing the [1987] March on Washington brought it to our attention. More and more of our friends are having wedding ceremonies. We've gone into preliminary discussions on having a ceremony ourselves. It's clear that we're going to do it, we're just not sure yet on the date.

Gil: I feel like, why not? As a gay couple, I think this kind of commitment needs to be expressed outwardly.

I would invite family, my brother and sister, who I've been out to for at least ten years. I'm not very close to any other family members, and both of my parents have died. But my concept of family goes beyond just blood ties now. It's really a whole set of people that have become my new family. A good portion of these are gay or lesbian people in different parts of the country.

Juan: I would challenge my family to advance themselves to that level, to understand my relationship with Gil in the context of a marriage. And I think they would respond. They might decide they can't accept it, but they'd have the discussion.

The increase in gay marriages shows me that there is a certain status attached now to long-term relationships. A lot of people are really impressed when they hear we've been together fifteen years. It wasn't much more than ten years ago that the mood was one of how many boyfriends do you have, how could you be with just one person for so long? I don't think it's just the AIDS situation; people are realizing relationships have something to offer.

I think by marrying, gays and lesbians help establish what our community is about. It shows that we have those kinds of relationships and we like to celebrate them, too. Marriage gives a certain stability to the community. We become part of other couples who've made the same decision. Publicly committing yourself also means that you don't go back in the closet. The concept of being able to float in and out, being straight in the daytime and gay at night, becomes less of an option.

No matter how we decide the contours of it, what's basic to any marriage is that you're committed to the other person for life. That's already the way Gil and I are. It's clear to me that this is the person I'll be with. At this point, having a ceremony would mean getting the public recognition of that, getting the acknowledgment that what we have is no different than what can exist between a man and a woman.

Gil: If Juan and I were to go ahead and have a ceremony, we'd have to define the parameters of the marriage. Would it include the heterosexual concept of being sexually monogamous? Is it purely a ritual, or does it become a demarcation point for a whole new level of interaction between us? Those are the kinds of things we're still discussing.

Juan: I don't link monogamy and a commitment to a lifetime partner. Our relationship is beyond just sex. A relationship is something you have to develop over time. That doesn't get replaced by an individual who comes in and out. Allowing myself to have sexual relationships with other people made it clear to me that my relationship with Gil is very special.

Gil: I had always wanted a monogamous relationship. In the beginning, I had to grapple with the fact that Juan was not going to be monogamous whether I said I wanted it or not. I felt very jealous, and I questioned his sense of commitment and responsibility to our relationship and to me. But we've managed to maintain our relationship with a lot of quality, and I don't feel the same threat I did before. I do feel the same jealousy, but I don't think it cheapens the relationship in any way.

What's kept us together over the years is communication. Even when things were strained and we lived apart for two years, the channels of communication were open. What's also helped is being able to recognize when you're wrong and being honest enough to admit it. On the same token, being able to hear what the other person is expressing, trying to gain the other person's vantage point and appreciate the perspective being expressed has also worked for us.

We come from different cultures. I'm Filipino, third generation, born here in this country. Juan is Creole, and identifies as a black man. He was born and raised in Louisiana. The experience of a black man growing up in this country differs from the experience of a Filipino many ways.

There are lots of things we've had to pick apart to try to understand over the years. Being able to see through Juan's eyes what it means to be oppressed as a black person in this society, my identification with being a minority, my experience of discrimination — that presents a lot to work through.

Juan: It's been a real challenge. Things that might not seem significant can turn into really big things. For example, in my experience, when you're dealing with interpersonal relationships, the thing is to be firm, up-front, and loud about it. Gil's culture is just the opposite. When we get into discussions, if I feel strong about a point, I tend to be very out there. He'll get more and more reclusive, and it just makes me so upset. I've learned that I have to work through it in such a way that he doesn't shut down. Because if he shuts down, we can't communicate.

Another big area of difference is the whole thing about how you treat sex. I think the reality for most black people is we live with a lot of variety of relationships. For example, many of the heterosexual people I know are not into a husband/wife kind of relationship. A lot of children are not from the same parents. Gil's experience is very different. Filipinos tend to be very closely knit. Gil's background is a Fundamentalist religious background, Pentecostal. I come from a Catholic background and spent many years in Catholic educational institutions.

Gil: My religious background brings into the picture a whole other framework for monogamy. Any extramarital affair is considered a taboo in a major sense. So we've also had to deal with that kind of religious hang-up.

Juan: What's helped me is I've always respected Gil a lot, even though we might have disagreed and I might have been upset and angry. I've never gotten to the point where I felt we weren't friends. After all, we've been through so much.

This past Father's Day I got Gil a Father's Day card when I was picking up one for my dad. I realized that in a lot of ways we've been brother and father to each other since we've had to grow up as adults. Because of homophobia, gay people don't have the same opportunity as heterosexuals to be ourselves when we are teenagers. A lot of times you have to postpone the experiences until you're older, until you come out. There's a way in which our bonds are very strong as a result of all of this.

Gil: I want to echo that being a friend is really important. I've had little "affairettes" with people over the years and, even though it was generated primarily by lust and infatuation, the lasting friendships with those people are very shallow. Friendship is the foundation that has stabilized our relationship so far.

We don't wear rings or any other forms of identification of commitment. But if we got married, we'd exchange rings.

Juan: We'd have the whole trappings. I'd appreciate the opportunity to serve as a model for younger people who are dealing with their sexuality so they can realize there are viable options. It's very fulfilling to realize that more and more, young people have the possibility of seeing these options.

As I think about my relationship with Gil, even though it's been really challenging, even though we're from different cultures, I think it's an example that it's possible for people from different backgrounds to form a lasting relationship. That's an important statement. I'm really proud of that. Gil is a great person. That we've been able to pull through these many obstacles is very fulfilling.

Gil: There aren't very many couples our age around these days that have been together for some time. The fact that we're survivors at this stage in a community that's becoming decimated more and more each day provides a role model for the generation of gay youth following us. They can see there's a stratum of the community that came before that's been able to nurture a relationship, that's gone through ups and downs. It gives the youth behind us a chance to say, Yeah, why can't we live like they did?

I expect to be with Juan the rest of my life. Whether or not a couple goes through a ceremony is a formality. The essence of the couple is really what it's all about.

9

Stevie Bryant and Demian

Seattle, Washington

---

*The gay community is the first impediment to getting
same-sex marriage legalized.*

Stevie, thirty-five, and Demian, forty-six, have been together for ten years. They are both involved in numerous
musical and artistic projects and have coauthored articles on same-
sex couples for both the gay and the mainstream press. In 1986,
they founded *Partners Newsletter for Gay and Lesbian Couples*, a national resource and forum supporting committed same-sex relationships, now expanded and titled *Partners Magazine for Gay and Lesbian
Couples*.

❧

Demian: Just before I met Stevie, I was seeing three men, and I
   was dissatisfied with all three. I made a chart of what I wanted in
   a relationship and saw that it was much more than these three
   very nice, wonderful men put together. The only way I figured I
   could get the ideal person was to let go of the relationships that
   weren't quite right. That was very frightening; I was letting go of
   a lot of security. As it happened, Stevie came into town, touring
   as a classical-music singer. I was amazed that this person fit everything in my chart so well. If I hadn't let go of the other guys
   first, I wouldn't have been able to see Stevie so clearly.

Stevie and Demian

Stevie was going to be leaving Boston, going back to Georgia, and I was planning a trip to Seattle to see about living there. I knew that if we didn't go together, we'd never see each other again. So I made a proposal to him. I told him that for us to tell if we would really be good for each other on a permanent basis, we'd have to live in closer proximity; I'd seen too many long-distance relationships fall apart. I suggested he come with me to Seattle and we'd see if this was a viable relationship. He came to live with me for a couple of weeks and thought about it, and then surprised us both and said yes.

Stevie: Subsequent to that, Demian came to the realization that it should be a lifelong thing, and I shortly thereafter agreed.

Demian: That realization was about a year and a half after we met. Taking care of each other didn't have to be a promise we made to each other; it felt inevitable. If one of us was poor, the other was going to take care of it. If one of us was sick, the other took care of the person who was ill. We were just doing that.

Stevie: We rarely celebrate anything — birthdays, holidays, anniversaries. We're not the ceremonial type. Neither of us practices within the context of an organized religion. I'm atheist and Demian is Buddhist. To us, marriage is a religious and a legal thing. We haven't been inclined to do any kind of religious ceremony, and, of course, with the legal option not available, it wouldn't have a lot of meaning for us. I want to emphasize that even though we're not the ceremonial type, I think it can be enormously valuable to couples who do have religious beliefs. They definitely deserve the same kinds of blessings and encouragement that other people in their communities get.

Demian: We'd be more inclined to have a party, invite people over to see my videos and have a dinner. We periodically do a state-of-our-union-address, sort of our life story to this point. We've done three so far. With our friends and relatives all over the country and in Europe, this is as close as we can get to any kind of — well, having everybody over for dinner.

Stevie: Early on, like many couples, we didn't expect or get a lot of support from our families of origin or from friends in the gay community. In time, we recognized that our relationship deserved some of the support and recognition that might be accorded our heterosexual siblings. So, we started developing some opportunities for our families to recognize our relationship.

For instance, when we decided to buy our house, Demian suggested we ask our families to help with the down payment as an anniversary present, or the wedding gift that we never got. And they all came through with one thing or another. We've also made a practice of always giving a gift from the both of us. When we talk to them on the phone, we refer to each other as "partner." Over time, they've come to recognize us as a unit and refer to us as such. My family now sends letters addressed to the both of us, or, at the very least, they ask me to say hello to Demian. That represents an enormous amount of progress. Most heterosexuals get that kind of treatment the moment they are engaged.

We've given the idea of having children a lot of thought. We both love kids. We would like to have a foster child, but we haven't done anything about it, partly because our lives are so full and our house is so tiny and jam-packed, we're not sure where we'd put the child. We both love children, we've both worked with children in many different contexts, at schools and day-care and all that. We just want to make sure that when we make that commitment, we're prepared to give the child everything it needs and deserves.

We have some legal protections — wills, powers of attorney, a relationship agreement in draft form, which we hope to finish soon.

Demian: That's been the hardest document to do. A relationship agreement has some things in it that are very hard to look at. It's mostly about how you want to construct your relationship. The heterosexual community does something similar in the form of a prenuptial agreement. This is more or less a pre-, during-, and postnuptial agreement, because there are no nuptials.

Stevie: The document is difficult because you have to decide on the exact terms of your relationship. And that's harder than walking in to your minister and deciding to hold a ceremony.

If we get to the point where we're not getting along and we're considering breaking up, we commit to undergoing some counseling with the purpose of resolving the conflict and maintaining the relationship. In our case, I have more income from an outside source, so if we were to break up, we'd have to set up some way of sustaining Demian until he can become more financially secure, things like that.

Demian: We've also made up lists of properties and who would get what. If we wanted to live separate lives, it could be very difficult to decide who would get what. Couples can get very angry when it comes to that part of a dissolution. So we've already thought out who would get the most value out of what when we're cool-headed and thinking clearly.

Stevie: As far as the terms we use for each other, we call each other "partner," or "life partner," to avoid any confusion with someone who might assume we're referring to a business partner. We don't wear rings because neither of us likes wearing jewelry, and also, it's a symbolic thing and we're not interested in rituals.

Demian: If marriage was legalized, we'd want a state marriage certificate, but we wouldn't have a ceremony. The certificate is extremely important. It's a matter of fairness, of civil rights, of equality in the face of the law.

Stevie: And it's a matter of dollars and cents. Married couples get a lot of economic advantages. Of course, you get responsibilities that go along with that. You don't get the option to pick *A* and *B* and leave out *C,* you get the whole package. But I think we'd be prepared to accept that.

We once thought legalized same-sex marriage was an impossibility, but now we think it's only a matter of time. Until the mid-1980s, the gay community was unprepared to ask for marriage. Now there's a great deal of ambivalence. A lot of it is their just getting used to the idea. A lot of it also is internalized homophobia. I think that the gay community will quickly become impatient with domestic-partnership initiatives, because they're finding that they don't buy us a lot.

The argument that getting married would be mimicking heterosexuals is just ridiculous. Marriage is not a heterosexual institution. If you look at the history of religious marriage, the Catholic

church was marrying homosexuals before it was marrying heterosexuals. It's simply a social contract that the government and the
partners agree to honor. There's nothing heterosexual about it.

Demian: The idea of aping heterosexuals is also a bit of hetero-
phobia. All the components of the traditional marriage or wedding ceremony are not necessarily appropriate for heterosexuals,
either.

The gay community is the first impediment to getting same-sex
marriage legalized. Unless the gay community has a clearer understanding of what same-sex marriage means socially, spiritually,
and economically, it won't happen, because no one's going to ask
for this besides our community.

Stevie: We recently surveyed gay newspapers, and radio and TV
stations, to ask if they're publicizing announcements of unions,
anniversaries or adoptions by gay families, and most aren't. The
almost universal response was they haven't offered or been asked
to publish such announcements.[1]

Demian: Four straight papers now publish same-sex wedding announcements. We don't imagine they're going to be swamped.
There are just too many people who would lose their jobs or get
harassment where they live.

Stevie: We feel it's a political act to make our relationship visible so
that long-term relationships are no longer hidden behind the
home portal as they have been for so long. In the next couple of
weeks we're going to be featured in the *Seattle Times* "Family
Talk" section, a family page in the Sunday paper where every
week they feature a family constellation and a short write-up on
how the family's organized and run.[2] They've attempted to show
some diversity, so we suggested ourselves, and they were very
eager to include us. And we're not a gay family with children,
which I think is an interesting distinction.

Demian: I think they've been browbeaten into it, since the *Everett
Herald* has been including gay folks in their wedding page and the
Seattle paper declined to do so.

Stevie: Couples are only now developing an identity of themselves
as a family. That is key to winning the support of others. We need

to build our own self-identity and raise our own levels of expectations from our families of origin, our employers, our government. Gay couples can't expect their parents to suddenly recognize them as a couple, to understand that they compare to their siblings and start responding to them in the same way. Parents of gays and lesbians need education and leadership on how they can respond to their child's partner and relationship.

Demian: The issue that has to be addressed is a very simple one — you have to come out. And that clearly terrifies people. Many people have said that coming out is a continuing experience. Although I've hosted gay radio programs, I've had experiences of publicly coming out which have made me feel so unexpectedly vulnerable, I find myself shaking! But I keep doing it. I tell myself, here's an opportunity to help people understand our community and help me understand myself. Gay people have to deal with the issue of self-discovery constantly. It's a privilege straight people don't always get to have.

We think it's very important that the families we create are supported and respected. And it's very critical that it be understood that there's tremendous variety in the gay community — so many kinds of families are formed.

Notes

1. The results of the survey are published in the Winter 1992 issue of *Partners Magazine for Gay and Lesbian Couples*.

2. The portrait appeared in the *Seattle Times/Seattle Post-Intelligencer* (June 9, 1991). The paper received about fifty letters and published a few favorable and unfavorable responses. Subsequently, it ran some of the many letters that came in defending "Family Talk's" inclusion of a gay couple against the criticisms in the negative letters published.

10

Margrete and Robin

San Francisco, California

Lesbians are pretty much invisible. Women's sexuality is invisible. To recognize lesbians through legalized marriage would shake up a lot of people in the heterosexual world.

Robin, thirty-five, and Margrete, thirty, have been together eight years. Robin is a research scientist and Margrete is a research associate. They commute thirty miles together each way to work every day, and everything in their lives is shared — including lingerie. They raise finches, cockatiels, and two large dogs and play on a women's softball team. They each plan to birth a child within the next few years using the same donor so the children can be blood relatives.

❧

Robin: We established early on that we believe in lifelong relationships. We believe they work. I needed to know right away that Margrete believed in that and that she wanted it, because I knew exactly what I wanted.

The first two years were the most difficult. I think we learned and grew a lot those first two years. We felt deep down that it was right. And I'm really stubborn, too. We face conflicts. We never go to sleep angry or sleep alone a whole night. We might fall asleep and then end up talking in the middle of the night. But we just never let things slide. Nothing ever seems so big that we can't deal with it. And we realize that we love each other and whatever's happening is just a transient thing. Then we can work on whatever the problem is.

Margrete: The first time we heard about a ceremony we laughed so hard. It was a couple of women jumping over a broom. It seemed so ridiculous! We laughed so much we thought we must have anxiety or something about ceremonies. They're just not quite right for us.

Robin: I don't think having a ceremony would affect our family or friends. Our friends already think of us as a couple, and our families . . . it wouldn't make them take our relationship more seriously.

Margrete: We don't practice any religion, so having a ceremony really doesn't tie in with our lives. But we would like to register as domestic partners. We'd do anything we can to help legislation. We'd at least like to help get on the books how many partnerships there are. It's important to make a statement.

Robin: We're planning to visit a prospective sperm donor in a few weeks. The wife is a close friend of mine, and over the years I've gotten closer to her husband. We've already talked to them and they're leaning toward wanting to do it. We have another possible donor that we've been talking to, a buddy of mine from school. He's coupled, but not married, and they have a child. They're interested in helping other couples in alternative life-styles. Whichever donor we go with, we're planning to store the semen and use it for Margrete later.

Margrete: I think there's a certain bonding that goes on between the birth mother and the child, and we both want to experience it.

Robin: And we think it would be nice for the children to be related by blood.

Margrete: Based on who we are, we'll assume different roles in parenting. We do that now. We assume different roles with our friends. I think that our personalities will naturally take over where they need to. I'll probably be called "mor," the Danish word for mother, and Robin will be called Mom, or Mommy.

Robin: Seeing how we've taken care of our dogs and birds, we're aware of the differences in the way we act in crisis situations, as well as in the everyday things. It's a good practicing experience.

Margrete: We're hoping to get a donation very soon. We want to scope out the doctors and get the donation in the sperm bank, then take an account of where we are emotionally and financially and plan when we want to do it.

We're in a grieving mode right now — a dear friend just died of AIDS four weeks ago. We need to work through that rather than rush into something different. In the meantime, we can do the legal things and get the sperm in the sperm bank so we're not stuck starting from scratch when we're emotionally ready.

Robin: We don't have any objection to the donor being known as an uncle or whatever, but he won't have any parenting role whatsoever. The two potential donors are fairly open to being known to the child at some point in the future, and both couples are excellent for guardianship should something happen to both of us.

The way the courts are right now, I'll be the only person who has any rights until the child is about three. Then Margrete can apply for a stepparent adoption. I understand that twenty-five of those adoptions have been awarded in the Bay Area. You need to wait until you can prove a parenting role, and then, depending on the judge, you may or may not get it.

Margrete: My family's response to our having children goes without saying — I expect my mother will be a total monster. Especially when Robin has her child first. She'll see it as a burden on me. Of course, once I have a child, it'll be favored over any child Robin would bear. It's going to be a lot of work for me and Robin. She's going to have to roll with the punches, too. We're going to have to put limitations on my family. They can't beat up on our kids emotionally.

I think Robin's family is going to be great, even though it's hard for her family to accept me; I'm kind of an oddity to them. They seem to have an unconditional love for children, but they won't bond as much with my child, because it won't look like a little Czechoslovakian!

Robin: When I told my mother, she said, "Tell me when it's done," meaning, when I'm pregnant. She wasn't saying it in a mean or nasty way, she just didn't want to know the details. She's going to treat Margrete with respect as a parent, I'm sure.

Margrete: My dad sort of treats us as a couple of girlfriends. He likes to buddy around with us.

Robin: But her brother and sister-in-law consider us family. Her brother made a statement to the family when I wasn't invited to his birthday party that I should be included because I'm part of the family. That was the worst thing he could have done, in their eyes. Our buying this house together has climaxed the scenario because it's such a sign of our commitment, it's really stirred things up in her family. So we have a lot ahead of us.

Margrete: November 30th is our anniversary, but we always forget it because it's around Thanksgiving. We get a second chance though, because we moved in together on June 15th. We occasionally celebrate that date.

Robin: We have a little anniversary dinner. Maybe champagne, but we don't involve other people in an anniversary party.

Margrete: Everything we have is shared. We did have separate savings and checking accounts before we got into the house-buying process, but now we don't. I was handed the role of accountant when I found out that Robin couldn't balance her checkbook even when she only wrote four checks a month! Women in our family have always handled the money, so I'm used to it; it doesn't bother me at all.

Robin: We give each other permission to spend money sometimes on something that's only for one of us. We just discuss it and can usually come to an agreement. We haven't kept track of who spent money on what since our relationship started. There were times when I was a student and didn't have any money; it just wasn't a problem, we never even considered it. When we got into the house-buying process, we made everything joint, we signed our cars over to each other because insurance was a savings, we put our names on each other's account. We have a will leaving the other everything, and powers of attorney.

Margrete: We've never had separate bedrooms, we've never separated clothing. We share a dresser and all our clothes and underwear.

Robin: I learned that style from my parents. They're very, very close. There's no separation of things. When you're a couple, you're a couple for life, and so everything is shared.

Margrete bought me a ring a couple of years ago. We've been waiting and saving for the rings we want to have as our relationship rings. I've never had any nice jewelry, which is how she came to buy me a ring rather than the other way around. I wear it on my left hand.

Margrete: The ring wasn't meant to symbolize marriage. It was more of a gift. The emerald stones reminded me of her eyes. I'm kind of superstitious, so when I travel for work I wear the ring. It's kind of a good luck, happy trails, hope you get through this trip okay.

I haven't come up with a name I'm comfortable with to refer to Robin. "Partner" doesn't encompass all the love and other aspects; it's sort of dreary.

Robin: We call each other "girlfriend," among women, because it's more understood.

Margrete: If same-sex marriage was legalized it would drastically change the laws. You'd have to get rid of sodomy laws, which would drastically change a whole region of the country. It would change our taxation in the gay and lesbian community, it would change so many things financially. It would change how we look at our golden years, our older years. Now, the way it's set up, you're like a single person, going through your whole life single. You don't get any retirement benefits from your partner when she or he dies. So you really have to plan your life differently in order to be secure. I also think it would validate our relationships. Right now we're on the edge.

Robin: Lesbians are pretty much invisible. Women's sexuality is invisible. To recognize lesbians through legalized marriage would shake up a lot of people in the heterosexual world. I don't know how many people would come forward and do it, though. I don't know how many people would be afraid.

Margrete: It may not happen in our lifetimes, but once you start validating relationships by saying it's recognized by the state, the church, and society, things would eventually change. I think it would bring more people out of the closet.

Robin: We've seen a great deal of change in our lifetimes, already. It would be a very powerful thing, politically. And it would be good for our children, too.

Margrete: One of the hard things a lesbian or gay parent faces is trying to help the child or children adjust to society. It's so difficult your first twenty, thirty years trying to figure out how you fit into this world, that if your parents aren't recognized in society it's going to be a lot harder. If we had a little more recognition in this world, if our relationships were validated through legalized marriage, parenting our children would be a lot easier.

11

Harry Hay and John Burnside

Los Angeles, California

---

*We have never contemplated investing in double rings or taking
vows of obligation to one another, because, as we say, how can
we commit ourselves to a tomorrow that hasn't come? Our
ongoing life is a celebration every day.*

John, seventy-five, and Harry, eighty, have been together
for twenty-nine years. The couple met in the mid-1960s, a
little more than a decade after Harry helped found the first gay
consciousness-raising discussion group, the Mattachine Society and
Foundation, in 1951–52. Harry describes the groups as "an aston-
ishing first blooming of self-respecting gay consciousness at the
height of Senator McCarthy's homophobic witch hunt."[1] John was
just beginning to explore his gay nature and venture into gay life
when he met Harry. Their attraction was immediate and their bond
soon followed. John left his marriage of many years and joined
with Harry within months of their meeting. Since then, they have
lived in New Mexico and Los Angeles; in 1979, they started what
is now an international counterculture spirituality group for men,
the Radical Faeries.

In the following interview, the couple discusses their almost three
decades of life together, their views of marriage, their perspectives
on gay sensibility, and the Radical Faeries.

❧

Harry: Most of the men I have known were what I call "flower-
faced men." I always saw them as flowers. They had a certain

Harry and John

delicacy about them. When I first met John, he was a mess! He had a crewcut and a perfectly ghastly, businesslike suit. He really didn't know how to dress. And so I had to take him in hand and dress him for a few years, cut his hair, and all the various things. And then all of a sudden — this was 1965 — he looked about twenty years younger. People couldn't believe he'd gone through this transformation. He was just darling. Since then, he's gently aged.

John: After a certain amount of that, I remember Harry saying one day, My goodness, all this time I've been dressing John . . . what about me! Over the years, he has produced the very beautiful being that he is. Lately he has been exploiting pearls and other forms of jewelry with wonderful taste, and produces very beautiful ensembles. Harry can't overcome the temptation to tickle the bourgeoisie, to outrage them, in a harmless way, of course, touching their prejudices.

Harry: A woman recently asked me why I wear the pearls, and I said, Because I like them.

John: We came together in December 1963, and we've lived together continuously since then.

Harry: Living together probably isn't hetero-imitative, because it doesn't seem conducive for the hetero male to live with a woman. He would like to possess her, but he doesn't necessarily want to live with her. We're probably closer to wanting to really live with each other than heteros are.

John: We live together because it has great value to us. It seems to be something in human nature. But I will say this also, that part of the nature of being gay is to not be confined to such a viewpoint.

We (lesbians and gays) are the people of insight. We are the people who consider all the various traditions and customs and question them — like marriage. We have a great responsibility here. The human race depends on us to do this. The traditions are the things heterosexuals do; they rarely question them. We question them, we bring changes to them. We have a tremendous surplus of creative energy since we are not reproducing the species.

Harry: We've had to grow up outside the chain-link fence of conformity because we are neither man nor woman. That's important to recognize. I always like to make the point that when I was eight years old, the boys used to say I threw a ball like a girl. So, I asked the girls if I threw the ball like a girl, and they said no, you don't throw a ball like a girl, but you don't throw a ball like a boy. Neither. Sissy.

"Sissy" to girls was different from "girl"; "sissy" to boys meant "girl." Because we're neither one, we don't want either hetero men or hetero women. One of the reasons we're friends with hetero women is because we don't want them as objects. We like them just as they are. They know that we see them as they would like to be seen. We can dress them, we fix their hair, we like them to look as nice as they want to look.

John: When we first met, I had been in the closet, and I was about to step into the milieu. But Harry came along, and we were so entranced with one another that we took up immediately being together. Harry felt that since I had a limited acquaintance with gay people, there was a danger that he would unintentionally shape me to his needs, and that was a matter of concern to him. Well, I wasn't concerned at all about that. Harry told me he didn't want to restrict me in any way in my life. If I was to take up with someone else, he would be hurt, but he would not prevent me.

We were exclusive with each other sexually, but completely promiscuous in loving. Of course, I don't know what Harry's response would have been at that time, because I didn't go with anyone else. Although I felt the usual male longing to break free and have all sorts of sexual experiences, I knew better than to start something because my relationship to Harry was too precious to me. It would have distracted me. When you undertake to do something, when you have a project going, you stay with the project, unless it somehow fails you. This was how I thought at that time.

It gradually began to dawn on us that there was no reason for sexual exclusivity. Joining together as we did to share our lives didn't require that we impose restrictions on ourselves or each other. Sensitivity to the values, to the important feelings, to the spiritual relationship and equilibrium in life, this was much more important than adhering to any single rule, and especially a rule that so obviously related to family dynasties and the importance of knowing parental lineage. Being gay gives you a marvelous freedom to question all the standard values.

Mine is not a jealous nature. That was not true of Harry. If he sensed that I was interested in somebody, that person was likely to have a bad time of it.

Harry: That was twenty-eight years ago.

John: Yes, that's true.

Harry: Jealousy belongs in a world where people possess one another. We're not concerned with possession; we're concerned with nonpossessive love. When we first came together, we were still strongly influenced by the heterosexual way of looking at things. It was all we had. The gay movement is still under the aegis of that situation. What we have been saying all along is we're not heteros, we have no business imitating them.

When John and I first came together, we were inclined to preserve the hetero-imitative patterns of monogamy. It wasn't until we began to examine it and live out what we began to perceive as what should be expected from Faerie-intercommunal relations that new ways began to present themselves. Sexuality, for instance? Since it was not a productive resource in terms of how it served the hetero community, did it or could it serve as some other, more far-reaching resource (besides the obvious function as a pleasure source)? Was it something we were supposed to search for and discover?

John and I have lived together almost exclusively for twenty-nine years. But that only tells you where we have or haven't been. We both will tell you that we have never contemplated investing in double rings or taking vows of obligation to one another, because, as we say, how can we commit ourselves to a tomorrow that hasn't come? John and I would have no problem with the tax breaks now becoming available to domestic partners; it could be an advantage. However, I still experience a horror at limiting my Faerie freedoms to any two-dimensional hetero-imitations simply for temporary or opportunist reasons.

John: When Harry and I came together, it was because we found a tremendous satisfaction and fulfillment in one another physically, mentally, in every way. The cement of our relationship is the existence of that affinity. A pledge or something of that sort would seem irrelevant to that. Our ongoing life is a celebration every day.

We go everywhere together and friends know we're a couple. We enjoy our friends' pleasure in it, too. They seem to find pleasure in looking at us as a couple, especially the younger people, because many of them don't know older gay people and don't know what old age is, what lies there. When they can see Harry and me as two very spirited people of whom it is true that every day our joy in each other only increases, it signals to them that the gloomy stuff that's often talked about doesn't have to be so.

Harry: I find the current popularity of hetero-imitative weddings pathetic pleas of the mindless, or spineless, professional cliques saying to the hetero mainstream, Look, families, dears, we're practically identical to you. This is heading into the new wave of assimilationism. We see it happening with the giving in to bisexuals (who want "in" with us because heteros aren't about to let them in, any more than they'll let us in until we drop this nonsense and go back to imitating *them* as we always had done historically). I adamantly refuse to identify in any way with bisexuals, because I refuse to reduce my beautiful totality of gay spirit to a couple of patterns of sexual behavior which can be practiced indiscriminately with anybody. (I turned down being Grand Marshal for Philadelphia's gay-pride parade in 1991 because I couldn't speak for the bi's.)

We have to be careful with all this rush to merge into mainstream acceptance. Because the more we indulge ourselves in this hetero-imitative bilge, the more we encourage the hetero majority to say, Well! Now that you've come back to our patterns of behavior this far, why don't you take the plunge, simply come back that final inch and abstain (openly at least) from sinful sex?

John: We were saying the other day we don't like this word "relationship." It's almost like a tumor, or something. There you are, and suddenly you have this relationship. We just go together, we walk together, as comrades. And that's not the marriage. The symbol of the marriage doesn't fit my concept of it. The connection itself provides me with abundance every day.

I think marriage is getting more popular because it's a reaction. Gay men once thought they had it made completely, they would have glorious sex all the time. This bumped up against AIDS, which suddenly made monogamy more promising. Monogamy suggests marriage, marriage suggests monogamy, doesn't it? So there's a tendency to fall back. If you get into difficulties, you tend to retreat back into something seen as safer. Marriage is the symbol of something safer.

Also, a great many gay men put a lot of value on property. In the straight world, the marriage laws offer a very valuable protection around property. My view of gay life represents the spiritual. I'm not concerned with surviving; I can take care of that very well with a minimum amount of effort. I'm concerned with everything that lies beyond that.

Marriage has everything to do with survival — of the couple, the species, the children, the family line — it all concerns hanging onto things, increasing. For me, time spent on that is time wasted. For those to whom the values of the world — money, position, influence, display — are attractive, well, we say of them, We wish there could be a cure for homosexuality, because their homosexuality is in their way.

It has been very important to us that our lives be more free, more open for creative productivity for each of us individually after our combining with each other. As free-ranging spirits, Harry and I are frequently engaged in completely different activities in different parts of the house. But the presence of one another is an ongoing sense.

We do have conflicts. It's inevitable, because we're both imperious queens at heart. One will say something, the other will battle, and we'll lock horns to change the figure. Harry's a rather terrifying being to some. He's well over six feet tall and has a mighty presence. But he's not intimidating to me because we're contemporaries. So when he thunders at me, I'm likely to say, Don't be ridiculous. It doesn't exactly please him. At first, Harry would say, This is the end! And he'd be gone for half a day or a few days.

Harry: The last time I left, I saw myself looking down a long road and he wasn't there. I couldn't stand it. And then I had to worry about whether or not he'd let me back in! I'd spent years already, looking for something — looking for John.

John: Of course, I was grieving the same way you were, you know. We finally caught on that it's unnecessary to part like that. As it's often said, for men and women alike, after a quarrel there's a deeper attachment than ever before. It took us years to learn that. At this stage, when we have the locking horns thing, we quickly let it go.

We should have more protections than we have established. I don't think we've really investigated it that much. Harry did, with respect to medical care, with the rights of nearest of kin. Harry takes a serious and responsible attitude toward these things. Of course, I tend to leave it to him for that reason. He goes ahead and takes care of things like getting our passports because he doesn't trust that I'll take care of it. I think it's very comic.

Any money that comes to us goes immediately into a shared pot. Harry is the one who takes responsibility for the money. He studies the market. He makes out our tax report each year, things like that. A relationship between us is such that I just simply dance about doing everything I enjoy and leave all the rough stuff to him!

I've always been greatly indebted to Harry, because his invention of the Faeries enriched my life. The forming of the Radical Faeries also greatly enriched our relationship, and gave us much work in common.

Harry: At Gay Pride Day recently, and at different times in recent years, someone embraced me and said into my ear, "Thank you for my life." It's very moving. But I have never felt I needed to speak for the queer movement, whatever it may have called itself in any particular time. The Radical Faeries of 1979 and the 1980s — like the Mattachines of the early 1950s — were the brothers and sisters to whom I could say, "I have a vision of how we could organize and develop continuity. If you like the ideas, why don't we walk together?" And, in both cases, they said, "Yes, let's."

John: The Faeries were a marvelous event, because all at once, from a life that was just with Harry and a few others, I suddenly found myself in a perfectly heavenly array of very wonderful people, very friendly and open, very ready to enjoy one another in the wide range of possibility.

When we came together at the first Faerie gathering, we didn't know what it was going to be. Harry conceived it as a conference, and called it that. It was my suggestion later that we change it to "gathering." It was done in the highlands of the Arizona desert. We prepared the site, we brought the food. We had to get more food when more people came than we thought would come.

In 1979, we came together, and within two days we realized that we had all gone through a door that we didn't know was there before. When we turned around, the door was gone; we had moved into an entirely different world.

At the gatherings, we have what are called circles, where we rap. The circle has no head and foot so you avoid hierarchy. We have what we call our "talisman," a lovely shell or glass ornament, which we pass. When you hold that, you may speak with no interruption, as long as you speak from your heart. In this situation, you feel perfectly safe. Therefore, you can reveal yourself. You can tell how you feel about things, your struggles and concerns. And the beautiful being that is there becomes visible to the rest of us, the struggling, heroic, loving being.

Much of this is already true of women's gatherings, we know from our dyke friends. We're happy to say they were long ahead of us in discovering what can happen when gay people get together in an area where they can really be themselves.

We have workshops on different topics that interest people. We love to dance, and we love to sing and play music. Food is a matter of concern, because the Faeries love to eat well, and we're all vegetarians. So many of the Faeries are splendid chefs. And we're likely to put on a show or two. We have a no-talent night and a talent night.

Faerie gatherings happen when several Faeries decide to call a gathering. When a call is sent out (we send out the calls pretty much to a mailing list now), there is a request for the Faeries to send in money to pay for it. We have the provision that no one's refused for lack of money. We tend to divide by region. There are Faerie gatherings in Utica, New York, every year, and in the North Woods area — Wisconsin and Michigan. There are gatherings in other countries, in France and Germany, Australia, New Zealand. These meetings are immensely important to all of us, emotionally as well as intellectually. And it isn't a matter of an organization anymore — it's a question of a marvelous family tie.

One of the things the Radical Faeries did was to introduce the custom of kissing and hugging on greeting. The Faeries represented to me the breaking of the bonds of gay-ghetto rules, which were that you were only interested in someone if they attracted you. Friendship always began as an affair. This new way was very delightful to me, and I made friendships with many, many people.

The Faeries are a good example of the potential of what gay men's lives could be if they could see the potential that lies in being gay. You could say, "I want to be part of society, and I have this yen for men instead of women, but maybe I can persuade the rest of society and then I'll do all the things they do." Or you can say, "Wow! This is amazing. I'm an outlaw! I'm somebody they don't control. And therefore, if I have something of a dream about life, something I want to explore on my own, I'm in the ideal situation." The Faeries are the latter group.

The Faerie approach, as I see it, is to savor and appreciate life, to enjoy it, to reach out for its many possibilities. A gay person goes to a gathering and finds what he wants, then goes back to society on a completely new basis. It may be a long time before he goes to a gathering again. Others of us find them so extraordinarily wonderful and productive that we go again and again.

When the Faeries got together, we found the wonderful common self we possess. We recognized that this is the path of the hero. The young woman who knows she's different must create herself. How is she to find the model when the models offered her don't fit? She must embark on a great journey and face many dangers.

So it is not for self-pity that we come together, but for the acknowledgment of courageous life. When people find they have this in common, a bond is established. How can you not love a woman or a man for the heroism of their life?

Note

1. For more information, see the biography of Harry Hay, *The Trouble with Harry*, by Stuart Timmons (Boston: Alyson Press, 1990).

Part Three

Public Ceremonies

12

Brian Binder and David Craig

Los Angeles, California

---

*We did it for all the right reasons. We didn't do it for taxes
or monetary purposes. We didn't do it for gifts.*

Brian, twenty-six, and David, twenty-seven, met at temple
in 1987, a few nights after David joined. They began living
together after one year. David is from North Carolina and now
works in the film business. Brian, a Detroit native, is studying nu-
trition in a graduate program. Their Jewish ceremony was held in
the fall of 1990 — at a PFLAG (Parents and Friends of Lesbians
and Gays) conference in Anaheim, California, with hundreds in attendance.

❦

David: I proposed to Brian on our anniversary. I handed him a
jack-in-the-box to "pop" the question. I had covered the puppet's
head with a question mark, and put a ring in its hand.

Brian: It took me quite a while to understand what he was getting
at, but even when I finally got it, I still made him say the words.
We had talked about marriage before. I'd always wanted a long-
term relationship and felt it deserved the same credibility as a
straight union, felt that some form of public commitment ceremony was the way to go. But David had disagreed.

99

Brian and David

David and Brian with their families

David: Brian comes from a large, tight-knit family. People have stayed together. Long-term commitment is exactly what it means. I come from a family where all the men have been divorced. I came to see marriage as a joke.

The other issue was my development as a gay male. I came from a very repressed world, which was partly self-imposed. I was very closeted back in North Carolina. Six months after I moved here, suddenly I was in this relationship. Up until that point, I can't say I had even a friendship with a gay person I respected. The idea of being in a relationship that was even a month long was inconceivable. So, in the two years before I proposed, I went from never having had respect for another gay individual to contemplating that this is an individual I could really commit myself to.

Brian: David's viewpoint of family also changed over the years. My family really took him in and gave him something he never grew up with. My brother's family, my parents, my friends, really took David in.

David: I don't think the ceremony solidified my place in Brian's family. I had already stood up at his brother's wedding a year earlier as part of the family. And I'd been to numerous family affairs where I was introduced as the brother-in-law long before the ceremony.

Brian's parents had expected us to have a wedding from early on. When we were together six months, his parents were talking about us getting married. They enlightened me that within the confines of a family there can be support, and nurturing, and unconditional love. That was hard for me to grasp until I met him.

Brian: And that's really what we felt we were doing in part by having the ceremony. We were creating our family.

My parents are very active in PFLAG. They got involved about two months after I told them I was gay, which was about four years ago. Their story is that when they went around the room introducing themselves, my mother said, "Hi, my name is Helen, I have a gay son," and then she cried for the next three hours. Three meetings later, they were practically running the meetings. They were on the board of directors of the local chapter in Detroit for two years, they were treasurers for the international PFLAG convention, and they've been very active in the speakers' bureau. They've recently moved to Las Vegas, after living in Detroit all their lives. I daresay that was the hardest part of their goodbyes in Detroit, saying goodbye to their PFLAG group. There is no PFLAG organization in Las Vegas, and they're thinking of starting one. While they're looking for an apartment and living out of a hotel, they're also tracking down AIDS organizations and gay organizations and trying to become active in those. That was on the same level practically as finding a house. We never could have imagined this would happen.

David: My mother and grandmother live together in Charlotte, North Carolina. I had come out to my mother five years before I met Brian. She said, "I don't care. It doesn't change anything as far as you and I are concerned, but I don't see why we should talk about it. I don't understand why you have to bring it up."

I was so closeted then, I couldn't ask her to seek help to understand my gayness when I wasn't seeking it myself. When I met Brian and he told me what PFLAG had done for his parents, I called my mother. She didn't see any reason why she should go. I told her she may not even realize what questions she had. I told her I'd never asked her to do something for me before; this was a one-timer. Within a couple of months she was secretary and my grandmother was treasurer. Now my mother's talking about how she'd like to be the contact mother that gay children who've lost their parents can call. She's been photographed for newspapers picketing outside Dan Quayle's speeches and [Congressman] William Dannemeyer's speeches with a big sandwich board that says "Gay is good. That's my boy." I don't know if I believe in fate, but if things are right, things will happen.

The PFLAG conventions are held annually, and each year they're more amazing. Imagine hundreds and hundreds of parents who all adopt you the minute they know you're gay and overwhelm you with acceptance and tolerance. Brian's parents organized the Detroit convention, and the next is scheduled to be in Charlotte, where my mother and grandmother are organizing it.

Before I proposed to Brian, I contacted PFLAG in Anaheim and asked them if they would be amenable to having a ceremony be part of the convention in October. I figured many parents wouldn't have the opportunity to see their children have a ceremony, and we feel like they're our extended family. They were thrilled with the idea. It would be held just as the convention ended. And because they already had the hotel, they offered us whatever they could in the way of facilities.

After Brian said yes, we went down to the hotel and met with the caterer. We were offered the large atrium, which we thought was very daring, considering the nature of the ceremony. Subsequently, we had problems when they wanted to go back on their word and get us out of the big atrium, but we told them they couldn't go back on it, we stayed firm.

Brian: For the ceremony, we wanted to create everything our own way, not to toe the line and do a conventional wedding. We designed the rings, we had a painstakingly worded bulletin that greeted everyone. We wrote the *ketubah* [the traditional wedding document], which now hangs in the dining room. We opted not to do the things that could have made the whole thing easier because we wanted everything original — not necessarily the classiest or the best, but truly from us. We were big on metaphors and symbols.

David: The ceremony was symbolic, so we thought it was important that our symbols be correct and right on. We wrote everything, with the exception of the rabbi's sermon. We wrote from our hearts, and that involved a tremendous amount of soul-searching, and rewrites, and time. The invitation was probably the hardest of all. I got the inspiration one night while I was sleeping. I got up and drew it and wrote the words.

Brian: We ended up with about 150 friends and relatives. We had placed an announcement in the PFLAG-dinner journal. About 300 came. We completely filled the atrium.

David: And that doesn't count the Disneyland tourists with their cameras!

Brian: After the ceremony, we had a private reception in another part of the hotel, and that was about 150 people.

David: We both wore black-and-white tuxedos. I wore Brian's tux with tails. Brian rented an old-style tux that was very classy looking.

We didn't know what the ceremony was going to be like until we sat down with our rabbi. She gave us a few options and told us the reasons for the symbolic things that are done. She walked us through the process and did some counseling with us.

We opted to have the *chuppah* [the traditional wedding canopy, which symbolizes the home] and the *ketubah*, to do the seven blessings, to exchange vows and rings, to drink from the wine together, and we definitely wanted to break the glass [the tradition that signals the finish of the ceremony, and one that has many interpretations]. We also wanted friends to sing a couple of songs.

Brian: The seven blessings were done in a way the rabbi suggested, as wishes. Instead of thanking God, they wished for us their hopes. The seven were divided as individuals and small groups of family and friends.

Our parents walked us down the aisle, which is traditional, following the rabbi. The wedding party that walked down the aisle with us were the *chuppah* holders — four people who'd been friends of mine since back in high school and before. They'd flown in from around the nation. We were so honored they came that we asked them to hold the *chuppah*.

David: All four were people Brian had taken to the prom at some point!

Brian: We also had two friends witness and sign the *ketubah* with us. While we do have tremendous support from my family and extended family, the sense of family-friends is important to us, as it is, I think, for many gay people. So it was important to have some of them included in our ceremony and the *ketubah* signing.

The rabbi greeted everyone. Then there was the blessing over the wine, and we both drank from the wine. Then we exchanged vows, which we had written out on cards, and we read to each other. Neither of us knew what the other was going to say until we said it. Following that, someone sang. Then there was the exchange of the rings. We said, in Hebrew, This is my beloved, this is my friend.

After the rings were exchanged, the rabbi read the *ketubah*, which we'd signed upstairs in a separate ceremony. After that, a friend sang, and then it was time for the seven wishes. The designated speakers came up and gave their wishes. Some wishes were long, some were short, no one knew what the other was going to say.

Brian: As a surprise to us, the cantor came up and sang a song with the rabbi, a beautiful song. He sang in Hebrew and she translated. Then we had the breaking of the glass, two glasses in one napkin. That was something everyone asked us, would we break the glass and, if so, how were we going to do it.

David: The rabbi offered an interpretation of the glass breaking that we really liked. In the beginning, when God created the earth, he had vessels of light. These vessels were broken, and the light permeated into our lives. The breaking of the glass was to symbolize our breaking the vessel and letting the light that comes from our relationship enter into the lives of everyone there watching.

Brian: After we broke the glass, there was a huge "*mazel tov!*" Then we kissed and walked up the aisle together for our private time, which is part of the Jewish ceremony.

David: I can't tell you what a great feeling it was to walk back into the atrium after we'd had a few minutes together, because everyone had waited for us, they were so eager to thank us for the way it had gone. We really felt like we had done something right by having it that way.

Brian: We had a tiered wedding cake, but there was no groom and groom at the top. After the cutting of the cake, that was it as far as rituals go. The cocktail reception was just for our family and friends.

In a way, the ceremony was kind of anticlimactic. The act of getting engaged and having a ceremony sort of heightens the drama of life and intensifies it to such a degree that immediately following it there is such relief. All the preparation beforehand does the character building and either tears a couple apart or pulls them together. There's so much weight and import. There were so many things that we wanted to accomplish through the ceremony that there seemed to be a lot at stake.

I think we have an unspoken bond between us that we really went through something special which no one can take away from us, something that gives us mutual respect and brings a different respect from friends and family. It wasn't like our commitment went deeper. It was like we went through a trial together, a very powerful emotional event. Once you've gone through that process, it changes you. That's why I think people may lose out when they elope.

David: We really tried to be careful with the wording to promise to cherish the moment in which we live, to highlight the fact that we focus on the value and quality of our life as we're living it, not just focusing on how long the relationship is going to last. And that comes from the HIV question. But I've always had difficulty with the concept of talking about what the future has to hold. We've laid the groundwork for a long-term relationship, but there are no guarantees. We weren't getting up there and saying, Look at us, ha-ha, we're going to last forever, and we're going to prove it by having a ceremony. We were coming up there to say, Our relationship is as significant or more so as anyone else who's come up and committed themselves to a relationship.

Brian: I have a lot of problems with what David is talking about right now. The way David's presenting it is as if we're not going to be together in two years, that's just the way it is. That's not the way it is.

David: It may be a nonromantic approach, but there just aren't any guarantees. And the HIV really makes that point. Brian is HIV-positive.

Brian: Isn't that ironic. I found out five years ago. On our first date, I ended up telling David I was HIV-positive. I knew that we were really a case of love at first sight. I knew it was something I didn't want to play around with, so I put it on the table.

I think it affects our relationship incredibly. For two people our age, we spend an unusual amount of time talking about mortality. And we talk about the different factors in living and how they affect us, our theories of life, what is important to brew over, loving another person, spending important moments with someone else instead of being with alone. The HIV forces those discussions. When you're HIV-positive, every single day you're facing the thought of not being around. It speeds up the maturation process. We don't make goals that are ten, twenty, thirty years away. We talk about wills. And cemetery plots. People in their twenties don't usually talk about wills and cemetery plots. We talk about things that couples in their fifties and sixties talk about. We still have our health, which we appreciate. Taking care of powers of attorney makes it more painful, because it's all so real. Still, although it's always lurking, we lead our lives pretty well.

David: I call it healthy denial. It's an overwhelming issue. It can be oppressive if you allow it to be. We try to talk about it matter-of-factly. He gets tests, we find out more about how the virus is progressing, and we just have to keep going on.

Brian: Our compatibility rate has to be up in the nineties. We disagree on some things, but far more we tend to agree or see similarly.

David: We're similar in values and work ethics and so many different things. Where we do have problems, our typical manner of handling it is of yelling, and then we go our separate ways for five minutes, and then we talk. We have patterns that may not be very healthy, but we rarely let the sun set on our differences.

Part of why we know how to work things through is where we've come from in our gay identity. We've had to be very honest with ourselves in many respects because of that. We've had to learn to ask ourselves the tough questions. So, when it comes to having to turn around and ask our partner those difficult questions, we're at an advantage. We're introspective enough to say, There's something going on here, there's something wrong, let's find out what's lurking under that. I don't mean to toot our horn, but I think we're very healthy emotionally, and there's nothing like HIV to give you perspective on life, and love, and relationships.

Brian: I always tell people that when it comes to our wedding, we did it for all the right reasons. We didn't do it for taxes or monetary purposes. We didn't do it for gifts; in fact, we didn't register, because we didn't want marrying to be seen as an excuse to get gifts. If people really wanted to give us a gift, we felt they should just give us money to help with the wedding since we're living off one income right now while I'm in school. We did it from our hearts and sharing it with families and bringing that into our lives together. Since our ceremony, three of our friends in couples have gotten engaged, and one couple has had a wedding. Our ceremony showed them what a powerful experience it can be to get married.

13

Nina Kaiser, Nora Klimist, and Kellen Kaiser-Klimist

San Francisco, California

---

*You can't be more "out" about who you are and about
wanting your relationship considered valid in society
than to get married.*

Nora, thirty-two, and Nina, thirty-seven, had their wedding ceremony in 1987, one year into their relationship. Both are parents of ten-year-old Kellen, and they plan to build a larger family. Nora, a therapist, and Nina, a nurse, share their mothering role with two other women, Helen and MK. Helen has lived with Nina and Kellen since Kellen was six months old. MK has been involved with Kellen since she was born, but lives separately. After years of calling all of them "mother," Kellen now calls Helen and MK "godmother"; at this age, she prefers not to have to explain that she has four moms.

❧

Nora: I'm monogamous, so I wasn't giving up something for this relationship. This is the first monogamous relationship Nina has had in eight years, so this was a big step for her. I had to put a lot of faith in her commitment, and that's a scary thing to do. The fact that she was willing to get up in front of people and make the commitment reassured me a lot.

Nina: One of the things we talked about at six months into the relationship is how to stabilize a family. We already had Kellen,

109

Nina, Nora, and Kellen

and we want another child. Nora was sure she wanted to have a child and didn't want to do it as a single parent if she didn't have to. She wants to carry the next pregnancy.

So, that brought up the discussion of whether or not we have the same goals. For Nora, it needed to be a monogamous relationship, and that was fine with me. It wasn't an issue of monogamy versus nonmonogamy, it was an issue of whether we have the same goals as a couple and as a family.

Our marriage helped Kellen feel more secure. In the eight years that I was nonmonogamous, Kellen saw a lot of women coming and going—well, not a lot, but too many, for her. I had two ongoing primary relationships for over two years before I was with Nora, and both those women played a sort of motherly role in Kellen's life, then took off. She didn't take too kindly to having to adjust, having to get used to new people, their rules, their way of relating to her. It was very clear that she was not going to do it with Nora unless Nora was sticking around.

Kellen: Before they got married, I was like, Don't let this person into my house. This is where I live, don't let her in. And then when they got married, I really settled down. I said, You can come in our house, you're part of the family now. When my mom was switching off, I got used to the people, and then they went away. And Nora hasn't gone away yet. The marriage meant a lot to me because I know that they're going to stay together.

Nora: There was a big difference in my relationship with Kellen after Nina and I were married. I think we got along better. We still have our battles, because I came in when she was five and here's this little person already with her own way of doing things. I'm very different in some ways from Nina in my way of parenting. Kellen's had to make adjustments. The first year was hard; she put me through the wringer.

Kellen calls Nina "Mom" or "Mommy." I don't get called "Mommy," she's made that clear, but I get called "Mom" all the time, or "Nora."

Nina: I took care of my baby needs with Kellen. Helen, who lives with us here, has lived with me since Kellen was six months old.

She has never been my lover. Helen and I have been friends for years, prior to my conceiving Kellen (which I did on a vacation, when I saw my opportunity). We would probably live together even if I hadn't had Kellen. Helen has a commitment to coparenting, to being involved in Kellen's life.

The woman I was involved with when I got pregnant, MK, was also one of her moms. The three of us haven't lived together at any time. MK also has kept her commitment and is still involved in Kellen's life. MK takes her for some time during the summer. She sees Kellen once a week, financially supports her.

Kellen celebrates the holidays with MK's family. In fact, Nora, Kellen, Helen, and I all go to MK's mother's house for Christmas. They come to her birthdays and celebrate Jewish holidays with us. It's very different from the traditional couple; it's a nucleus, and then we have this extended version. When Kellen started kindergarten she had four, five, six moms.

When I first had Kellen, both MK and Helen said they saw me as the primary mom. I had unilateral decision-making power. Now, we all are involved in decision making. First, I discuss the issue with MK, then we discuss it with Helen, then we all talk about what we think about it. In the beginning, I planned that MK, Helen, and I would raise her and be together; we all made that commitment when I was pregnant. It's been a little trickier maintaining that.

It was tough to make sure that Helen and MK didn't feel replaced by Nora, seeing that Nora was now my permanent partner and new mom in a relationship to Kellen. They needed to know they weren't going to become insignificant. I don't think it's true in other families, either, that when somebody remarries or becomes involved with somebody new other relationships just fall off the face of the earth. It's been somewhat hard for Helen and Nora to adjust to each other.

Nora: They'd been living together since Kellen was six months. When I moved in, I got the whole family!

Nina: We had a bunch of different responses to our wedding announcement. Some were positive, some people wouldn't come if you paid them, some couldn't come but sent a gift to show they supported us. My family didn't respond at all. My sister wrote and said, "This is my last chance to try to talk you out of being a lesbian." I'd been a lesbian for fifteen years before this relationship, and she'd known all my lovers, but to her this meant the final commitment to lesbianism rather than to a particular person.

Nora's father couldn't understand why we would want to do something "so traditional and oppressive." He said he thought she was a feminist. It was wild. He wouldn't come to our wedding. But then he wanted us to come to her brother's wedding the following year. Three of Kellen's friends came to the wedding, even one whose mother is Fundamentalist Christian.

Kellen: And she came anyway.

Nina: She's a good friend. The mother doesn't support the idea of any validation of our relationship because she sees us as a threat to the family, which is interesting, because the reason we did this is for family support, for structure.

Nora: The friend who was my witness had definite problems with it. This was very patriarchal to her, not an okay thing to do. But she agreed to be a witness because she loves us both.

Nina: I had built a community of people who support nonmonogamy. A lot of my friends were used to seeing me in a nonmonogamous context, and the fact that I was settling down and making a commitment upset them. When you turn around after eight years and all your community still supports a nonmonogamous life-style, they all flip on you at once.

Nora: We were married by a gay rabbi in a temple. The ceremony included a combination of Jewish and Native-American rituals. Before anyone arrived, we smudged the temple. We walked around the temple with smoking, burned sweet grass to cleanse the area. The rituals in our ceremony were lighting candles together and drinking from a Navaho wedding vase, which has two spouts to sip from. Then we went under the *chuppah* [the traditional Jewish wedding canopy, which symbolizes the home]. We had two witnesses, a close friend of Nina's and one of my best friends. Kellen was our flower girl.

Kellen: I was the only one in the whole ceremony who was wearing a dress!

Nora: That's true. Some guests wore dresses, but no one else in the ceremony did. We wore beige suede pants and ivory-colored silk blouses and corsages. Kellen's dress was white and long, with blue bows.

We wrote our own ceremony with our rabbi. We had six meetings with him over four months in which we would sit and talk about who we are and what we wanted. He gave us three different ceremonies to choose from. One was a very religious ceremony, one was sort of interfaith, and one was Reform. We took all three, pulled out what we wanted, and created our own ceremony.

Our rabbi gave a monologue about who we are and what we were doing and how important it is to make commitments and have the support of people in your life witnessing and partaking in that commitment.

Nina: We had a *ketubah* [the traditional Jewish wedding document]. One side is written in Hebrew, which our rabbi changed for us so it took out the things that didn't apply to us as women, and he wrote in our names and the date in Hebrew. The other side is in English. We had the *ketubah* signed and witnessed, and we have it framed and hung over our wedding altar.

We asked people not to bring gifts unless they wanted to bring something for the wedding altar, things that meant something to them. We did ask people to bring food for the reception. There was an incredible spread. A friend who used to be a caterer did a wonderful job helping set everything up. We had a wedding cake, and dance tapes.

Nora: I'm a romantic. I always knew I was going to get married, but I didn't know it would be to a woman. For me this was a very political thing to do. You can't be more "out" about who you are and about wanting your relationship considered valid in society than to get married.

The marriage hasn't changed how out I am. I'm out to anyone bold enough to ask if I'm a lesbian. If people notice my ring and refer to my husband, I correct them by simply saying "my part-ner." Nina's and Kellen's pictures are on my desk at work.

Nina: We've made a few changes since we've been married as far as handling legal issues. For custody issues in the event of my death, an attorney suggested that we establish in as many ways as we can that we are a couple. So, we joined our checking ac-counts, we buy things in common, we plan to buy a house, we have arranged power of attorney for serious health matters. We did that probably a year after we were married. Nora's on Medi-Cal because she can't get on my insurance from work. They wouldn't even let me pay for it. Now the state ends up paying for it.

Since we've married, I take our relationship and the conse-quences of my behavior more seriously. Before we got married, people asked whether we thought this would keep us together, and I said I don't think an agreement keeps you together, I think it sets a tone for what kinds of agreements you're willing to make. It was very scary for me to make that kind of solid commitment to somebody. Was I ready to say in front of fifty people that I am going to try very, very hard to stay with this woman? In front of my friends, who are not of this tradition, that I am going to be monogamous? It's much easier to just live with someone and say, Okay, we're together as long as we're together, as long as it feels good. There's a lot more room to get out of it.

Nora: Whenever you make a big commitment like this you always wonder if you're going to be able to do it, if you're setting your-self up to fail. All your doubts come up—is this the right person? Nina had a fever that day—I mean, we were stressed out! But it felt good, too. Having done it, I feel more relaxed. I don't worry as much as I did the first year and a half of our relationship about whether we'll stay together or whether she would be tempted by someone else. Whatever anyone says, you get up in front of fifty people and it's real hard to back down. You break up and there are all these people who knew what this relationship meant to you—it's real different.

Financially and emotionally, it's gotten more complicated, which is as it should be if you're a family. Straight married couples set up a financial being together; if they break up they have a lot to deal with, and so will we if that should ever happen — let's hope it doesn't. You have to push past your fear. It's easier to do knowing that someone is committed to the relationship and isn't going to turn around and leave when it gets hard, and it does get hard. Long-term monogamous relationships are a lot of work. And there's a lot of joy in it, too.

Nina: I think that we carry a certain sense of hope for our friends and for people who want to see that there is such a thing as long-term relationships in the lesbian community, that relationships can stand up under all the social pressure. Our friends want us to make it. Maybe that's because they were part of that beginning ritual. When we're unhappy, we can go to our friends and tell them we're having a hard time and they say, "Let's work this out. Don't quit." They want us to get through hard times.

Nora: Before we got married, friends asked why we wanted people to be there. To me, you have as many people as possible join a ritual to add their energy and affirm what the ritual is about. The rabbi talked about how part of what we were doing was making a statement of hope, optimism, self-affirmation, and affirmation of ourselves as a couple. We asked people there to bring that affirmation to life.

Two Years Later

Nora: A year before the first interview, I'd miscarried a child at six months. The following year, I got pregnant and miscarried a few days after I found out I was pregnant. This year, we've managed to stay pregnant! The baby is due in two months.

We put an ad for a donor in a gay/lesbian paper, basically asking for somebody who was willing to do this but who didn't want to be a parent. We found someone who fit that bill really well, a gay man who's seen a lot of death, who's lost a lot of friends. It was very altruistic; it was about wanting to do something about life. So, we'd drive over there, pick it up and inseminate. It took me five times over six months. It was scary, because of my history. This last trimester psychologically has been better because I've gotten past twenty-three weeks and it's a great relief.

The first year, I'm going to be more responsible for the child, but things will even out. It won't be like "This is Nora's kid," that kind of thing. Things will even out as Nina becomes more available and I'm less available, because I'm going to go back to work part-time in six months. And I'll be breast-feeding. It used to be that I'd take Kellen to school in the morning and Nina would pick her up. Now I take her to school, pick her up, take her home. I spend more time with her because I'm not working.

I had to go back on Medi-Cal in the middle of my pregnancy because I lost my job. To make life simple, I had to get off Nina's accounts. It's a rigmarole you have to go through over and over again. It's a real drag.

Nina: We registered as domestic partners the day it started, on Valentine's Day. One of our reasons for doing that is that I'm a veteran, and there was a rumor that vets and health-care professionals were at risk of being called up if they decided to reinstate the draft [during the Persian Gulf War]. When they sign people up they ask if you've ever had homosexual tendencies. If you say yes, they'll ignore it if they need people. We figured they couldn't ignore it if we registered as domestic partners because it would be a legal document that could serve as evidence. I know the military, and I had no doubt they would take a lesbian during a war and then, after the war, kick her out. So we went down and did it. It's the only form of legal recognition of any sort we have; it's the first in-road into legal rights.

Nora: Registering was a political statement for us, whatever we can do to keep the issue in the foreground.

Nina: It's amazing how little has changed in the last two years. In a family-therapy session recently, Kellen said exactly what she said two years ago — that it was originally really hard for her to accept

Nora because other people had come and gone before, and after we'd gotten married she realized Nora wasn't going to leave and she was going to have to work out her issues with accepting Nora. Kids change their opinions, but nothing has changed there.

Nora: My parents live in Israel and had never met Nina or Kellen until a couple of years ago, when they visited. Since then, they've been much warmer. They had basically ignored Nina's and Kellen's existence before they met them, and, after that, they've changed a lot, at least my mother has. She treats Kellen as a grandchild, sends her presents and talks to her on the phone occasionally, signs postcards "Grandma." They sent Nina a birthday present last year.

Nina: Helen plans to retire in a few years, when she's around seventy, and go live on her ranch up north.

Nora: Helen recognizes that this second child will be Kellen's sibling and she'll need to treat this child equally. The attachment will occur naturally the way attachments do, but she doesn't see herself making a lifetime commitment to this child because she knows she's going to be leaving eventually. When she moves away, Kellen will be fifteen. She sees them as being able to continue their relationship living separately; she doesn't see that happening with a five-year-old. We'll go up and visit, and Helen will come down occasionally; it's not like she'll just completely drop out of this baby's life.

Nina: Both MK and Helen see Kellen and this baby as inseparable. If anything ever happened to me and Nora, both kids would go to whoever was going to be the guardian mother.

Nora: There will be provisions in the will for Nina having custody if something were to happen to me. If anybody were to contest the will, that would cut them out of it automatically.

Nina: We still keep our wedding altar. We have things that we used from the ceremony, our Navaho vase, crystals we were given, pictures from that time, a copy of our invitation, some other family photos, a ritual rattle we received as a present. We add things to it, gifts that are special to us.

We celebrate two anniversaries, from when we got together and when we got married. We haven't really decided which is more important. This year was our fifth anniversary. I took her some flowers and chocolate and a card. We celebrate our wedding anniversary alone, often with a weekend away, but we usually celebrate the anniversary of our meeting together with Kellen, since that was a new and important time for all of us.

Editor's Note: In August 1991, Nora gave birth to a healthy boy, Ethan Andrew.

14

Thomas F. Coleman and Michael A. Vasquez

Los Angeles, California

---

*If we want support, we have to be visible. We have to
be who we are in the mainstream of society and participate
as gay people.*

Thomas, forty-three, and Michael, forty-two, have been together since 1980. Their ceremony, in 1981, was held on a
ship in international waters to symbolize that same-sex marriage is
not recognized legally in any state. Thomas is an attorney, professor at USC Law Center, and executive director of the Family
Diversity Project. Michael, a California native, is administrative assistant at the Family Diversity Project. Although the couple had an
elaborate wedding ceremony, Thomas is opposed to a focus on legalizing same-sex marriage.

❧

Thomas

Michael and I went through dating and courtship, and then we
decided on marriage. We were both raised Catholic, and it's kind of
a natural thing to do, to get married. We also felt that a lot of the
success of relationships is having a support system.

When we decided to make a lifetime commitment to each other,
we had to select our vows and then decide how we would go about
formalizing our commitment. We didn't want to plug in to tradi-

Thomas and Michael on their wedding day

tional vows. We wanted what we felt would make our relationship satisfying for our lives. So we decided on a lifetime context, on vows of honesty, togetherness, emotional and financial support of each other, and fidelity. Fidelity was the one that we added at the end. We struggled with that one a little bit. Do we need to, do we not need to? We decided that monogamy was important for us. We didn't think our relationship would last if we were to get involved with other people.

The person we selected to officiate happens to be a Catholic theologian, but the ceremony wasn't in the context of a particular religion. He helped us clarify our vows and put together the ceremony we wanted.

We invited our families and some extended blood relatives. Michael invited a lot of his extended family, and many of them came. A lot of my family lives out of state, so many of them couldn't come. But two brothers did, and my mom and dad.

At first my dad wasn't going to come, and that bothered me. As we were getting closer to the date, I thought, Something's gotta give, this doesn't feel right. Someone suggested that I tell him how important it is to me, so I went ahead and called him. I told him, "I really want you to be there, Dad. I can't imagine you missing the wedding of any of your children. I can imagine you being uncomfortable with homosexuality, but I can't imagine you not being at my wedding." And he said, "Okay. I'll be there."

The ceremony was held in Long Beach. When we thought about it, we realized that there's no nation on the planet where we could go to have our relationship recognized in a same-sex marriage. And then, bingo, came our theme: "Recognized by No Nation, Married in International Waters."

We chartered a three-decker Catalina Island boat, taking advantage of the fact that the United States had not entered into an agreement yet as to where the territorial limits were. We declared that they were the three-mile limit, and we went three miles out to get "married."

Our invitations were framable posters with a picture of a big art-deco steamship and a little tugboat in front of it which read

"Recognized by No Nation, Married in International Waters" and had our names and the date. The invitations were sent in a poster mailer.

We had an eighteen-piece swing band, which happened to be a gay band. We figured that style of music would help some of the older people feel more comfortable as well as being romantic. I remember my dad trying to teach me how to dance to some of this music. That is a special memory.

We hired a limousine to take us down to the dock. While the boat was prepared after its return from the island and people were decorating it, we waited in the limousine. We arranged it so that before each person got on the boat, they received a carnation to keep until a certain part in the ceremony. People were up on the side of the boat, waving the flowers. There were about three hundred people all cheering for us!

We didn't start the ceremony until we passed the three-mile limit. And it got very scary, because after we got out from the breakwater area it became choppy. Really choppy. You could hear noise from the lower deck, people were holding onto things.

We both dressed in white tuxedos. A friend of Michael's, a woman, was our ring bearer, and we had ushers, friends of ours. The ushers led our parents to seats where they would be able to see our faces. The guests were seated around us in a semicircle. Michael and I faced each other, with the officiator off to the side a little. The two best men each had a lei draped over a shoulder, big, fat leis, four inches thick, with three hundred red and white carnations on each. At a particular point in the ceremony, they were used as well. A 1920s guy and girl group sang while everything was getting set up. Meanwhile, the boat was rocking wildly back and forth.

Then the officiator came up, and here is all this noise and everything, and everyone is wondering if we're going to go ahead with the ceremony in all this turmoil. He made the announcement, "The ceremony is going to begin. It's time for everyone to get calmed down." And somehow, mysteriously, everything suddenly calmed down — including the sea.

He said a few words about marriage and then, before we exchanged vows, instead of asking if anyone objects to this union, we asked that anyone who wanted to affirm this union come forward to the bouquet stand nearest their part of the boat and place their carnation. Out of that, several bouquets of flowers were created. Then our best men transferred the leis to our shoulders. We exchanged our vows and then exchanged our rings — simple gold bands. We took our lei and placed it around the other's neck, and we finished the ceremony. After that, we went out to the back of the boat on the top deck to be alone for a few minutes, and we took our leis — we didn't want to part with them, they were so pretty — but we threw them together into the sea. They just happened to land side by side as they floated away. We talked about how happy we were and how beautifully everything had gone. It was mostly just being together and beaming, and kissing and hugging.

There was music and dancing for the next few hours — four hours went so fast. The limousine was outside, ready to take us to the *Queen Mary*, where we spent our honeymoon night. Just before we left, Michael's dad came to the window to say goodbye. Michael rolled the window down, and his dad gave us a bottle of champagne. The two of them kissed. Fortunately, the photographer was there to get that. It was just so beautiful, the love between them.

Since the wedding, our family relationships have become closer. The family could share another dimension of our lives and have a label for it other than "roommate" or "friends," or whatever name people give to relationships when you don't define them yourselves. Almost all family members treat us as sons-in-law. There are only a couple of in-laws who seem to have trouble thinking of it as a marriage. Terminology is always difficult. We just don't have the right words.

A bonding has definitely occurred with the nieces and nephews. We don't lie. The kids are growing up, they're asking questions, like why do we have a ring. I don't care what the parents have told them. When they're six or seven years old, we tell them we're married to each other. Michael says we're honeys. And they say, "Naw, naw!" and snicker a little bit, and then the next time, it's not an issue, because we've been honest with them.

In referring to Michael, I use the term "spouse." I suppose being technical-minded as I am I would feel more comfortable saying "husband," but I don't want to perpetuate gender stereotyping. In public, I have to decide all the time whether to correct people if they assume I have a wife, or just let it go by. It depends on how much time I want to spend with the person. It's gotten me into some long discussions on the Bible, but generally, if I have the time, I'll correct the misperception. I'll affirmatively disclose it by using the term "spouse" and then a couple of sentences later, use the term "he." I try to say it in the least offensive way possible while still being truthful.

We've gone so far as to have our cemetery plot picked out. We can even see it from our house. We're so into life and the spiritual dimensions of our lives, it doesn't create an ugly symbolism. We want the ceremony when one of us dies to be as beautiful, thoughtful, and meaningful as our wedding ceremony.

❧

Michael

The card read, "Finding you, I found love too. And a life that's beautiful, and a world all new." And inside: "Michael, I love you. I am committed to you. I want to marry you. If you accept my proposal, I'll be the happiest man in the whole world. Your honey, Tom."

When Tom proposed to me, I was very excited. I knew that someday I would fall in love, and that would be the person I would spend my life with. I hadn't thought about going through the whole ritual process, as we eventually did. Years ago, I didn't think I would get married or have a ceremony. It was like a dream come true.

Having a ceremony shows the public that two people, regardless of their sexual orientation, can make a life commitment to each other. I have the same feelings that my siblings have for their spouses. I felt that commiting to this relationship was just as important as a heterosexual marriage.

We moved in together after a few months of commuting between Oxnard, where I lived, and Los Angeles, where Tom was living. Our courtship lasted about a year and a half.

It was exciting telling my family about the wedding. My parents were there, my sister and two brothers. They all were very supportive. They welcomed the event with open arms.

I remember something that touched me very much during the ceremony, when we exchanged rings. My side of the family was seated behind Tom and his was behind me. When Tom put my ring on my finger, I recall looking at my dad, and I saw a tear rolling down his cheek. And then he smiled. He knew I was looking at him, I caught him out of the glance of my eyes. That was really touching because, in the Spanish culture, there's so much of that macho thing. Latin men have to be strong, you have your wife and your kids, the whole stereotype. But my family, speaking for most of them, is not like that.

My parents were accepting of me as gay since I was about seven or eight years old. I knew that I was gay even then, and my parents and brothers knew, because one weekend I'd play baseball and football with my brothers, and the next weekend play Barbie dolls with my cousin, stuff like that. My parents didn't discourage it. They knew I liked dolls and feminine things as well as the masculine things. They saw it as my choosing, and allowed me to be myself, and I really thank them for that. If my father had wanted me to be Mr. Macho, I don't know where I'd be right now.

Within the family, Tom's considered a son. But during introductions, my mom will call Tom "a friend of the family." I asked her once about it, and she said she does it to avoid conflicts, or conversations. She isn't sure what certain individuals in her circle would think and she'd rather be quiet about it. I would think she'd be proud and introduce him as her son, but she doesn't. My dad is the same. They're proud and they respect Tom and love him like a son, but in public, if anyone asks who Tom is, they call him a friend of the family. Nieces and nephews on both sides of the family refer to us as "uncle." Cards come to us as "Uncle Tom" and "Uncle Mike." When I visit my family, the nieces and nephews come running out, "Uncle Tom, Uncle Tom!" They like him better than they like me!

I introduce Tom by the name I call him: my honey. I don't usually say "this is my spouse" or "this is my lover," I just say "this is my honey." I think I picked that up from my parents, especially my mom. I've rarely heard her say "this is my husband," unless it's at the doctor or something. When Tom's mother sends birthday cards, she always signs "Love, Mom." On a couple of occasions, she would refer to herself as "mom" when she called the house.

On forms, I check off "single," since we aren't recognized or legally married. I can't put down "married," because then I'm required to write the spouse's name and maiden name. In the beginning, I was more of a fighter, and I told Tom I wanted to check off "married." But Tom pointed out that since it's not legal, it doesn't mean anything.

We talk about having children. I've always wanted to adopt a child, more so than Tom. We've had discussions about the responsibilities, the commitment, changing my personal program as far as what I like to do at night, because it would be a full-time responsibility. And then the questions: Do you adopt a child that's four years old, or ten years old? All these questions started popping up. For now, it's on hold. I don't want to rule it out, because I love children. We're just waiting to see where our life is in another five or even ten years, and at that time, we'll see if we're seriously ready to change our life-styles and commit to raising a child. The reason it's on hold — coming from a large family, there are always problems and crises, and we have friends who also come to me with their problems and they want my suggestions. So I thought, why have any children, they're all my children. There's no point in having a child right now.

We have wills and powers of attorney, but no relationship contracts. As far as finances go, we share everything. Our whole household, our whole life together, is one. It's all ours.

If marriage was legalized, I think we'd probably have another ceremony. I don't know what type it would be. Some couples go back and do their vows again. I think I'd do something like that, but I wouldn't change what we did at the beginning. That was our personal ceremony.

For our tenth anniversary, we haven't talked about it yet, but I'd like to have a little celebration at our house. I think it'd be great to get a big boat, tie a little tugboat on with a motorized thing, and float it in the pool with flowers and candles, because the boat is our symbol.

We don't have many conflicts. Basically, we'll sit down and share our thoughts and feelings and try to brainstorm together to try to see how we can resolve it. It's never been like "you go into one room and I'll go into the other, and goodnight." We won't end the day without a hug and a kiss and saying goodnight. Because that makes it complete. You never know if you'll fall asleep and might not wake up, or who knows what. It feels good to know that your honey next to you is right there and has said, "I love you, goodnight, sweet dreams." If there was something bothering us, we couldn't go to bed without dealing with it before ending the day.

I feel that if same-sex marriage was legalized, I would be for it. I can understand Tom's political viewpoint and his thoughts, but I'd like to see it happen.

❧

Thomas

I have some philosophical issues with marriage. I struggle, because I believe that discrimination on the basis of marital status is wrong, and I'm fighting that. If we slightly enlarge the preferred class, would we drop out of the movement for equality and forget about civil rights and women's rights because we would then get the goodies? The whole notion of rights and benefits for married couples, of rewards and punishments to beat you into submission — you will get married or we will withhold and you'll get paid less — is wrong and discriminatory.

And there are problems with the model. The model is based on the oppression of women by men, historically. You could rape your wife without being prosecuted. Your wife couldn't vote; she had to vote *through* you, so to speak. All the trappings of battery could be done against the female spouse and the law wouldn't do a thing. We don't personally identify with that, obviously, since we're not women, but, vicariously, I understand and empathize with people who feel that way.

I think having people acknowledge the relationship as a family relationship is what we can do now, and make incremental changes. We fit the primary definition of family under existing law, generally speaking: people who reside together with intimacy and mutual interdependence. The secondary definition is husband, wife, and children. The third definition is all blood relatives. So, if we have intimate relationships with interdependence, we are family. Why not build on precedent and not pick a battle if we don't have to? Other people would say, "Fine, that sounds good, but we should be able to make the same mistakes as everybody else, we should have the marriage option open to us, even if we reject it."

Historically, marriage has been a man and a woman. We're bucking hundreds, if not thousands, of years of tradition in Western culture. Second, we're bucking religion, which is so intermingled that we're inviting the other side to pour in millions of dollars to fight us. And I don't know that we have the money or the resources or that it should be a priority now with the other battles and everything else that's going on. If we focus on this, our energy is taken out of the national movement for decriminalization, privacy, employment rights and protections, child-custody rights — we still have those battles. Third, the timing isn't right for it. This country still has twenty-five states that criminalize our relationships. When 70 percent of the public is against it, legalization of marriage is the cart before the horse.

Progress will more likely be made when we reach people on basic gut issues of fairness like inheritance rights and health insurance benefits, things the majority of the public would agree with. Someday, as we move incrementally along and get various rights, the gap will become so small that the average person will say, Why don't we just legalize same-sex marriage, we practically have it now. The name of the game is to narrow that gap, getting the health insurance benefits at work under the theory of pay equity rather than standing firm on gay marriage — now or nothing.

I suppose because religious and social tradition is so ingrained in our society, marriage is something many people aspire to. Public-opinion polls show that most people want to get married. About 90 percent of people aspire to that, almost more than having children. So, as gay people in this society, we're going to have the same feelings, because we're members of society.

And as part of society, we're going to have to stop being separatist. I don't go to a gay church; I go to the neighborhood Catholic church. I don't go to a gay political club; I'm a Democrat, period. It's not that I'm against it, it's that I've done enough of that and I don't feel a need to surround myself exclusively with gay people. I believe it's good as a phase until you can work through your feelings and feel strong and accepted. But by and large, I don't believe in ghettoization. I believe in cross-fertilization of ideas, in coalition building, of going to the neighborhood groups. I encourage people to get out there, because if we want to get support, we have to be visible. We have to be who we are in the mainstream of society and participate as gay people.

Since the gay-rights movement began, there have been shifts in our goals personally and politically. Among my peers, back in the early 1980s, I heard rumors that some people thought our wedding was silly. Through the 1960s and 1970s, it was academic to think about integrating into mainstream society. The focus was on de-criminalization and police harassment. Women were focused on getting custody of their children from previous heterosexual relationships. Artificial insemination wasn't much a part of the scene. Now there's more of a focus on integrating into society because we're starting to gain rights, respect, and recognition. There's more focus on relationships, on family. Though we may have some uniqueness and differences because of our sexual orientation, we have more in common than we previously thought because we were made to feel isolated, different, less than, and so on.

The other day, my best friend (my best man at our wedding) asked me whether I would go through a ceremony if I had it to do all over again. And I said I would; I wouldn't change a thing. The *system* is one I don't agree with, but I did want a ceremony because I do believe in permanent commitments.

The vows we made were very important to me. Besides my relationship with myself, my relationship with Michael is the most important dimension of my life. I've found that if there's ever anything that doesn't seem to be working well in my life, I can usually trace back through the vows and find out why I'm anxious, or unhappy, or whatever it is. I believe in telling the truth, I believe in fulfilling commitments, and I believe that I'll find happiness in that process. If I'm not happy, that probably means that there's some deviation that's occurred, that I'm not in alignment with my vows. I believe that if I'm in alignment with my vows, I will be happy. But I'm willing to go through the rest of my life, if necessary, without having marriage legalized.

15

Ed Swaya and Randy Fitzgerald

Vashon Island, Washington

*This was the first same-sex wedding Dad had done. He
was very pleased that his first was his son's.*

Randy, thirty-one, and Ed, thirty, have been together since
the summer of 1988. Their ceremony, officiated by Randy's
father, was held in 1990 at an outdoor retreat center in central
Oregon. Both are therapists (Randy specializes in male survivors of
incest and sexual abuse), and they share an interest in sea kayak-
ing. Together they facilitate workshops for male couples called
"Loving Men."

Randy: When I came out at twenty-two, part of the process was
grieving the loss of a childhood dream, which included having a
wife and children. Over the years, as I became comfortable being
gay, really liking that I am gay, I started to reclaim the idea that I
could have a marriage.

When I moved in with Ed, we decided to be monogamous.
Around that time, I said I'd like him to marry me. It was a statement of love, and ownership of gay pride, and that I like rituals.

Ed: My long-term relationships prior to this have been with women.
But I'm bisexual, and I'd assumed that when I found the person I
would spend the rest of my life with, I would marry that person. I

Randy and Ed on their wedding day

Randy and Ed talk with Rev. Fitzgerald before the ceremony

had worked through my fear of intimacy and was ready to have a life partner and make a commitment. When Randy and I met, something very magical happened. It became clear to me that not only was I psychologically ready, but Randy was a good person to move on this with.

Randy: I wasn't looking for relationship when we met and wasn't planning on starting a lifelong relationship then, though that lasted about three weeks.

Ed: We had wedding rings made, a gold band that we wear on our left hand. We sent out invitations. We invited guests to stay the night with us at Breitenbush Retreat Center, which is located on a natural hot springs in the old-growth forest of central Oregon. We closed Breitenbush down for the day. People stayed in cabins, then had breakfast and lunch the next day. We invited probably 300 or 400 people, most of whom we wanted to make an announcement to; we didn't expect them all to come. We had probably 125 people.

Randy: My brother and his wife came up from San Diego, my sister and her family came up. My brother, sister, and mother spoke in the wedding. My mother is dying of cancer and initially said she couldn't come; it was a real statement of support that she drove down. And her best friend of fifty years was there.

I invited my extended family and, typical of them, there was a sort of nonresponse. My one surviving grandmother sent a gift. My father was terrific, he did a great job and was very much a part of the emotionality of it all.

Ed: Although my brother and his wife, who live in the area, came to the wedding and were very supportive, the rest of my family is not. My brother was my best man. It took a lot of courage for him to be there, considering the strength of my parents' and other siblings' responses.

I'd come out to them several years earlier as a bisexual man. I was getting involved with a woman at the time, but felt I wanted to tell them I was bisexual. They didn't really respond.

When I first told my parents that I was involved with a man named Randy, my father's response was, "You're a schmuck." It sort of went downhill from there. I got a very clear message from them not to tell my extended family that I was in this relationship. I decided to tell my extended family, which included elderly aunts and uncles, that I was getting married, and I got a pretty positive response.

When I told my parents I was going to get married, they thought it was terrible that I told them, I should have just done it. They knew that Randy's father was going to officiate the wedding, and proceeded to attack Randy's father, saying he's obviously not a real minister because no real minister would ever do that. We're Lebanese/Syrian Orthodox Christians, but their religion wasn't what fueled their feelings. They didn't speak to me anymore about it and really haven't spoken to me since. My brother was really mad at me for having this wedding. He thought I should keep it quiet. My sister didn't respond to the invitation at all.

I consider Randy's parents to be my in-laws. I support Randy very much in the work he's done with his mother's dying.

Randy: We had a group of friends we called the Guardian Angels as our wedding party, people who agreed to support our relationship in the future, possibly as a group if need be. Especially if a divorce is imminent, we'd ask them to come in and do some work with us.

We wore top hats and tuxes with tails, black with burgundy cummerbund and tie. The Guardian Angels didn't wear matching outfits. My dad wore his traditional minister robe and sash.

The pianist played the Beatles song "Here, There and Everywhere" as we began the wedding. My dad led the procession, his brother followed, then my ex-lover Bill and two good friends of ours walked down. Ed and I walked across the grass and down the aisle behind all of them, holding hands.

Ed: We had a bouquet with early fall flowers, picked from the area. We had bowls of water on the altar, which we used to rinse each other's faces as part of our ritual. We poured hot and cold water over our rings as a blessing of them. A lot of the water was from the natural hot springs on the grounds. We talked about the old-growth forest and how we want it saved, talked about the healing nature of Mother Earth and her water, talked about the general philosophy of peace and the community and being vegetarian.

Randy: My father was helpful in keeping the tone of emotionality, humor, grace, and reverence. He brought to life what we'd written about what this marriage meant to us. He also talked about what it was like for him. This was the first same-sex wedding Dad had done. He was very pleased that his first was his son's. He allowed us to cry and had tissues in a little pocket for us. He basically provided the lead-in for us to do our talking and for friends and family to talk to the group.

We wrote our own vows and read and signed them in front of everyone. Dad asked for the entire audience to say "I do" if they support us. We kissed at the end—and Ed's hat went flying off his head! Everybody stood and applauded, and then we had a receiving line with my family and our Guardian Angels.

We had wonderful Thai food for dinner, a three-tiered, deep-chocolate cake, a great marimba band—we laughed and cried all the way through it.

Ed: I think we'll celebrate our wedding anniversary rather than the date we celebrated before the wedding. We'll also have the top tier of our wedding cake made fresh again at Pacific Desserts in Seattle at our one-year anniversary. They give you a little certificate for a free cake at your one-year anniversary.

When we went into the shop to choose the cake, the woman asked which one of us was getting married. We told her *we're* the couple, we're getting married. She just said, "Oh," and went right on.

We registered for gifts at a bridal registry—which we'd like to see called "wedding registry"—and we were treated very well there also. After the woman at the registry asked which one of us was getting married, she apologized! She said, "I'm sorry. Excuse me for assuming that."

Randy: I use the term "partner" because it seems to be the local term, but I find it a little cold, businesslike. I haven't yet gotten comfortable with using terms like "husband" or "spouse." "Husband" is so loaded; it implies there's a wife.

We didn't change our name, but we're going to change it, legally. We want a family name that's ours. We've tried to come up with a combination of our last names, but we're unwilling to accept the other's suggestion, so we're going to come up with something totally new.

Ed: We have durable and financial powers of attorney, wills and living wills, and rights of survivorship on the home we own.

We're going to have a child, possibly as soon as within the next two years. A woman who lives at Breitenbush offered to carry a child if we wanted to. She said she's wanted to give this gift to somebody. She tried working with agencies, but it seemed too impersonal. We were absolutely stunned.

Randy: Basically, she said she was just waiting for the right couple to come along, and we were it.

Ed: She likes the fact that we're two men, because her father wasn't involved in her life and to give a child to two fathers who really want one feels very healing to her. Also, she'll be able to relate to our child as she wishes. She won't make parental decisions, but she'll be able to love that baby without making another woman jealous.

Randy: Ed and I will be full parents and she'll be involved more on the level of an aunt, so the child will know who its mother is.

Ed: We're both planning to inseminate so we can both feel like biological fathers during the pregnancy. We look very different — Randy has blondish red hair and I have darker skin and dark hair, so the father's identity should be pretty obvious once the baby is born.

Randy: Whoever isn't the father this time will be the inseminating father for the next child. I plan to use a syringe. Ed is thinking of inseminating through sexual intercourse.

Ed: Both her partner and Randy would be present for the conception.

I'm not actively having sex with women, but I'm still bisexual. I'm sexually attracted to both men and women. I want a monogamous relationship, and I would do that with either a man or a woman. I'm dealing with my own grieving process around that as I continue my monogamous relationship.

Randy: Ed doesn't want to go into invisibility and state that he's gay when it's not true for him. He's in a gay relationship, and the sex he's been having up until he has sex with this woman is exclusively homosexual sex. But that doesn't determine his orientation.

If marriage was legalized, we would do it for the political statement. I think gays and lesbians have the right to all the legal benefits that come with a marriage license. I'm also in favor of it because, even with all the legal protections we have, Ed's parents can still challenge us in court and we'd have to pay all the legal costs. I have a client who didn't make a will with his partner of twelve years; his partner recently died, and it looks like my client will lose the house and car, which wouldn't have happened if he was with a woman.

Ed: And the adoption issue. We'll be taking on a court case for the nonbiological father to be the adoptive father.

Randy: I'm very in favor of gay marriage. I've never understood why gay men don't think marriage is a good thing to do. It doesn't mean it's inherently bad just because it once was a heterosexual institution.

Ed: After all, there's a possibility we can make that institution healthier.

Randy: I'd like to tell people, if you're thinking of having a wedding, have it! The process of doing the invitations, the rings, the registry, getting tuxes, securing the location, getting the cake, and then a four-hour celebration, was tremendous! Our relationship is stronger because of the wedding. Preparing for it brought up emotional issues we've dealt with that otherwise wouldn't have come up. The rings really work as a symbol of our commitment. It was good before the wedding, and it's only gotten better.

16

Mollie and Morgan Sidhe

Portland, Oregon

---

*To be handfasted at Beltane is to become joined as
one with nature, the earth, and each other, which is
exactly what we wanted.*

Mollie, fifty, and Morgan, thirty-four, were married in a
Wiccen handfasting ceremony one year into their relationship, which began in 1985. (*Wicce* is the practice of early female
spiritual traditions, or witchcraft; *handfast* is an archaic definition of
betrothal.) The couple met at a lesbian s/m support group in Los
Angeles. Mollie, a high priestess, teacher, and European shaman,
has four children, one of whom had a handfasting in which she
officiated. Morgan, a Los Angeles native, is working toward a B.S.
in adult education and plans to teach specially abled adults. The
couple lives with Morgan's two children.

❦

Morgan

As Wiccen traditions differ from each other, so do the meanings
of handfasting differ. Any definitions offered here should be considered mine and shouldn't be construed as speaking for all Wiccens.

Handfasting is simply another word for marriage. The marriage
is made between the two people involved and doesn't require paperwork or approval of a third party.

139

We were handfasted at Beltane, a pagan spring festival which lasts from sundown April 30th to sundown May 1st. It's the planting season, when the seeds saved from last year's harvest are planted in this year's fields with the expectation that something will grow out of it. Beltane was the traditional time for marriage of Celtic people in the pre-Christian era, because it was then that the Goddess in her earth aspect joined with the God to bring forth new life. Couples would join in the festivities, and later slip away from the fires at night, doing what comes naturally to people in love.

Beltane is, therefore, a time of union, when all of nature participates in life and renewal. To be handfasted at Beltane is to become joined as one with nature, the earth, and each other, which is exactly what we wanted.

Handfasting literally means to make the hands fasten together, to join two people together hand in hand. We used colored ribbon to bond ourselves during the ceremony. The ribbons were removed without untying. (That would have constituted an act of divorce.)

It's usually rather solemn, but it does have some humorous outcomes. One couple we know had their hands joined in such a way as to make it very difficult to remove the lacings after the ceremony. This caused a lot of glee among the other members of the wedding party, as the couple had a hard time maneuvering, bound as they were, in order to privately consummate their union.

Wiccen ceremonies call for the cleansing and preparation of a ritual space, the circle, and the blessings of and from the four directions: east, south, west, and north. In our tradition, this means clearing out any negative influences from ourselves and our surroundings. We call upon the elements of air, fire, water, and earth, respectively, to bless us with their presence, to guard against negativity and create harmony and balance. We try, to the best of our ability, to live that way, and we felt it was appropriate that our ceremony reflect that.

Mollie and I made our vows to each other in the front room of her Valentino-style apartment, with its 1930s arched doorways and French doors. My daughters were flower girls, and Mollie's grown children called and sent good wishes and flowers; they live out of state and couldn't be there.

Our altar had been laid out especially for this occasion. I'd gone down to the florist a couple days before and, when they found out what it was for, they loaded me down with flowers. So we not only had a spray of flowers over the altar, but anywhere else they would fit in the house. The basic spray was red and white roses set off by gladiolus. We were decked out in red and white rose garlands twined in purple ribbons, which I made.

We both carried flowers. And, aside from our cloaks, we wore nothing else. That's how we perform rituals in the Wiccen tradition, and we saw no reason to change it for our ceremony. Besides, it's sexy! Everyone else was dressed in either jeans or skirts.

There were eight of us that evening, and all participated. Our Priestesses cast the circle, and we all followed them to each of the four directions. Our officiator then read a piece called "Pan's Invitation."[1] Here is some of it:

> I want you to want me. I want you to forget right and wrong; to be as happy as the beasts, as careless as the flowers and the birds. To live to the depths of your nature as well as to the heights. The Crown of Life is not lodged in the sun; the Wise ones have buried it deeply where the thoughtful will not find it, nor the good, but the Gay ones, the Adventurous ones, the Careless Plungers, they will bring it to the wise and astonish them.
>
> All things are seen in the light — how shall we value that which is easy to see? But the precious things which are hidden, they will be more precious for our search; they will be beautiful with our sorrow; they will be noble because of our desire for them.
>
> Come away with me, Shepherd girl, through the fields, and we will be careless and happy, and we will leave thought to find us when it can, for that is the duty of thought, and it is more anxious to discover us than we are to be found.

Mollie and I wrote our own vows. After the officiators finished, we exchanged those vows, which mainly concerned the type of life we would promise each other. They ended up being somewhat flowery, somewhat serious, and filled with a lot of ironic humor. Part of my vows went:

> On this day we stand in love. We love each other but it doesn't bind. It moves between us like the ocean's heart. I will only give

> what I am so that what is between us becomes strong and power-
> ful. I have given my vow to She who holds the Cup of Life. When
> I have drunk that cup and the sun rises no more, I will walk with
> you in Summerland, under the moon and in the stars.

Mollie said, in part:

> I cannot promise you a future of "happily ever after." I can prom-
> ise you a future shared. That I will always be there for you until
> you go beyond. I promise to share forgiveness, to comfort you
> when you want it and to let you know when I do; to groan at your
> puns; to not snore in your ear; to stay in trouble often enough to
> make it enjoyable. I can't give you the whole world, I can only give
> you mine, while happily sharing yours.

We didn't set any time limits on our relationship. However, the
rings we exchanged have the infinity symbol, an elongated figure
eight, carved on the face. The inside of both rings is inscribed:
"Above and below, together we go." This is an adaptation of a
Wiccen adage. The gold ring worn on the left ring (heart) finger,
the infinity symbol, and the wording inside the rings express our
feelings that this union will last beyond our time together here on
this earth.

Mollie and I were not able to move in together until six weeks
later, and we spent that time discussing how we felt about the
handfasting. We both were very emotional during that time, as well
as having to deal with the usual hassles of work, home, and kids. I
remember thinking that our rite acted as a sort of anchor, or focus,
during a period of upheaval, both emotional and physical.

In going back over our memories, Mollie and I find ourselves
grinning and shaking our heads at the same time. We've had over
five years together, and just about everything we promised each
other has come true, including all the rotten stuff. Looking back, I
think we were fairly realistic about our expectations. Our relationship is still growing along these lines.

The two of us call each other "wife" or "spouse," the latter being
the usual one. All the kids call me "Mom," including Mollie's kids,
who do it rather jokingly. Her children are very close to me in age,

but they're pretty accepting of the relationship. To my two kids, Mollie is "stepmother," "Mom," or "Mollie," depending on the situation. Collectively, they refer to us as their parents, even in school.

Our household is put together much the same as other married couples'. Our incomes are pooled into a joint account and bills are paid from that. Mollie is the financial planner as far as month-to-month accounts are concerned. We have yet to fill out our wills, but we've made out medical powers of attorney that have already proved useful.

Some time before Mollie and I were married, I went through a child-custody case with the state of California. I was very open about my sexuality with all of my attorneys over the four years it took to settle the case. I was eventually successful; I do have the children back. I hired both gay and straight people to work on the case, and I didn't find much difference in the way they handled it. Being open and honest is what got me through the whole thing. It was largely my parenting skills that were considered important, not my sexuality.

I really don't have a position on legalized same-sex marriages. If it was possible for us to claim the tax, survivorship, veterans', Social Security, and pension benefits that heterosexuals have, Mollie and I would sign up like a shot. Other than that, I don't see how third-party recognition would make us any more married than we already are. All the people in our life who count—including ourselves—accept us for who we are, and that's what's important.

Mollie

I didn't believe in marriage for a long, long time, for a couple of reasons. I know very few people who can make a commitment and stick to it. There aren't many people who believe in that kind of honor. You really have to be friends before you are lovers. Usually, if you're lovers first, it's such an intense emotion that it overshadows the friend part of it. It can be done, but it's harder.

The promises in the vows aren't meant to be weapons. They're something of our essence that we're giving—a commitment. I feel very strongly about this because most people cannot do that. They take their vows, they think it's wonderful, but when things start going wrong, when they start feeling antsy, they tend to bolt. They don't look at the commitment they made. How much honor does a person have if they don't live up to a commitment? And you don't keep it grudgingly; you keep it because it's part of your essence.

Morgan and I had been together nine months, and we were having a really good yelling fight in the car in the parking lot behind the bar where we used to go. Out of the clear blue sky, I asked her to marry me. I honestly looked up and said, "Where did that come from?" because I didn't believe in marriage! I know that I'm directed many times by the Goddess, so when something like that happens, I have to follow it because it's so important that it interrupts what I'm doing. We believe in the Goddess, by whatever name—a female force. We also believe in a male force, a God image.

From the time we got together, I found that being with Morgan triggered memories. I am what some would call a medium and an empath. I can pick up emotions. In the past, in other lifetimes, things have happened that have stopped our bonding. We've needed to bond. I think that's probably why I blurted out and asked her to marry me. The ceremony finalized and solidified the foundation. It created the basis of this connection we have together everlasting.

I have officiated at two handfastings. One was for a gay couple, the other was for my son. The handfastings were similar in intent, similar in the bonding of physical, mental, spiritual, astral—all of the elements. What Morgan didn't touch on in her description of the handfasting is the broom, a very ancient pagan symbol. The broom is a cleaning instrument. The circle is swept clean with this ritual broom and then the broom is laid in front of the couple as they state their vows and say what they need to say. The symbol of jumping over the broom is the symbol of starting fresh, starting clean. It doesn't mean that one person becomes the other person or tries to; it means that both people are new in their relationship with each other and they're creating this new relationship, almost like a third entity.

We had drinks after the ceremony, a medieval drink which I make out of honey, mead, cinnamon, cloves, and some other ingredients. The reception was held for us at a gay and lesbian bar in the area, and there were presents and a cake. I actually had a white wedding dress, which my son helped me pay for. I never did have a real wedding dress before. We had a wonderful party.

After that, we spent three days at Big Bear Lake. Any marriage needs that honeymoon ("honey moon" means "sweet month"). It's a time for the couple to have the sweetness of a marriage before they get into the nitty-gritty of work, bills, kids, whatever.

We still have some of the things from our ceremony. We keep the rainbow streamer hanging in our room, and the garlands we wore in our hair. We have a notebook of our memories, with our invitations, the guest list, the poem Morgan wrote for me, our vows, and a note she left me in my apartment before we married.

We always celebrate anniversaries. We celebrate the handfasting anniversary. We go out to dinner, or go in the bedroom and lock the door. I always give her a different kind of a rose. One is made out of silk, one out of china, one of leather, another from sea shells. It's a tradition. Our anniversaries are very important to us because they show us that we've grown, that we've developed, and that it's getting better. I bought a twenty-five-year anniversary candle for us at a card shop. Every year on our anniversary I take it out and we burn it down to the next year. That's very special to us.

I call Morgan my wife, my spouse, my honey. I don't like the word "partner"; it sounds very cold. I don't like "companion"; it sounds like a nurse. My favorite is "spouse," because it means the wedded one. My kids all call her Morgan because they're close to her age (anywhere from two to eight years younger). The grandkids call her Aunt Morgan, or Grandma.

We don't have separate bank accounts. The family's bank account is the family's bank account. We're not gearing our finances or anything else to the possibility that this is not going to work.

Morgan's helped me to be better with money, and I've taught her not to be so scared of it. We're striking a happy medium. It doesn't take that legal paper to make us married. If this country agreed to make same-sex marriage legal, which I doubt will happen, I'm sure Morgan and I would go down and sign the papers and do all that crap, because there are too many financial and legal assets for "legally" married people. But that doesn't make a marriage; that would be our taking advantage of the system. We *are* married.

Morgan believes as I do where commitment is concerned. When she finally gives a commitment, it's lasting. And that's what made our marriage, our handfasting, very solid and very real. We don't have problems as lovers. Yes, we look at women sometimes and drool, but we don't have any thoughts of going out and having a sexual relationship with another woman.

We have had problems. I've had medical problems, we've had financial problems. And because of that, sometimes the friction is really great. And I have an Irish temper; I blow up and then forget it. She's learned how to argue in a positive way. We yell and we fight; I'm not going to say we don't. If people say they don't, they're probably suppressing a lot. But there is no physical abuse whatsoever. The important thing is to not hurt when you're fighting, to avoid saying hurtful, nasty things, and to try to be open.

What's saved us is that we're old enough now to be kids. We have two stuffed animals, Bear and Puppy, and they've become personas. Bear is "Mollie Bear." Puppy is "Bousha Puppy." They go through all kinds of adventures together. It really deflects things, at least until we can get some distance, some perspective, to get back into that persona when we get into a problem. It helps us remember to be joyful and helps us see clearly, as only the young can.

Note

1. James Stephens, *The Crock of Gold* (New York: Macmillan, 1912; reprint, New York: Macmillan, 1960), 45–46.

17

Terry Tibbetts and Don Wright

San Francisco, California

I have the same feeling I had for Don twenty-two years ago,
like I first met him.

Terry, fifty-two, and Don, forty-six, met in 1970 and were married in San Francisco the next year with 450 guests in attendance. They raised a son, now twenty-one. They own and operate a western-apparel shop in the Bay Area.

Terry: We've been together twenty-two years, faithful. I met Donald at a coffee shop and invited him over for dinner. It was our first date. I've still got the flower he gave me that first night, a bottlebrush flower he got in the park and brought me when I was working, before we went to my house.

Don: I came over for dinner, and then I kind of moved in.

Terry: I asked Donald to marry me. I asked him to marry me and he said yes. He went out two weeks later and had an engagement ring made for me. We got matching rings.

I wanted a wedding because I felt that was the way I would get Don. I'd been at a gay wedding before ours, and I said to myself then, Someday I'm going to have a wedding, someday I'm going to meet the right man.

Don and Terry in their western-apparel shop

*Terry and Don during the cake
ceremony at their wedding*

Don: Terry said, Someday I'm going to meet Mr. Wright — and he did!

It wasn't as important to me to have a wedding. Just telling people we were together, we were united, was enough for me. But it was fun. Lots of fun. It was a big step to take in those days. You didn't see a lot of weddings back then. In those days, it wasn't a family-type thing at your house, it was more of a costumey thing. You hardly ever saw two women or two men in tuxedos. One was generally in drag, the other was in tuxedo.

We were engaged six months, from April 5th to October 21st. I handwrote the invitations. I went through Terry's phone book. About 450 people showed up! My boss was the best man, his wife was the ring bearer, and his daughter (who has since come out as a lesbian) was the maid of honor. It was an almost-true-to-life wedding.

Terry: I sent all my family invitations, but of course they didn't come. They thought the world of Don, they loved him to death. But I told them I was getting married in a wedding dress, and they just didn't want to see that.

Don: My family comes from a little town back in Illinois, and they're the type of people who've only heard the word "gay." They don't know what a gay person is. My mother came out to visit a couple years back and met a couple of people she knew were gay, and she loved them. But if she knew I was gay, she would have big problems. I couldn't be out to her for her sake.

Terry: I am God to her. I can do no wrong.

Don: She knows we sleep together.

Terry: She knows we do everything together. But she said to me last time she was here, she said, "If Don is gay, then I want to put him on an island where the people with AIDS and gays all belong. If he's gay, I want to hear it come out of his mouth." And I said, "Well, I won't say."

Don: My mom and one of her sisters have had this argument for fifteen years. My aunt says I'm gay and my mom says I'm not. They've even had a fist fight over this point. I'm not going to create one problem to solve another. Also, it's not their business to talk about it. My sister knows, and she accepts it. But it's not something I want the rest of my family to know; they just couldn't handle it.

So anyway, we used the traditional ceremony and wedding vows, except it was, "Do you take Terry as your lawful loving partner" — not wife or husband. The whole ceremony lasted maybe ten minutes.

Terry: They played "Here Comes the Bride."

Don: Afterward, instead of playing the wedding march, "There Goes the Bride," we just played music, like "Oklahoma."

Terry: During the planning, Donald grabs my shoulder one night and says, "Don't I have a say in this wedding too?" I said, "Oh, what do you want?" He said he wanted "Oklahoma" played. That's the only thing that wasn't traditional. People thought it was a little tacky because it was an elegant wedding, but that's what he wanted.

Don: It was different, but then the wedding was different.

We had a mini reception at the house with champagne and cake.

Terry: The cake was gorgeous — fresh orange and yellow flowers.

Don: There was also a bride and groom.

Terry: I thought I didn't want a bride and groom, I wanted flowers.

Don: There was a bride and groom.

Terry: Okay. Well, it was six or seven huge tiers. Someone stole the top cake, so we didn't get to see it for very long. We had gifts, we threw the bouquet, we did the reception line — all just like a straight wedding.

Don: I hadn't seen Terry yet before the wedding. I'd gone out to get my hair permed.

Terry: Oh, he had gorgeous hair and then he went out and got a perm. I was surprised.

I wore a white wedding dress, a Spanish-style dress with lace and lots of pearls. We went into Emporium downtown, went up to the bridal department, and I said we wanted to buy a wedding dress and some bridesmaids' dresses. And she asked, "Who is it for?" I said, "For me." There was a lot of money involved there, so she agreed. She was very nice. They even sent us a thank-you card.

Don: The lady that worked there used to be in the men's department downstairs and she recognized us from there. When we first walked in, she said, "I know you."

Terry: She was a nice person. She said she could lose her job, but she went ahead. I couldn't try the dress on, I couldn't go in a dressing room.

Don: So they had to makeshift a fitting room, just for him.

Terry: I wore everything, the whole shaboom. I wore the garter, the bra — everything. I even used hair remover on my chest. I'm not into dragging, though, I don't like drag. Actually, nobody knew ahead it was a drag wedding.

Don: But that's how it was done in those days, and I wasn't going to wear the dress! My arms are too big.

Terry: And I wanted people to know I was marrying a man. I was very proud of Don. I had lots of friends, and all we used to say was, "I want a husband, I want a husband." But we do not have roles in our relationship, there's not a wife or a husband; we're lovers.

Don: We were up real late the night before the wedding. We hand-dyed the carnations, made the boutonnieres for the wedding party. We had twelve people at our house dyeing flowers. Terry's favorite color was blue, so we dyed all the tips blue.

Terry: It was something to see. We had a four-story house with a winding stairway, a parquet floor. We walked up the stairway. Don waited at the top of the staircase. And when he pulled up my veil, I had tears in my eyes I was so happy. It was really hard for me not to cry. The guests were up the stairs in the dining room and other rooms. We had lesbians, we had straights, we had gays, we had prostitutes, we had everybody. I like everybody.

Don: The officiator, who was with the MCC, was the first reverend to come out and say he was gay. He was with a Baptist church, but he was asked to leave.

Terry: I told the minister we didn't want to have it in a church because I have family, Don has family. We had to be very careful.

Don: In those days, you could lose your job if people knew you were gay. So we kept the wedding very private in our home.

Terry: The news was there — Channel 4, Channel 7 — but we would not allow them to photograph us. We had a hard time getting into the limo. I told them we have nothing to say. They hit on us again when we got to the hotel. They wanted to know was I a sex change. I said, "I have nothing to say. This is a private wedding."

Don: A neighbor had seen the limousines parked up and down the street, so he called the press and they wanted to know, Well, who is this getting married? So they came on down. We told them we couldn't allow any names to be used in the news. In those days, if you said no to the press, they took it for no, they wouldn't just photograph you and say okay, we won't use your name.

We tied the wedding in with the Beaux Arts ball, the Halloween ball which they held on October 21st that year. We had the reception at the ball. There were three thousand people at the reception!

We went back to the ball the next year for our anniversary, and Terry wore the dress again. We were written up in the local gay papers. We had write-ups about our rings, our ceremony.

The next morning, we went on a honeymoon. On the way, we stopped in Livermore to have breakfast. I thought, Why are all these people looking at us? We look like everyone else. Well, it turned out, we'd gotten up in a real hurry and Terry still had some eye makeup on. It was pretty funny.

Terry: We love each other a lot. We've been through a lot, but we love each other just the same. If something bothers us, we talk about it.

Don: We've known each other long enough where if I'm telling him a fib, he's going to know. I can't lie to him.

Terry: He can't lie. I know when he's telling me a story about anything.

Don: In this business, we're constantly in close contact. We spend ten hours a day together and then spend the night together. We're together sometimes twenty-four hours a day. It really doesn't bother me at all, until he starts eating my M&Ms!

Terry: The only problem I have is when the younger guys come into the store and say something about Don coming on to them. I go to Don and tell him I don't think it's true, but I have to hear it from you. We don't go out on each other. That was something we both agreed on before the wedding.

Don: We have friends that have other partners, or they both have the same partner, and we haven't seen any of them work out. There's too many problems that lead to lying and cheating and too many risks involved.

We've built up trust. If Terry's going shopping at Emporium, he doesn't come back with a bag from Macy's. If I say I'm going to spend a day at the stables shoveling horseshit, I'm at the stables. If he needs to get hold of me, I'll be there. It's not like I say I'm going to be at the stables, but I'm really going to go pick somebody up. We're not deceitful.

Terry: In the early years, a lot of people respected our relationship, but we also lost a lot of friends because of it.

Don: They were bar friends, they were hobnobbing friends . . . they weren't real friends. We're real selective about the friends because for the past twenty years we've had a child at home. We didn't make a big thing about being gay with the child. He knew, he understood it, but it wasn't like we'd bring a lot of gay friends over and have a party. We would associate with our friends away from home.

Terry: We share everything. When Donald moved in, everything was his too. We never put names on anything. We own the business, we own our home, our cars. We have wills, powers of attorney. The only thing we didn't have was a child. I wanted a child so badly. And it was pure luck that we got our son. He came to us through a member of my family. We got legal custody. It was very difficult. We raised our son with me more the mother role and Don the father role. Don went with our son to school when he needed to go in for anything, I was more the problem-solver.

Don: Twenty years ago it was difficult for one man to get custody of a child, let alone two men. I wasn't going to have the mother

saying she wanted the child back after all the love and the invest-
ment, the time and everything else.

Terry: We're very close with our son. He calls me "pop" and he
calls Don "uncle" or "old man." All of his friends call me the
"stepfather." He's never seen us fight. We never fight in front
of him.

Don: He hasn't seen us kissing. These are things that just aren't
important in front of children.

Terry: We're talking about being grandparents now. That's what
we want.

Don: I'm not in any hurry to have grandchildren.

Terry: I want grandchildren. I want a granddaughter and Don
wants a grandson.

Don: Only if he likes horses!

We celebrate our anniversaries every year. We celebrate April
5th, the day we gave each other the engagement ring, and the
21st of October, the day we got married. It's like the twelve days
of Christmas. We celebrate from April 5th to October 21st.

We didn't register as domestic partners with the city. It may be
beneficial for the people who need it, but it isn't something Terry
and I need. I remember the days where, if you were arrested for a
"sexual offense," you had to register as a homosexual. I don't
think it's any of the state or the federal government's business to
know we're gay. I don't think we should be listed under "g" for
gay and "s" for straight. I'm not saying the government is plotting
to put us on a list, I just don't feel it's their business. And I
wouldn't do anything different if marriage was made legal. If that
was the case, we might as well go down to city hall and register
right now.

Terry: I feel differently about it, We would have more laws protect-
ing us if something were to happen.

Don: We've seen the community change a lot in San Francisco over
the last ten years. There are a lot more long-term relationships,
and a lot more weddings. I think with the emotional problems
going around, people are taking their relationships more seriously
and making them last longer. One way of making them last longer

is to form an agreement or a bond between the two people. And things between gay men and lesbians have really changed. Ten years ago a woman wouldn't go into a gay man's bar, and twenty years ago a man wouldn't go into a woman's bar.

Now that I'm Mr. San Francisco Cowboy — my new title — that's one of my obligations. (Mr. San Francisco Cowboy is president of a cowboy association, responsible for handling and raising funds for whatever their cause is. Mine is visiting nurses and the AIDS emergency fund.) One of the female judge's questions was what would I do to unite gay men and women. I said I didn't know if I could answer that question, who could? All I could do was make the invitation, and it would be up to the people to decide whether or not they're going to get together. I was just elected two weeks ago, so I have nearly a year ahead.

Terry: I signed him up.

Don: Another question they asked was whether being Mr. San Francisco Cowboy would interfere with my being married, and I said no. Everywhere I go now, I'm introduced as Mr. San Francisco Cowboy and his partner of twenty-two years, Terry.

Terry: We're going to have another wedding on our twenty-fifth wedding anniversary. I want to do it so we can do our vows again. We want to show people what we have. Our son will definitely be in the wedding. It will be another formal wedding, but not drag. We'll wear white tuxes. It'll be traditional.

Don: His version of traditional means say the vows, exchange rings, kiss, and live happily ever after. My version is probably a little different. We may change it a little bit and write our own vows this time.

A big wedding now wouldn't be so important because we're more secure than we were in those days. Back then, we were saying this is who we are and this is what we're going to do. We don't need to do that anymore. I'm more concerned about showing each other what we have, and the rest of the world can acknowledge it or turn their back or do what they want to do.

Terry: I want to do it because I want to show that there are two people who truly love each other and they're still together. People are amazed all the time when they hear we've been together twenty-two years. They always want to know how we did it.

Don: My answer is, It hasn't been all that easy.

Terry: And I say I love him and we've had a lot of ups and downs.

Don: The way we get through the downs is, if it doesn't work to-day, tomorrow it might. If it doesn't work tomorrow, we'll try something else, we'll try again.

Terry: Don's the most unusual person I've ever known. He's very understanding about anything. He's much easier to talk to and share anything with than anyone I've known.

Don: The basis of a relationship is communication. If you don't talk about it, you're not going to get anywhere.

Terry: It's true. Because I'm a person who'll clam up. And he'll say, Come on, let's talk. Donald makes me more — God, I feel like I should have a trophy for him! — but really, he's so easygoing, he's so easy to talk to. In twenty-two years, we've only had two real fights. That's saying a lot. When people ask me how we've made it work for so long, I usually say to them that we talk everything out and that we trust each other. That's the most important thing, trust.

Don: I've seen a lot of people's relationships go sour because one person's pride was too much to say, "What did you mean by that?" or "I'm sorry I said that." That's what I told Terry years ago. If you walk out the door one time, if you can just say "The hell with it" and leave, that means you wanted to do that, and basically, that's it. If you're going to make a commitment, then it's time to grow up and live up to the commitment. If people say to hell with it, then they didn't have a relationship to begin with, or at least they don't want to make it work.

This has been a twenty-four-hour thing for twenty-two years. I like to spend time with Terry when we have time off from work. Generally, if we have the same days off, we'll go down to Terry's brother's house, and Terry'll visit with him while I go down and work with the horses. We'll have dinner together.

Terry: And I have the same feeling I had for Don twenty-two years ago, like I first met him.

18

Diane Bernstein and Andrea Yates

Los Angeles, California

---

*It was a really nice feature I didn't expect, the coming out over
and over, the assumption that there was a groom, the questions
about "him," and my correcting it. And always the decision:
Do I say something?*

Together five years, Andrea, thirty-eight, and Diane, thirty-
four, were married three years into their relationship. Diane
is a psychiatric social worker and has a part-time private practice.
Andrea works for the police department and operates a private tax-
accounting and bookkeeping business. Theirs was a mostly traditional Jewish ceremony, held in the backyard of Diane's parents'
home.

❧

Diane: Andie and I first met in 1981, when we were both involved
with someone else. When we met again a few years later, we were
both single for the first time since we'd known each other. We
didn't have a true commitment to each other until about a year
and a half into the relationship.

We started thinking seriously about getting married a couple of
years ago, at my brother's wedding. It was hard being there because Andie and I had been together longer than he and our sister-in-law had been, and here they were with all this hoopla. I felt
like this would be nice for us, too.

Andrea and Diane stand under the traditional Jewish wedding canopy during their ceremony, held in the Bernstein family's backyard

Since I was little I've thought that I'd get married when I grew up. Andie has a lot more difficulty with the concept of forever and ever. I felt that if she was willing to do this, it would really say something to me. Also, we're very close to our families. I saw that there's a lot of attention and support given to the couples in our families, and I wanted us to have that too.

Andrea: Getting married was mainly something Diane wanted to do. I'd never thought about it before. I never really pictured myself being married. But the more support we got for doing it, the more I welcomed it.

Diane: At my brother's reception, both of our aunts and my mother's best friend approached us at different times and asked when were we going to do this. It was the first time an outside person had said anything like that. Not long after, when Andie's stepbrother got married, he and his wife asked when we were going to get married. At that point we knew there was support from our families. That was the beginning of the process.

Later that year, we told my family what we wanted to do. My mother said she'd doubt the seriousness of our relationship if we didn't do it. Then she pulled out a piece of paper and started listing the guests! My father's mother, who is ninety, was the only person in my family who didn't know I am a lesbian. So my mom turned to my dad and said, "Well, dear, how do you feel about inviting your mother? This means you're going to have to tell her." My father doesn't talk to his mother about serious things, but he said, "Sure."

It was really cute — my mother prepared him a speech, and he went to Miami a few days ahead of us on our vacation. When he met us at the airport, the first thing out of his mouth was, "I did it! And I didn't even use the speech!" Grandma said of course she'd be there.

Then we met with Andie's family, and they were all very supportive. All the parents said they'd financially support us. It was very important to me that my parents support our wedding financially just like they'd supported my brother's wedding. Not the dollar amount, but that it was the same gift.

Diane: We planned all year until August. The only sure thing we knew right away was the rabbi we would have. We sent out eighty or ninety invitations. We didn't want to write "daughter of" on the invitations, partly because we have six parents between us, but we also wanted to make it clear that our parents were giving this wedding for us. The invitations read: "Diane and Andrea, along with their parents, invite you to join them in celebration of their commitment" — and then the date, time and place, and reception information.

The wedding was held at my parents' house since they have a wonderful view of the canyon. About sixty-five people came. Family came from all over — aunts, uncles, cousins from New York, Andie's brother from Ohio, everybody.

Andrea: The easiest thing about our wedding was that there was no question it would be a Jewish ceremony. Diane's brother — actually, all our siblings — married non-Jews. This was a piece of cake. My family did have a hard time with the word "wedding," though.

Diane: For some reason, our parents weren't seeing it as a wedding, and we had to get to the bottom of that. My mother kept using the term "commitment ceremony." But the more we said it, the more they became comfortable with it. Once, my dad said "for your party," but he finally stopped referring to it that way.

During preceremony preparations, the rabbi told us there were several choices for the style of the ceremony. We could prepare our own, follow a traditional outline and add whatever we want, or just follow the basic outline. Since neither of us is very creative as far as writing goes, we decided to stay with the basic outline.

We had the *ketubah* [the traditional wedding document] ceremony in the den before the main ceremony. Our mothers hold it up and the rabbi does a little spiel and then they present it to us.

We both wore above-the-knee, fun dresses. We'd each bought a special dress that we really loved, something fancy. I wanted something with beads; Andie's was silk. It was just a coincidence that the patterns were so similar. We had rings made, which we designed; they're very similar to each other.

We walked in together, without our parents. The *chuppah* [wedding canopy] holders were two good friends, my brother and Andrea's stepfather — family who were very close to us. There was the opening prayer and the blessing over the wine. Then our fathers came up and poured a glass of wine. For the seven blessings, the four *chuppah* holders and three guests each read a blessing; that's how we brought our families into it. Then the cantor sang and a friend from the temple choir joined for a duet.

After that, the rabbi said something sort of humorous and personal about us, which she wrote after meeting with us four times before the wedding. She read the *ketubah,* and we did the ceremonial sipping of the wine and breaking of the glass. We each broke a glass instead of just one of us doing it, because we think of it as a very sexist tradition — the man breaks the glass and everybody claps as if he's just won something. We broke the glasses holding hands to show that we were doing it together. Then the rabbi said, "I pronounce you lifetime partners." The pianist played while we did a receiving line, and then we went to the reception area and had cocktails.

We picked and chose from traditions. We didn't have a wedding cake — we had pastries from a bakery we like. We had gotten corsages and boutonnieres for our parents and ushers, but we didn't want to hold a bouquet, so there was no throwing of a bouquet and there was no garter, none of that. We did have a first dance, though, a country-western song, "I'm Going to Love You Forever," sung by Randy Travis. We also did the chair dance, the tradition where you put the bride up in a chair and dance. They put us both up in a chair. I fell out of mine.

There was a real diversity of people at our wedding — ex-lovers, my ex-boyfriend, straight people, gay people. The people who helped with the reception were mostly lesbians: the deejay, the bartender, the caterer. Couples dancing were opposite sex and same sex. My grandma took a picture of me and Andie dancing together and put it on her fridge.

I consider myself married, and I say I'm married. Using the word gives it more validation. When we closed out escrow last month on our house, the form said: "Diane Bernstein, single woman," "Andrea Yates, single woman." I said to the escrow officer, "This is wrong, we're married," and she laughed and told us, "Just sign it." I knew it was a joke, that they weren't going to say that in a deed, but we make a point of saying it and making it known.

Andrea: It's another opportunity to let people who wouldn't normally think about it know that we don't consider ourselves single women.

Diane: It came up so many times during the preparations. Whenever I talked to people I made sure to say "Andrea," because I knew if I said "Andie" they'd refer to her as my husband. I'd tell them we're both brides.

Part of planning the wedding was registering, which we did at Neiman-Marcus. That was a learning experience for the lady in the bridal-registry department. I'm filling out the papers and I come to the part where I have to fill in the name of the groom. I could have written "Andie Yates," but I didn't. I said, "There is no groom. We're two brides. We're two women who are getting married." The woman hesitated a minute, then she said, "I'm sixty-three years old. I've never seen this before, just give me a minute. Okay, now what was that pattern and how many settings do you need?" She was great. She wanted to see the wedding pictures. The bridal-registry woman at Robinson's didn't miss a beat; she'd done same-sex-wedding bridal registries before.

It was a really nice feature I didn't expect, the coming out over and over, the assumption that there was a groom, the questions about "him," and my correcting it. And always the decision: Do I say something? I like the idea that we started some dialogue about it. The more straight people can see we're like them, the more we'll break the stereotype.

Andrea: I don't think we had any outward negativity. What people said when we walked out the door may be another story.

Diane: My parents refer to Andie as their daughter when they talk to people. And we talk about the in-laws. We use those words.

Andrea: But that didn't change because of the wedding. I've always felt supported and accepted by her parents.

Diane: And I've always felt close to Andie's parents. I suppose on some level it made a difference for me that they were so enthusiastic about the wedding. Actually, it wasn't the wedding in particular, I think it was buying this home, and then the wedding, and now working on having a baby — all of that.

Our folks are excited about the possibility of having a grandchild. I'm going to be inseminated by an unknown donor. My mother wanted us to use someone known, but I didn't feel comfortable with that.

Andrea: I've never been very interested in being a parent. But I've known from the beginning that Diane was interested in it, and I've readjusted how I think about my life.

Diane: That came up in our counseling sessions with our rabbi. I made it clear that I was planning to do this. The rabbi made it clear that she wasn't going to marry us if she didn't think we were both very committed to it. Andie said if it was a major problem, she would take whatever steps were necessary to work it through. That's as much as I can hope for. I'm aware that she may not be able to handle it. But I think her paternal instincts are going to come out. I'm banking on it. We're all banking on it.

This kid's going to have a lot of family. We have about twenty people right here in L.A. that are family, and then there are all the friends. The only thing I'm concerned about is that the kid is going to get some crap at school. But they'll deal with it. I went to junior high and high school in a very anti-semitic neighborhood and I know how it feels to get teased. It wasn't pleasant. But when I went home and my parents assured me that things were okay, I got through it and it wasn't devastating. We know a lot of lesbians who are having or planning to have kids. By the time this child is old enough to go to school, it will have a lot of support from family and friends, and it will know many other children of gay parents.

Andrea: We didn't make many changes because of the wedding in terms of how we do things or share things. We don't have wills, but the house and car are in each other's names. We have a durable power of attorney for health care, we have life insurance policies, most of what we own is in joint names.

I handle all our finances. Diane just tells me to write her a check when she needs it. We maintain a joint account for the house and put money into it on a monthly basis. We keep private accounts for our private businesses. We have our large investments together. When we go out for dinner, there's no division; whoever has cash pays.

Diane: We celebrate our anniversary of getting together, January 31st. My parents usually send us cards. When the January card didn't come, I asked my mom about it and she said, "Well, your anniversary isn't until August." She thought we should change the anniversary to the wedding date in August. But since we've always measured our relationship by when we were first together, those anniversary dates and that period of time is what's important. Andie and I had never made it to three years with a lover before. I'm not into starting over and making this coming August our first anniversary. The fact that we're in our sixth year together, *that* is meaningful. I imagine our families will recognize the wedding date.

If marriage was legalized, we'd probably have a party, hold up the banner, so to speak. If we could register as domestic partners, we would. Anything that gets us closer to gaining some equal rights. I feel so strongly that insurance companies need to acknowledge gay people. We both have good insurance through our jobs, but if we didn't, I'd be very upset and probably take it to court, or something.

Andrea: Being married to Diane, I've gone through a real learning process about looking at myself and what I've gotten away with all these years. The things I have to deal with for self-improvement are going to come up whether it's with Diane or anyone else. This relationship has helped me change some things in myself, because I want the goal of being together for our lives.

Diane: I feel the same about Andie as before the wedding, but there's a little more stability and security there. The process we went through preparing for the wedding brought us closer. We had to make a lot of decisions about how we were going to do it — our vows, who we'd invite — and we had to write our *ketubah*.

Our *ketubah* hangs in our den. If there's a problem, I tell Andie to go and read it. I tell her, "You signed it." I think it helps.

Andrea: In the past, if I was feeling restless in a relationship or didn't think it was the right thing, I'd end the relationship. With Diane, I tell myself this is the right thing and what can I do to be sure it's okay? The wedding made it more concrete for me that problems get worked out, problems don't get pushed away.

Diane: We never have that major of a conflict because we're pretty in synch on the important stuff. Family. Having time for ourselves. How to handle a situation. We feel exactly the same about money and savings and how we spend it. We're both very clear about being monogamous, so we don't fight about it. We keep some separate friends and separate activities. Our values and goals are the same: we plan on being together forever.

Getting married isn't something of the patriarchy, because I did it with a woman. Plus, we did it in such an equal way — no one gave me away. I suppose we imitate a model, but we also imitate a model by living in a house. I feel we did something important by doing this very public and pro-gay thing.

19

Alvin Hukins and Darryl Fenley

Minneapolis, Minnesota

I felt we weren't just living together anymore. Granted, there was no legal piece of paper that sanctioned anything, but it made me feel we were somewhat recognized.

Alvin, thirty-nine, and Darryl, fifty-five, celebrate ten years together. Alvin, originally from Louisiana, lived in California for fourteen years before relocating to Minnesota. Darryl, a Sacramento native, served in the navy for five years, until it was decided that his sexual orientation was not suitable for military service. After two heterosexual marriages, Darryl acknowledged his sexual orientation. The couple was married in Stockton, California, a year after they met.

❧

Darryl: I remember the night Alvin said he would like to get married to me. I had never heard the term "married" used in the context of a gay relationship and I wasn't sure what he meant. It was early on in our relationship, and I felt threatened because we were moving along real fast. But as we began to plan for it, I felt more comfortable with it.

Before Alvin, I was married, once when I was twenty-five and once when I was thirty-seven. Following that, I was in a very negative relationship with a man. When Alvin and I met, I told him flatly I was not ready for a relationship. But one thing I

Alvin and Darryl

learned very quickly is that Alvin is innately very honest. He's not deceptive. I began to find that I trusted him. It was easier to trust him because he was so trusting himself.

We met in August 1981, and we've lived together since Halloween of that year. We were married April 24th, 1982. Part of the reason for the marriage was that I felt the need for that commitment. It was also a very significant part of my coming-out process: I didn't feel bad about who I was, and I wanted to share all of myself.

Alvin: For me, it was to show and share with people that we were committed to each other. Without legally being married, that was the best we could do.

Darryl: There were no engagement rings, but I felt it was an engagement period because there was that precommitment commitment. We sent out invitations. With some of the people we invited, it was a coming-out process. And it wasn't because I wanted to shock, it was because I wanted to share with them. They all came.

It was held on a Saturday. We spent most of the morning fixing food. Alvin's sister-in-law made the cake — it didn't have a bride or groom, but it was a wedding motif and had our names on it. Afterwards, we ate out on the patio — roast beef, salads, and rolls, things like that.

My sister and brother-in-law were invited, but she had a long-standing work-related commitment she couldn't get out of and she couldn't come. But at that time, and since then, she and my brother-in-law have been very supportive of us.

Alvin: We didn't invite my parents, mainly because they lived so far away, in Louisiana. I have a gay brother who didn't show up. He says he forgot. I know it doesn't make sense, but he's very homophobic. We had only one gay couple there. The rest were all straight people.

Darryl: We didn't know very many gay people in Stockton. We're very much homebodies. We'd rather be home and have people in for dinner and music or conversation or go to somebody else's home than go out.

Alvin: A friend officiated. She stood up with us and made the announcement that we wanted to show our commitment to each other in front of people. We had written a little service, which she pretty much followed as far as the order of what we would do, and then we exchanged our rings, which we still wear. Darryl read a poem and I read a passage from a poetry book.

Darryl: We used one section from Kahlil Gibran's *The Prophet*.

I had told our friend who was officiating that I didn't need a written copy of our vows, but when it came time, I couldn't remember anything! Our vows paraphrased the standard vows to where we were comfortable with them. Part of the commitment was that there be fidelity, honesty, openness, and supportiveness.

I lived in San Francisco in the mid-1970s when holy unions, so-called holy unions, were starting to come into vogue. You'd go to the bar Saturday night and somebody would be having a holy union, and the next week they'd be having another one with someone else. There was no sense of commitment. And that's what I didn't want. I felt that this had been a long journey, and I would really like to settle down and feel comfortable with Alvin and feel that sense of commitment.

The ceremony affected our relationship very positively. I don't want to minimize anyone else's relationship, but, for me, I felt like we weren't just living together anymore. Granted, there was no legal piece of paper that sanctioned anything, but it made me feel we were somewhat recognized — even though we weren't.

This is the first honest marriage I've been in. I was filled with self-doubt when I was first married at twenty-five. That was before anybody discussed questions about their sexuality. I didn't know who to talk to. The message was grind it out and maybe you'll change. I entered my second marriage for all the wrong reasons. I knew at the time the ceremony was taking place that it was a mistake. In my relationship with Alvin, I guess I've never felt more secure, both with myself and with the relationship.

Alvin: I think it's real important to point out that when Darryl was straight married he was also alcoholic, which I think was a big factor in his marrying and a big factor in denying his sexuality.

The alcoholism was in part from not accepting himself. I think a big reason his marriages didn't work was because he wasn't accepting himself. He was sober when we met, and that made a big difference in our relationship.

Darryl: I met Alvin the day I was released from a nine-month recovery program. When we first met, it was obvious I had recently moved. I was terrified to tell him where I'd been. It wasn't until several weeks later that I did tell him. I figured that would be the end of whatever might develop. But it wasn't. I'm not saying that my actions were dependent upon his reaction, but it helped me find some strength within myself at that point. Because I was still vulnerable, being that early into recovery.

For too many years, I lived a shame-based existence, not fully understanding who or what I was; but whatever I was, the world said I wasn't okay. That would nullify any relationship I ever got into because it would be just a further extension of that shame-based existence.

Alvin: We've had some bad times, like any relationship will have, but for Darryl to have gone through the public ceremony makes me feel he has more of a commitment. When it's done in front of people, it makes you think about not just walking out. I think the ceremony strengthened the relationship. But I don't know if it's my maturity or the ceremony that makes the relationship stronger.

Darryl: We deal with conflicts in our relationship by generally just kind of blundering through. But we do a pretty good job of not letting things fester and hang around and go unaddressed, so there isn't a lot of garbage to carry around.

We've gotten a lot of support for our relationship since we've lived in Minnesota. One of the greatest things that has ever happened to me happened after my office Christmas party. Alvin had gone with me the two previous years, but one year he decided he didn't want to go. The wife of the senior partner where I work called me within several days with a concern. I know her pretty well, although we've never discussed my relationship with Alvin any more than we've discussed her marriage. Evidently, I had sent them a Christmas card where I'd signed only my name. She called me and said, "Is everything okay at home? Alvin didn't come to the Christmas party, and you signed your Christmas card alone. I just wondered if there was another message in there." I appreciated her concern, which I told her, and then we talked about relationships, without talking about any sexual boundaries. Once in a while she'll call, asking for her husband, who's running late, and she'll say to me, "Marriage is really a job, isn't it?" I appreciate that. It makes it easy.

Alvin: My parents knew we were together, but we never talked about it. I had a relationship with my parents that you just didn't talk about it. My mother said to me one time, "You're my son, I love you. Your sexuality doesn't have to be discussed. I'm not saying I approve of your life, I'm not saying I disapprove. You're happy, you're living your life the best you can live it, and that's all that matters." Darryl told my father we'd had a ceremony.

When my father was dying and in the hospital, my mother called and said that I should come if I wanted to see him. The first thing he said when she told Daddy I was coming was, "Is Darryl coming?" She asked him why he wanted to know and he said, "Alvin can't come by himself. I sure hope Darryl comes."

Darryl: She stayed with us one week not long ago, and we go down all the time and stay in her home. I've never felt anything but real acceptance. Just this morning at the end of her phone conversation with Alvin she said, "Tell Darryl I love him." That's very important to us, too. We don't have that additional hassle with family that some do, and I know that some have a very bitter battle to fight.

I have four children from my first marriage, who I've never had the opportunity to sit down and discuss any of this with. Part of the problem was that my ex-wife had taken it upon herself to tell the children about my sexuality, and evidently not in a positive way. There are a lot of issues there that have never been dealt with. I try to stay in contact with them. It's been pretty much a one-sided thing. I've tried to adopt the attitude that if it's ever going to be, it will be, and it may not be on my terms. My sister in California maintains pretty close contact with them, so I'm assured of their welfare. That's what I'm mostly concerned about. They're all grown now; my youngest son is twenty.

We'd like to see marriage legalized for the benefits of taxes and survivorship. Now that domestic partnership passed here, and there hasn't been the backlash that some expected, there's been talk in the local gay community that legalizing marriage is the next thing they're planning to work for. One of the main reasons we registered as domestic partners is so that if something happens to me, Alvin will have some rights to our possessions and visitation rights if I should be hospitalized for something.

The term we call each other really depends on the group we're with. I don't like using the term "lover." We usually use "partner" or "spouse." Sometimes I put down "married" on a form. I was shocked a few months ago when I ran a credit report on myself and found that Alvin is listed as my spouse on my TRW! What a ground-breaking event! We've got some legality somewhere, and nobody realizes it!

Alvin: I usually introduce him as "Darryl."

Darryl: I don't care whether they're straight or gay — people realize we wear matching rings, they know that we live together. We own our home together, we have wills together, everything we have in the way of assets is commingled.

Alvin: Our friends, whether they're gay or straight, look at it as a relationship. It doesn't matter to them whether we've had a ceremony or not. Of course, our friends are pretty liberal. The people in this area seem to be more liberal than they were in California.

Darryl: I find that people in our area seem to place more credibility in you as a gay person when you're in a relationship.

Alvin: We belong to the Metropolitan Community Church's couples group. People from that group sometimes send anniversary cards, and we do that for them.

Darryl: We really don't know which anniversary to celebrate. I go by the day we started living together.

Alvin: We usually remember our anniversary a week or so after it passes! We say "Happy Anniversary," sometimes give each other a card.

Darryl: The main local paper, *Star Trib,* recently changed the "Wedding Announcements" section to "Celebrations." They also list gay and straight domestic partnerships. As we've talked about our upcoming tenth anniversary, we've discussed announcing it in the paper, but neither of us feels we really need to.

Alvin: Our friends already know we've been together ten years and see us as a couple. I don't need to announce it to strangers.

Darryl: Things are really changing. I'm the organist and choir director for a Presbyterian church. I think I'm their first real exposure to the world of gays. The minister has been to our home for dinner; he's fully aware. About a year ago, the pastor of a mainline church in the area was quoted in the newspaper as very homophobic and very anti-gay and lesbian in his sermon and statements to the press. I talked to the Presbyterian pastor about it the following Sunday because I knew they were colleagues. He said he'd told the minister he was going to have to wake up and realize that times are changing. He thinks we're all going to live to see the day when we are actually celebrating gay and lesbian marriages within our mainline churches. There are many churches back here, including some of the very conservative churches, Baptist churches, that advertise in the paper that they are gay- and lesbian-sensitive.

Alvin: Being involved in the MCC and being recognized as a couple by them really strengthened our relationship. Quite a few members of the MCC church are heterosexual. A number of them are in PFLAG [Parents and Friends of Lesbians and Gays], and that has helped the relationship a lot, too.

Darryl: I guess I didn't fully realize going into a gay marriage that basically our life wasn't going to be a lot different than the couple's next door. That we were going to have bills to pay, have health crises, have interpersonal conflicts, that the lawn would still have to be mowed on Saturday. I used to reflect on the old Peggy Lee song, "Is That All There Is?" But today, I wouldn't trade my life for anything.

20

Ruth Mahaney and Nina Jo Smith

San Francisco, California

---

*My family took the wedding more seriously as a wedding
than I did. I related to the demonstration part much more, saw
it as part of the massive protest.*

Together since 1979, Ruth, forty-seven, and Nina Jo, thirty-
eight, participated in The Wedding at the October 1987
March on Washington for Lesbian and Gay Rights to make a political statement. They started the writing of names in chalk on the
pavement in front of IRS headquarters during the mass wedding
ceremony, to mark the spot and to give participants a sense of the
power inherent in naming. Ruth, involved in progressive politics
since 1967, teaches women's studies at San Francisco State University and is a member of the Modern Times Bookstore collective.
Nina Jo has been active in the women's movement for two decades
and works now as a martial artist and self-defense instructor. She is
also a graduate student in physical education. In 1991, they registered as domestic partners in San Francisco and so have another
anniversary to celebrate: February 14 (the first day of domestic-
partners registration).

❧

Nina Jo: I wanted to do this wedding because it sounded like it
would be fun — and it was fun! It was a public statement of our
relationship, and gay and lesbian relationships in general, that

174

Nina Jo and Ruth

At the 1987 mass wedding in Washington, D.C., Nina Jo and Ruth pulled out boxes of chalk and started what became the writing of hundreds of same-sex couples' names in front of the Internal Revenue Service building

we're here, and we're here to stay. And it was a way to celebrate our relationship without having to be the center of attention.

We subsidize a lot of heterosexual relationships. It seemed like a way to make that public. It also helped me get that across to my family. Even though they're supportive and they know a lot of gay people, they aren't aware of details like not being able to share health benefits.

I think lesbians have lower expectations about deserving the benefits and recognition that heterosexual relationships receive, and we don't imagine we can get that. The Wedding felt like a way to tell ourselves and our community that this is a relationship everyone should take seriously. The demonstration felt very full of pride. It validated that we are good.

Ruth: For me, it was part of the historical struggle. The right to get married has been vocalized as far back as the 1950s, and even before, long before feminism. The negativity about marriage within the lesbian community comes from the 1970s' women's movement, which had a simplistic analysis of the family and marriage. As with a lot of stuff, if you take it from heterosexuals and "blop" it onto lesbians, you miss something. I think marriage has a different meaning for lesbians and gays.

Nina Jo: The Wedding was held on Adams Street, in front of the IRS — it still makes me laugh! There was a stage that went into the street where the "dignitaries" stood. There were about ten thousand people there, watching and supporting.

We'd preregistered after seeing some fliers around the neighborhood. I think they were trying to put together a registry of couples to show the march organizers that there was enough interest. But there were also sign-up booths at the gay-pride march in June. So we rounded up two other couples and sent in our registration forms for the information packet. There was a small donation to cover costs.

We didn't dress in any particularly special clothes. All I remember about what I wore was that it was too hot — I was wearing wool. Other people were very elaborate — men in gowns and men in tuxes, women in bridal gowns and tuxes, people in jeans, and everything in between. Two of our friends found us, miracu-lously — and they were wearing pink circles pinned on their shirts that said "Bridesmaids." That was really sweet.

Ruth: Before the ceremony there was a rally with speakers. Rev. Troy Perry and [comedienne] Robin Tyler both had their part-ners there and talked about why they were doing it. Then Karen Thompson [the Minnesota woman who has fought in court eight years for guardianship of her lover, Sharon Kowalski, who was severely disabled in a car accident in 1983] talked a little bit about how she and Sharon had exchanged rings, and how she wished Sharon could be there. Then the minister got up and talked.

There were so many people there, we didn't really look at each other during the ceremony. We looked at everyone around us. We did exchange rings during the ceremony, though, matching rings with silver hands holding a stone. It can either look like a heart or two hands. But we didn't exchange vows.

We were very restless during the ceremony. I mean, this was a rowdy group, and the minister was long-winded and taking it all too seriously for us. We were ready to have a short ceremony and party! At one point, it sounded like it was done and everyone started cheering, and they let the balloons go. And the minister told everybody to quiet down, that it was still going on.

Nina had brought a box of fat pieces of colored chalk, and she pulled them out during the minister's talk. We wrote our names on the street, then passed the chalk around to other couples. Peo-ple were delighted. There was something so wonderful about it.

Nina Jo: It's such a ritual — couples writing their names together — yet I think gay people don't get much of a chance to do it. I wanted to be able to leave a record that we'd been there, to make it personalized and public at the same time. It was so sweet, all these couples bending down under the crowd and writing their names. When the street cleared, it was so wonderful. The chalk had passed through hundreds of hands.

Ruth: My parents always remind me of our wedding-anniversary date. Nina's family doesn't relate to it much, but my parents have totally latched onto the fact that we got married. So we get anniversary cards that always remind us of our October anniversary. We celebrate the anniversary of our first date, in June.

Nina Jo: Ruth's family was happy she was no longer "living in sin." My parents accepted us before the wedding, so it really didn't make much of a difference to them.

Ruth: In a sense, my family took the wedding more seriously as a wedding than I did. I related to the demonstration part much more, saw it as part of the massive protest demonstration. Surprisingly, it was my parents' response more than anything else that made me feel the wedding made a difference in the relationship. They have a lot more confidence now in the relationship than they did before. They'd seen me go through relationships and break up. I think it helped them realize there was not going to be any other wedding for me, so they decided to celebrate this one.

Nina Jo: The treatment by her family is probably a big element of why I feel closer to Ruth since the wedding. They accept me more as family. I became Uncle Nina to her nephew! We are Aunt Ruth and Uncle Nina.

Ruth: I feel like we're not really married, but I keep getting from my family that we are. Just the other day when I was talking to one of my nephews, he said something about my being married, and I said, "I'm not married." He said, "Come on, you're just as married as anyone else." I liked it. It was sort of like, Who cares if the state doesn't recognize you, I recognize you as much as any marriage I've ever known.

I always put "single" down on forms, unless it's something I'm angry about. Like insurance. When I get insurance applications in the mail, I always write down that I have a spouse and that when they start recognizing it, I'll be glad to buy their insurance. I'm constantly writing nasty little notes in the margins of these things and returning them.

Nina Jo: I'm ambivalent about the institution of marriage, heterosexual or otherwise. I thought I probably wouldn't get married if I were heterosexual, so it was odd to do it as a lesbian. But to do it as a political statement at that time and at that place made a lot of sense to me.

Ruth: I think we were too shy to think about doing a private ceremony. I've been to many lesbian and gay wedding ceremonies, and I've loved all of them, but I didn't want to do one myself. We had a tenth-anniversary party at the house, but we made it a domestic partnership campaign fund-raiser. People thought of it as our anniversary party, though. We passed around a little book for people to write in, but there were no toasts, no cake, none of that.

　We're very excited about the domestic partners bill in San Francisco. We understand there's controversy about it, but we consider it an important step in the acceptance of gay people. We've had huge fights with some people who are scared about the danger that a public list could bring — losing jobs, things like that. Some people against it seem to feel that you get the financial responsibility without any of the benefits, and worry that people don't realize this before they go into it. But we'll register, knowing there are risks, because we want to help build the names on that list. I've come to love studying gay history, so the idea of having ourselves recorded feels important.

Nina Jo: After all, we are family to each other.

　We've set up some protections for ourselves. We have durable powers of attorney, and I wrote up a will when we traveled last summer. We're joint owners of our house.

Ruth: We have a joint account for the house payments and we share the payments, but we keep our own bank accounts. We do that mostly to avoid arguments. Our class background is pretty similar, but the way we think about money is different. I come from a family that's terrified of not having money because they didn't have much during the depression. Nina's family is younger and the depression didn't have quite the same impression. She's more apt to spend money and I'm more apt to save it. So it's better not to mingle it.

Nina Jo: We don't plan to have children biologically, but we may someday adopt or have foster children. We have two children in

our lives that we take care of every other weekend, and have for
the last twelve years. They think of us as family. Sometimes they
call us "mom." The older boy used to call us "specials."

Ruth: We've never made vows to each other, but we do plan a
future together. I've come to distrust forever promises. When you
make those promises, it's still about how you feel today, not how
you're going to feel in the future.

When I envision my future, I very much envision it with Nina.
We still haven't said we'll be together forever and ever. We go
day by day. And it works.

21

Demetri Williams and Dwain Ferguson
Cleveland, Ohio

---

*I had told Dwain no when he asked me the first time because
I didn't know how the public was going to react to it. But,
after I got to thinking about the wedding, I said, this is what
you got to do, this is your life.*

Demetri, twenty-eight, and Dwain, twenty-five, married
two weeks before this interview, after being together for
four years.

❧

Dwain: It all started a couple years ago. I asked Demetri to marry
me. We never got around to doing so because we was just playing
at the time. The second time, he asked me to marry him to see my
reaction. Then, a couple months ago, we asked each other, and
we decided to get married. We was really serious about it this
time. Our love had got stronger, our honesty had got stronger,
our trust in the relationship had got stronger. So everything got
strong and we just feel that this is it. We wanted to commit ourselves because we wanted to do the same thing the heterosexuals
do. I felt thrilled! It seemed like the best thing that had happened
to us.

Demetri: I had told Dwain no when he asked me the first time. The
reason I had said no was because I didn't know how the public
was going to react to it. I knew that a lot of people would find out
about it, the kids would find out. I was so worried about what

Demetri and Dwain on their wedding day

The wedding cake with two
grooms in a heart

other people would think and say. I'm not like Dwain, I'm kind of low profile. If somebody ask me, I don't deny it or nothing like that, but I don't publicize it. But, after I got to thinking about the wedding, I said, this is what you got to do, this is your life. Can't nobody make this decision for you. And I got a lot of support from different people. It was a real nice turnout at the reception and a fairly good turnout at the church. There was a lot of support there. I invited a lot of heterosexual people I work with, and I'm finding out they feel that gay people deserve the same rights as heterosexuals.

Dwain: We didn't buy the engagement rings at the same time. There wasn't no engagement because we was talking about it for a while. And we'd been living together for four years. Each time he got mad at me, he'd take his ring off. The last time he took that ring off, I took it and put it on my finger. When we was back to luvvy duvvy once again, he asked me for his ring, and I looked on my finger and the ring wasn't there! During that day I was washing clothes . . . the ring was gone. But I wear the ring he gave me every day, on the right hand. I wear the wedding band on the left hand.

We invited at least seventy-five people. We had about thirty people at the wedding and about a hundred people at the reception. The second week in May, the Channel 25 auction came on and they had wedding invitations on there and I bid for the invitations and I got them. I took them down to the shop and we had them drawn up with the reception cards. It was a mixed crowd, gay and straight. Everybody had a wonderful time.

I did not invite my mom and dad. Well, I did invite them, but they didn't want to come. My two sisters came, and they enjoyed theyselves tremendously.

My parents accept my being gay and they accept my relationship, but the wedding part was a little bit too much, because they're a very religious couple. But they treat Demetri like he's their own son — their only son! Because he do a lot of things with them around the house and I'm the lazy one of the family. It's terrific!

My mother asked me why I wanted to do this, and I said because I love Demetri. Then, because she was upset, she gave me
an example of what if she wanted to marry Mrs. Williams across
the street, what would she say? I told her that it's her life, you do
what you want to do. I don't have no say-so about her life, just
like she have no say-so about mine; I'm the only person who has
to live it. So that was it.

Demetri: The majority of my family is in Alabama. I didn't send
invitations to none of my family members. I have never sat down
and told them me and Dwain is lovers, but they speculate and
assume. When you've been with a person for going on four years,
and your mother knows you're staying with a man and you're
staying in a one-bedroom apartment, it's only natural she's going
to know even if you don't say nothing. It's never really crossed
my mind to tell her. I'm a very private person.

Dwain: We both have kids. My boy is going on seven years old.
Demetri kids are ten and five. I treat his kids like they're my very
own. I take his kids lots of places — bike riding, to buy an ice-
cream cone. I enjoy being around his kids as much as I enjoy
being around my kid.

Demetri: I had the kids for about a year. Then, the way my work
schedule was, they had to go back to their mother.

Dwain: Demetri had a common-law marriage with her. So this was
the first wedding for both of us.

It started out where I was supposed to take care of the ceremony and everything else that goes with it and he was going to do
the honeymoon. But, after looking at what I had to spend and
everything else to do with the wedding, it was a little bit too much
for my blood, my budget. I thought about asking him for some
help, but I really didn't want to. I was so glad he came around
and said, Dwain, I tell you what. Why don't I give you a little
hand with the wedding and we'll just hold off the honeymoon
until we get up to financially able. And I thought to myself,
Hmm, you must have known what I was thinking all the time.

But when he helped me out with the wedding, he didn't think
there was a lot he'd have to do! It came out really nice, though. I

took care of the pop, the beer, the rings, the cake, the tuxes, and half the invitations, and he was in charge of the food, the liquor, the Lincoln Town Car we rented, and he paid for the wedding.

Demetri: With the invitations, Dwain went directly to the invitation place and told them what it was for and how we wanted it worded. I went with him, but he did the majority of the talking. With the cake, Dwain told them exactly what he wanted. He wanted two mens and a heart on the top. He let them know right then that it was a gay wedding. The one cake place refused to even do it. The next one we went to was all for it because they had did it before. It was a regular wedding cake with three tiers, and there was two grooms on the top in a heart ornament. It was white and maroon with flowers. It matched the tuxedos and the wedding invitations. Everything was just about corresponding.

It took place at Christ Community Church. The church has a gay service in the evening and a heterosexual service during the day. The music we used was "Here and Now" by Luther Vandross. We wore double tuxedos, white and maroon. The two best men walked up the side aisles, they came together at the middle, then came down the center aisle to the altar. When they made it halfway, me and Dwain came across the back part, and when we met we held hands and walked up to the altar where the two best mens were. Prior to us walking out, we had lit two candles. There was a total of three candles, two smaller candles and one big candle. We lit the two smaller candles. Then we went through the ceremony. First the reverend said a few words and prayers, then we said our vows.

Dwain: We did not write our own vows. We left that up to the pastor.

Demetri: After the vow services, we took the two smaller candles and we lit the one big one, and blew out the two smaller ones. Then we came back to where we were standing at the altar and finished our vows.

It was also a ring ceremony. We placed the rings on each other's fingers, then we kissed, and we exited through the center aisleway to the back, and that was where we greeted everybody and thanked them for coming.

The reception was at a house. We changed clothes upstairs and waited for the majority of the people to get there. They had a champagne toast for us, at that time with about sixty people there. Then everything progressed from there . . . the food, the dancing, dinner . . . the bar was in the basement. We had excellent people helping us, they really helped put it together well. We did a first dance and we cut the cake and gave each other a piece.

We bought decorations for the car, but I felt we shouldn't decorate it after all because the church was situated partially in a gay community and partially in a heterosexual community. The heterosexuals in the neighborhood knew that this was partially a gay church and that they had gay ceremonies. But to keep down any confusion or anything that could mess up our day, I chose not to have the car decorated and not to throw rice when we was leaving out the church. We didn't want our wedding day ruined by somebody not accepting it.

Dwain: We're going to throw a big anniversary party for our first anniversary next June. We celebrate our anniversary every year we've been together. But since we got married, we start over.

Demetri: I didn't want to do it that way. I wanted to keep the four years, even though it is a new start for us with the wedding. But if he want to do it that way, it's only right, so I'll just go with the wedding. And it's only proper to start with the wedding.

Dwain: For our anniversaries, he'll try to give me hints of what he wants, or what he needs, or has to have, all these different kinds of things, and I'll go out and buy it for him. And he do me the same way.

Every now and then — and this don't have anything to do with our anniversary — every now and then when I'm out and I'm thinking about him, I'll pick up a nice card and some roses. In the past four years, I think I've given him about fifty beautiful cards. They are so romantic, and they're well put. I get a card on my birthday. But he's not the card type, or the flowers type.

Our relationship is growing every day. With us making this commitment together, I guess it just assures us that this is what we want, and he loves me as much as I love him. Now, we have had our ups and downs plenty of times, but we handle the ups and downs and we learned how to work together on the problem. We sit down and talk about the problem. Most of the time, Demetri always have a solution. It's always him that asks us to sit down, but I'm always open to it. I'm a very open-minded person.

Demetri: We sit down and map out some kind of strategy. I used to keep everything inside and let it build up and burst out, but now I've learned how to control that and sit down and immediately work on the problem and come up with some solution, because that's going to be the only answer. It took close to three years for us to really be able to work on different problems we had. It's harder with two men being together because you both have that stubborn independence. But you work on it. It's like anything else, it's a learning process. You always learn something new.

We have a real close relationship. We get along excellently. Having the ceremony hasn't changed the way we feel for one another. The ceremony was to say we're faithful, we're going to be together, this is it. But, it could have been without a ceremony or with a ceremony. We just chose to have the ceremony.

I see a lot more gay people starting to come out. But what I been noticing is a lot of heterosexuals is accepting it better than I had anticipated, of gay people being together and gay people getting married. I had invited a lot of heterosexuals I work with, and I'm finding out they feel gay people have the same rights as heterosexuals, especially when you look at people being together for four years. Once you've been together four years, you've been through the rough times and the bad times, and you know each other. There was a lot of support there.

Dwain: I believe that a lot of gay couples is coming out now to be married because something tell us that a bill will be passed for gay rights. The reverend had told us that he's married four gay couples in this month! Saturday, they had a march downtown for gay rights, and there was more than fifteen hundred people downtown marching. Last year it was only something like two hundred people. It was a great improvement.

If marriage was made legal, I would take my piece of paper [the church-issued certificate of holy union] downtown and say I want a legal license right now.

Demetri: But I consider that we had a wedding. We took the same vows and the same commitments as heterosexuals take, with the exception of the pastor pronouncing us "spouse" instead of "husband and wife." We've got a cute little thing, we say "husband-wifeband." It's a combination of a husband and a wife. We use both of them. If you asked us about our spouse, we'd say we husband-wifebands.

The one thing I feel bad about is we don't get to take each other's names. They make it really hard. We'd have to go through the legal change, go down to the court and all that instead of having it just change automatically. We're not going to do that.

We're on each other's insurance policies. We keep separate checking and savings accounts. The one thing we going to have to work on is learning how to put the money together and use it as *our* money instead of "this is yours and this is mine." But he have access to everything I own, I have access to anything he own.

Dwain: I do feel more secure because of the wedding. But having a ceremony hasn't changed what we do. We don't want an open relationship, that is a no-no. I don't know what else to say except I love this man a whole lot and there's nothing in the world I wouldn't do for him, and I'm sure he feels the same way about me.

Demetri: It's a little hard to explain why I wanted to have a ceremony. I felt that we deserve to have the kind of ceremony straight people get the pleasure of having. This is a ceremony I would have missed because this is the person I plan to spend the rest of my life with. I didn't want to miss having a ceremony because I'm gay. And I am gay and always will be, and we are together, and we are in love.

22

Frances Fuchs and Gayle Remick

Santa Rosa, California

I said, "Would you marry me?" Right there in the middle of the movies.

Gayle and Frances, both thirty-seven, have been together since 1978. They had a commitment ceremony in Santa Cruz, California, in 1981, and a renewal ceremony four years later. They are now planning for a recommitment ceremony to celebrate thirteen years. Frances is a therapist in private practice. Gayle works for the county and is a part-time stand-up comedienne. Since 1985, Frances has been an ordained Universal Life Church minister; Gayle was ordained in 1989, and they both officiate marriages.

The first section of this chapter is from an interview conducted in 1989; the second section is from an interview done two years later. In the last two years, Gayle's opinion of marriage has taken a big turn.

❧

Fall 1989

Gayle: Within my home I feel married to Frances, but I don't consider us "married." The marriage part is still very heterosexual to me. One of the reasons I don't like to associate with marriage is because heterosexual marriage seems to be in trouble. It's like

189

Gayle and Frances

booking passage on the *Titanic*. Frances is my life partner; that's how I'm accustomed to thinking of her.

Frances: I feel married and I like to use that term. I like stretching the meaning of the term, taking a term that has traditionally been heterosexual and changing the meaning for us. Our wedding was very different from a heterosexual wedding. It has to be very different just by the fact that it's a lesbian wedding. On doctor's reports or when people ask if I'm married, I say yes, unless it's going to legally get me in trouble, like on my taxes. It's important for me to challenge those things.

I think ceremonies and rituals have a wonderful effect and purpose, and just because heterosexuals do it is not a good reason to throw it out. It was saying, We've made it through tough times, we're going to make it. It was also a statement that I'll be damned if I'm going to forego the good parts about heterosexual marriage — the support of the community, the support of our friends, the public acknowledgment, the fun. It was saying, I'm going to be with a woman, and I'm going to be with this woman in particular. I grew up thinking I would go through a wedding. I was not going to deprive myself of that experience.

As a lesbian, for me to marry, I get to embody all the good parts of that institution. I can choose which parts I want. It's not legal, it's not regulated by the state. There's nothing possessive or buying into the patriarchy as far as I can see. It's much more of a personal statement.

Gayle: Getting married was the ultimate coming out of the closet. In 1981, we were a very, very small handful of lesbians who got married. We took a lot of flak from other lesbians, as well as heterosexuals. In 1981, we didn't know any other lesbians, not a single one, who had had a ceremony in Santa Cruz, and a lot of lesbians live in that city. Everybody was on our case about it. They said, What are you doing, How heterosexual. We really had to sell it. A lot of people were curious as to why we were doing it. We did it because it's okay to be lesbian, okay to celebrate, okay to be festive, okay to step out and say, Yeah, we're normal, what about it?

The engagement began a year after we were together. Frances designed engagement rings for us. They're silver and gold with two bands at the bottom, then a big space and one band at the top. It means together and apart, a couple and individuals. When she gave it to us she was really excited about it, made a big presentation, a big dinner. That was the engagement, I felt.

Frances: I didn't think of that as our engagement!

Gayle: What she said to me was, All right, we both have a ring, and it really doesn't mean anything — but it could — but it doesn't really mean anything.

Frances: I don't recall saying that. I consider those rings to signify that we were at a certain level of commitment. I think of the formal engagement as when Gayle asked me to marry her. We were sitting at the movies, watching some ridiculous movie — *Sir Lancelot* — and Gayle turns to me and says, "Will you marry me?"

Gayle [to Frances]: Do you remember the exact moment in the movie?

Frances: When the Lady of the Lake was coming out of the water.

Gayle: That's it! The scene was so beautiful, and I was watching Frances watch her so lovingly. I thought, I better bag her right now. Because I don't want her watching another woman like that. So, I said, "Would you marry me?" Right there in the middle of the movies.

Frances: And I said yes.

Gayle: Yes.

Frances: After the movie, we went into our Volkswagen van and we planned. From the time that she asked me to marry her to the time we did it was about six months. We had a bachelorette party at a friend's house. We did silly things and had a good time, had champagne and cake.

I designed our wedding invitations, and we sent out quite a few. I sent an invitation to my sisters and my mother. I was too scared to send invitations to my father and stepmother, I just didn't think it was going to be okay for some reason. I found out later that it would have been okay. My dad was even upset that I hadn't invited him. My mother didn't come because she wasn't too fond of Gayle at the time, so that was difficult. Neither of us had any family members there. Nobody flew in for it, which they would have done if it had been a heterosexual wedding. But I was actually more relaxed because none of our family was there.

Gayle: I sent invitations to my two brothers and my sister. I didn't send one to my parents, who were still hostile to Frances at the time. All my family lives on the East Coast. Nobody came, though they did send me cards with their regrets that they couldn't be there.

Frances: Our families have really come around, they accept us really well right now. My parents see us as legitimately married. My father acknowledges our wedding anniversary, sends us presents. We celebrate the full time we've been together when we celebrate our anniversary. We like to acknowledge the entire time because the first three years were rather significant.

Gayle: All in all, we invited about a hundred people; about sixty came. We did it in Aptos, California, in a national park, in a ring of redwoods with a huge stump in the center that was our altar.

Frances: We followed some of the format of a heterosexual wedding because we wanted some of those things in it. The ceremony was led by a Universal Life Church minister. We wrote our own vows, and we had music, lots of flowers everywhere. It was beautiful. We both wore silk pants and white tops made of flowing rayon with silver threads. We put flowers in our lapels.

We had a rehearsal. We had "best women," who came down first. Then Gayle came down and was "given away" by a friend. Then I came down with a good friend of mine who gave me away. We each had two people.

Gayle: I was nervous before the wedding. Even though it wasn't a legal marriage, I thought, This is it. I can't go back. It was terrifying, even though I really wanted to do it.

Frances: First we had the minister's opening statement. She talked about how she knew us, and what we were like as a couple. We had written our own vows and we said them to each other. We also did the vows of "Do you, Gayle, choose as your partner in marriage, Frances?" and said that stuff. And we shared a cup of wine as a symbol of sharing life together. We exchanged rings — we had rings made for each other, gold rings with single stones in them. Then we did the Jewish ritual where one person smashes a glass underfoot, and the ceremony was finished.

Gayle: Then there was lots of milling about, lots of hugging and "That was incredible," "That was great."

Frances: After that, we went back to the minister's house at the ocean and had a potluck reception. A band played for free, and we had a three-tier chocolate layer cake with flowers all over it. A friend found a little crescent moon figurine with two little angels kissing underneath it for the top, which was perfect.

Gayle: Some people wondered if we'd change our last name. We talked about it, but Frances was concerned her father would be real upset if she changed her name, and I love my last name. So, we kept our names.

Frances: I never would have changed my name if I'd married a man, so actually, I really didn't consider it.

Gayle: We decided that if we had a child we'd hyphenate our name. We wanted children when we were first together, but that's changed. We're not going to have kids.

As far as being "out" about my marriage at work, I talk about Frances and our marriage. I bring her to the parties. I've always had to deal with the controversy at work. I've always been "out" on the job since being gay is such a big part of my life. I fit one of the stereotypes. People assume I'm gay.

But I rarely call Frances my wife. Only at home and only with friends. I've used it as part of my comedy routine: "My wife is here in the audience tonight." I've used it as an educational device. But mostly I call Frances my partner. And she's a good buddy, too. She's a lot of fun.

Frances: I don't really feel that our relationship has changed because of the marriage. Although, in some ways, I feel more secure and more able to be myself. But I don't feel that any assumptions changed about who we are or what we expect from each other.

Gayle: I think the relationship was definitely changed by the marriage. I was always the one that didn't want to make a commitment, never wanted to be 100 percent attached. So, when marriage came up, it was really hard for me because I wanted that security, I wanted the commitment, but I was afraid of it at the same time.

When I actually did get married, the vows I said had incredible meaning to me. I was making a promise to be honest and true with Frances as my partner. It meant that I was going to be with this person for the rest of my life. It was scary to think about having sex with the same person for the rest of my life. I wondered if it would be boring, I don't know. So it was scary, but I was also very happy. It was a real balance.

Both of our weddings were fantastic. The second was much more casual, more fun.

Frances: We did it campy. I wore a hat with a veil and a kind of Madonna-style white top with pearls all over it, a merry widow, and a long white skirt, and Gayle wore a leopard-print jacket, white pants, shades, tuxedo, black tie — it was a real kick. We did it at a gay resort in Guerneville, at the Russian River.

Gayle: We exchanged new rings, black onyx rings, and new vows. I did my vows on the spot, Frances had hers prepared, tucked away in her merry widow. She whipped it out in front of the entire crowd, which was delightful. It was a totally different ceremony because we were in a totally different place.

Frances: We had some Jewish elements which we didn't have the first time (my cultural background is Jewish). We had a *chuppah* [the traditional wedding canopy], and we both smashed glasses under our feet at the end. Some of the elements were the same — we shared "wine" (it was juice) and had a friend lead it. Her words were changed, but some of the original elements were there. It was a lot of fun. It was also a lot of work. And it was expensive. There was no "bride's" family to cover expenses.

Gayle: But what the heck. It was worth it. I couldn't ask for a better life than what I have today. I am by far the happiest I've been in my whole life. I feel so proud of my strengths, and of

Frances's strengths. I delight in seeing Frances every day. I'm very attentive to her. I tell her, You're good at this, You're good at that, I love to see you wear this or that. I'm glad you're spending this time with me. I want to share my life with you, I want to compromise, I want to work on things. My marriage is better than I ever expected it could be.

Frances: That's beautiful.

Gayle: Well, I love you.

Frances: I love you, too.

　　　Every year Gayle asks me to marry her again.

Gayle: And this year, she finally said yes!

Frances: I was just kidding.

Gayle: You were not kidding, it was just a couple weeks ago!

Frances: Maybe at our twenty-fifth anniversary.

Gayle: We're going to do it again.

Frances: Well, we'll see.

❧

Spring 1991

Frances: We're going to have a small renewal of vows this year, on our thirteenth anniversary.

Gayle: We're going to wear "Star Trek" uniforms. It's a uniform party, but it's a cover. For me, it's a marriage. For Frances, it's a summer party.

Frances: We're going to make it a kind of "Star Trek" take-off, and, at the same time, say nice things to each other.

Gayle: Frances and I really enjoy being big kids a lot of the time. That's what this thirteenth anniversary is about. We like to play. It's one thing that's really kept us together. We love to play with each other and laugh and have a good time.

Frances: We haven't decided on it yet, but I think we'll have a friend officiate. I'd like to be in a circle, and have the officiator in the middle with me and Gayle. I'd like to say nice things to each other about what we've been doing and what we'd like to keep doing.

Gayle: The concept of marriage has changed for me in the last few years. Since I have become a minister, I've done a lot of same-sex weddings. Now when I think of marriage, I think of lesbians. I consider us pioneers, and I think we're good role models. I think straight marriage is a total failure.

It empowers me to marry gay people. I also marry straight people, legally. I turn in the paperwork, I go down to city hall. It makes me angry that they get insurance benefits and all the privileges, and Frances and I take a beating financially. We both pay for our insurance policies, but we don't get the discounts that other people get, and that's not fair. The state won't acknowledge us, the federal government won't acknowledge us. So I feel that as long as I have the power to perform ceremonies, I'm going to affirm that for people.

Frances: I don't think that heterosexual marriage is a total failure, and I don't care if lesbian marriage is associated with heterosexual marriage. I think the concepts of marriage are still the same, concepts of commitment and devotion, respect, honoring, and getting support for doing that, getting cultural sanction. Of course, we don't have cultural sanction; we have to create our own.

Gayle and I think about things in a bit of a different way. I don't consider that being a reverend with the Universal Life Church empowers or disempowers me. I would perform ceremonies whether I had that or not. It only allows me to do it for straight people in a legal way and it gives a little added boost. But when it comes down to basic values, we agree on almost everything.

More lesbians are marrying these days because internalized homophobia is diminishing. I see it as part of the movement that's developed out of the feminist and gay movements. As the movement becomes more public, we're willing to take the risks, to acknowledge that we don't have to throw the baby out with the bathwater since we're not embracing heterosexual tradition. Early on, there was a very reactive time against marriage by gay people, like when we had our first ceremony. You don't find that anymore.

It seems that more lesbians have wedding ceremonies than gay men. In the local gay paper's wedding and anniversary announcements, I see many more women than men. The wedding page in that paper started in 1990. Ours may have been the first wedding-anniversary announcement.

We celebrate one anniversary a year. We celebrate our meeting, our coming together, and our weddings all on the same date. Gayle always wants to do more. It's gotten to be kind of a sweet joke. Gayle asks me to marry her on a regular basis. I think she would do it every year!

Gayle: I think people don't celebrate enough! People process stuff, get together and talk about problems; that is very commonplace and comfortable. I say, put that stuff aside and go out and show people your good side!

I have incredible respect for Frances as a woman, as a lesbian, as a therapist — there's nothing about Frances I don't respect. There are things I sometimes don't like, but that's not her problem, it's my problem.

Frances: Sometimes it's both of our problems.

Gayle: I had a life long before Frances. We're making a life together, but I don't expect her to like everything about me. And she lets me know when she doesn't like something. I rely on that to keep the communication going.

Frances: We believe in a few very basic principles, and we work on them over and over again. The first is honesty, and the second is direct communication without being abusive. We've worked on our communication skills a lot over the years. We try very hard to listen to one another and understand the other's perspective. When we get into a reactive state, we take time out. We have our little explosions and our little tiffs, but we never let them get very far. We'll say, stop, that's enough, let's come back to it later. We really use some of those tools. We don't believe in just beating it until it buries us with it. If there's an issue that's a serious conflict, we'll take a little piece and work on it, then go away to get perspective and come back to it later. And we may have to do this a number of times. We really try very hard to attend to our own problems.

Gayle: We have some basic rules and understandings. We made a pact that we would tell each other the truth to the best of our ability. We agreed that we weren't going to cheat on each other or go out with another person or do anything that would do injury or harm. I have trusted that from the gate.

We have systems set up to guarantee communication. We have a monthly house meeting and a Wednesday night which is our time together. I trust that if there are any issues or problems, it will be brought up at that time because it's our personal time together.

Frances: At our house meeting we have what we call our calendar comparison. We plan for trips we want to take together and we plan our time frames because we're both very busy. This way we can make sure we have time for ourselves. Then we talk about the bills, since we take turns paying the bills every other month. We talk about our budget and how things are going financially. We talk about chores and if there need to be changes in any of the systems we have or if someone's unhappy with something about it. Feelings is the fourth category. If there are any feelings that aren't being addressed about any of the three items or anything else, then we look at what needs to be attended to. We try to do it in the first week of every month.

For money, we have a three-pot system. We both have an individual account and we have a household account. We contribute to our household account based on a percentage of our income.

Gayle: Frances handles the math; I'm inept at it.

Frances: We've been doing the house meetings for years. Our Wednesday night is new. It's when there's no TV and we just hang out together.

Gayle: The Wednesday nights were my request. I was getting really grumpy in the relationship, and partly because I felt I wasn't getting enough time with Frances, so I asked for that Wednesday night. Our lives get so busy that sometimes we have to remind ourselves that we are important, that it's coupledom, that it's our responsibility to pull ourselves back together and say, hey, wait a minute — what am I doing this forty-hour-a-week job for, what am I making this incredible house payment for, what's this all about? It's about wanting to be with Frances. All the rest is secondary. If I don't get the quality time and enjoyment with Frances, then I'm an unhappy person. So, I'm willing to fight for that time and to bring it up.

Frances: I work late, and after my job is done I don't feel like communicating very much. Weeknights are more parallel-activity time; we don't make a lot of connection. Gayle goes to bed a lot earlier than I do. Wednesday night was an attempt to have something in the middle of the week that said, hey, we're a couple and we like each other and need to connect.

Gayle: If marriage was made legal for us, I'd do it for the recognition and the affirmation. It's my entitlement as an American citizen and what this country stands for. I'm not a flag-waving type, but I do think about the Bill of Rights and individual rights, and I think it's real important to go after them.

My marriage is a tool I've used to let people know who I am. I'm a very loving person. I could never be loving enough. I would like to encourage women and gay men to get married and be who they are and do it as much as possible. If they want to get married every year, fine, I'm available, I'll do the wedding. It's my pleasure.

Frances: If there's one thing that I could complain about, it would be that Gayle is so superlative in the way she expresses herself that there's nothing left for me to say. Though I'm much quieter about how I express it and it's harder for me to say it out loud, I love Gayle terribly deeply. She is my soul mate.

Gayle: I've never been as happy in my entire life as I am right now. I like the recommitment ritual because I never believed I could be so happy, I never believed I would be so fortunate. This relationship with Frances is way beyond my wildest dreams. I'm proud of it, I like to share it. If other people get something out of it, I'm really blessed. And that's the truth. If I can share this with people, it means so much to me, I just can't begin to tell you.

23

Ted Gaiser and Chuck Hornberger

Boston, Massachusetts

---

*I don't harbor any illusions that legalizing gay marriage would
give us instant recognition. What it can do is similar
to what the civil-rights movement did for the black community:
provide an opportunity to educate and give us grounds
to fight in the courts.*

Ted, thirty, and Chuck, forty-five, have been together since
1983 and have lived together all but two months of that
time. Their ceremony, in 1985, was held in an Episcopal church
and conducted by an Episcopalian minister who had never officiated a gay holy union before. The two work in the same hospital
and are in graduate-degree programs in business administration.
Ted gave up a potential career in the ministry to have the ceremony.

❧

Ted: By having a ceremony, we were offering both our gay friends
and the straight community a model of what could work. For our
heterosexual friends and family, it was a model of seriousness and
commitment so they could understand it on a personal level, compare it to themselves, and realize what we mean to each other.
For our gay friends, it was a model of a lasting relationship. It
created some political trouble in our community. Some people
were angry, some saw it as assimilation. Others were brought
closer to us because of it.

202

Ted, wearing a green clay complexion mask, receives a morning kiss from Chuck

Chuck: It wasn't that I thought a ceremony would make any real difference in our relationship or that I wanted to prove to anyone that I was serious about Ted—I was serious one way or the other. The ceremony was a means of announcing that to community and family, inviting them to be a part of it and to celebrate our relationship.

Ted: I also wanted to do it because I needed to acknowledge my relationship in the context of a spiritual community. In part, we structured our ceremony to make sure that community was involved. We had an open Eucharist, where the entire congregation was welcome to join us, and they did (in the passing of the bread and the wine).

Chuck: The minister who officiated was the minister of our parish. He was eager to do a ceremony like this, but he wouldn't commit the parish itself. The ceremony was held at a neighboring parish in the small chapel.

Ted: A lot of big churches have a little chapel on the side for smaller private ceremonies and christenings. We chose the little chapel because it was very pretty and quaint. We would have been dwarfed in the main sanctuary. I think the size and sweetness of the space added a sense of intimacy.

We met with the minister several times beforehand to formalize the ceremony. We confirmed that it was just a blessing of our relationship, although we structured it very closely to the marriage ceremony in the Episcopal prayer book.

Chuck: We sent out about forty invitations; about twenty-five people came. Our wedding attire was matching suits—white slacks and navy blue, double-breasted jackets. The service started with music—I played the piano and Ted sang. After three musical numbers, we walked forward and began the ceremony. There was no "best man" or anyone else, it was just the two of us.

Ted: We took the ceremony directly from *The Book of Common Prayer* (the Episcopal prayer book) and just changed the words as necessary. We had some Scripture readings. The vows were structured very similar to a traditional wedding.

Chuck: Here is the beginning of it:

Good friends, we have come together today in the presence of God to witness and bless the spiritual union of these two friends who wish to vow lifelong commitment. This is not a marriage. Such a union between two men is not yet regarded as marriage by either civil law or church tradition. But recognizing that human love is a sacrament, an outward and visible sign of God's grace in our lives, we are here to ask God's blessing on their love and on their promises.

There is a bit more, and then the usual, "Will you have this man," et cetera.

We said the vows and exchanged rings, and the minister draped his stole over our hands as a symbol of the union. Then there were prayers. We didn't discuss it ahead, we just opted not to kiss at the end of the ceremony. I think we shook hands. We may have embraced. And then we did another musical number while the minister set up the Eucharist. Ted baked the bread for the communion.

Ted: The minister was a little nervous. I know that he had gotten some flak in the diocese from people who heard that he had done this. But nothing dramatic. I think the bishop was actually somewhat supportive and basically only said what he did because he had to say something, politically. I think the kind of official word the minister got was, "Now, now, behave" — end of discussion.

Chuck: It was a wonderful time for us, and for my friends and family. Afterward, we all walked back to the house, where we had our reception, catered by Ted. We did some of the traditional things, like cutting the cake, having toasts, the presents, the food.

The cake was made at a bakery just down the street from our house, an old Italian bakery. That morning, my dad went down to pick it up. It's always crowded on Sunday mornings. So my dad asked for the cake for Ted and Chuck, and everybody there was getting kind of snickery. But he picked it up just the same.

My parents were very accepting. My two brothers didn't come. My older brother didn't come because he didn't feel comfortable with it; the other probably didn't come because I didn't go to his second wedding.

Ted: Chuck had come out to his parents ten years ago, so they had ten years to decide how they felt about his being gay. My family was still trying to determine how they felt about my being gay when I announced we were going to be married. I had been living with a woman my first two years of college, and then they discovered I was living with a man — Chuck. Shortly thereafter, I announced I was getting married.

My mother had a thirty-year class reunion the same weekend, and she and my father decided not to come. But my father struggled and struggled, and decided at the last minute that he would come. My mother was upset about my father having gone after they'd decided not to go. We've never discussed her feelings about the wedding, but it's become apparent over the years that she's more accepting of us as a married couple. We get cards at holiday time. She invites us to do things with her in ways she didn't used to.

My older brother was in the service in Japan and couldn't come. My younger brother came, and my sister came with her baby. She arrived early and, along with Chuck's mom, helped me with preparations for the reception. She called me up the night after the ceremony and said she'd thought about the wedding all the way home and just wanted me to know that it was the nicest service she'd ever been to. That was real powerful to hear, because my sister was still trying to deal with my being gay. She came because I'm her brother and she loves me, but she was still struggling, and it really meant a lot for her to come back and say that. It was, in a sense, a validation of why I'd done the ceremony in the first place.

Chuck: Our parents met each other for the first time at the ceremony. They found they have a lot in common and that they're a great support system for each other. Ted's parents invited my parents up to Vermont to spend Thanksgiving with them just a few months after the wedding. They had such a good time that we all celebrated Christmas together the following year.

Ted: We still celebrate the anniversary of our meeting on Valentine's Day. The official anniversary, in July, gets another celebration. Often it's a private celebration. One year we chose to do a reception for an AIDS healing service that took place in our parish on our anniversary night. We made it clear to one another and to the community that we were celebrating our relationship in the context of participating in this service, which meant a lot to us. So that was an alternative mode of celebration.

Chuck: Ted and I don't agree on the subject of children. I have very little patience with children anymore.

Ted: I haven't entirely given it up yet. I have some good nurturing skills and I'd like to use them. But ethically, I don't think one should bring more children into the world, so if we decided to have children we would only adopt.

Chuck: We share our money in a completely joint way. We always have. We haven't put together a will yet, but we're planning to do it.

Ted: I think we won't get motivated until something forces us to, like we've seen happen with friends being denied access to visit a partner in a hospital. We're very busy — we're both graduate students, we both have full-time jobs, we're active in the community. It leaves us very little time to work on things unless we have a very strong motivation.

Chuck: We're very busy, but we manage to see a lot of each other since we work in the same hospital.

Ted: I took the job on purpose because I knew that with our busy lives, we'd never see each other. This way, we can make lunch dates, or if one of us plans to stay late, we can tell the other and both decide to work late, or have dinner together.

We work out any problems pretty well. We're pretty good at talking. We haven't had major conflicts, there haven't been any crises where we've slammed doors or windows and yelled at each other.

Chuck: As a rule, I'm more the quiet type. If things go wrong, I'll tend to clam up. Ted can sense when I'm "clamming."

Ted: I'll say, "Excuse me, you're clamming up. I want to hear what's going on."

Chuck: But those times are few and far between. We know what we can and can't expect and what we can and cannot change. And I think we've pretty much learned how we're each willing to bend and shape and be shaped. The amount of give and take has increased through the years. That's why we work so well together, because we know how to read each other.

Ted: Chuck is very accepting of my diversity. For example, last summer I quit my job and took off for Nicaragua for three weeks. Though he's supportive of that, Chuck doesn't always understand what it entails and why I'm willing to quit my job and take off. His support, his willingness to have me go away for three weeks — I think that's an example of his being able to support me in what I do even though it's not his central interest.

Chuck: Another reason we get along so well is that we're complete opposites. Ted is very extroverted, where I'm very introverted, so we're not fighting for attention.

Ted: In public, I'm a little more uptight about appearing as a couple than Chuck is — holding hands at the movies or walking down the street. But I don't think my attitude would change if marriage was legalized, because I don't think society would change much very soon after. I don't harbor any illusions that legalizing gay marriage would give us instant recognition. What it can do is similar to what the civil-rights movement did for the black community: provide an opportunity to educate and give us grounds to fight in the courts. Same-sex marriage educates people regardless of whether it's legal.

There is one exception where we do touch each other in public: in church. It's important to us to worship together. At the passing of the peace, we embrace. We frequently sit closely and hold hands. It's the one place in the straight community where we have the opportunity to touch and be emotional with one another. Granted, that's on a different plane than cooing, but it's a place where we can embrace and acknowledge our intimacy.

I had considered ordination in the church as an Episcopal priest. I graduated from seminary in 1988. I knew that marrying

Chuck was a guarantee I could not be ordained, at least for some time. But I still chose to attend seminary because it was important to me. At present, I wouldn't have a clear conscience sacrificing the integrity of my relationship by joining a club that says I'm not able to have this relationship (the priesthood). So, in a sense, I was going into a willing exile that I felt was unjust, but an exile I needed to take because my relationship with Chuck was worth it. It meant that much to me to demonstrate my love for Chuck.

Chuck: In the ceremony, we included a reading about exile from a book called *Embracing the Exile*.[1] We wanted to include a reading that acknowledged what we've gone through being gay. Since that ceremony, I don't think Ted and I really feel exiled. Our ceremony and our union helped dispel the exile that we felt individually and that society places upon us. This is where we've come from, this is what we're dealing with, this is what we're trying to get away from. We don't wish to be exiled.

Note

1. John Fortunato, *Embracing the Exile: Healing Journeys of Gay Christians* (San Francisco: Harper & Row, 1982).

24

Pat and Karen Norman

San Francisco, California

---

*The only time I was against marriage was when I thought
you had to marry a man. It never occurred to me that I
could still get married.*

Pat, fifty-one, and Karen, thirty-three, have been together
since 1983. Karen is an attorney teaching AIDS law. Pat, a
longtime activist, created the position of coordinator of lesbian/gay
health services in the San Francisco Department of Public Health,
the first position of its kind in the United States. She was the founder of the Lesbian Mothers' Union in 1971, a time when many
people did not acknowledge, or even realize, that lesbians are often
mothers. She is now executive director of a statewide training program for AIDS intervention. Pat is the mother of four and grandmother of eight. At the time of this interview, Karen is pregnant
with her first child.

❧

Karen: My friend Norman introduced me to Pat at the Castro The-
ater in 1983, the opening night of the lesbian and gay film festival.
We happened to run into each other the next night and went out
afterward. I drove Pat home. She said she never wanted to see me
again after she found out how old I was, which was twenty-five.
We were married the following year.

211

Pat and Karen

Pat: There were a number of reasons to make a commitment in public. To say to people that we felt strongly enough about our relationship that we wanted to have witnesses to support our commitment; to invite our families to participate because we wanted them to acknowledge our bond and support us; and to have fun, to be joyous in our celebration. Also, we are traditional in terms of religious and spiritual experience and wanted to have the universe involved as well.

We had a minister who's since died of AIDS—Rev. Jim Sandmire, one of the first pastors of the MCC—and a Buddhist priestess. So we had not only the more traditional ceremony, but we also did the washing of hands to cleanse ourselves of past commitments and affiliations, we burned any of our insecurities and jealousies, all that kind of stuff. It was very meaningful to have both Western and Eastern perspectives.

We had about eight people at the ceremony. I didn't want everybody in the world seeing this commitment except people I felt very trusting of. Then we had about 150 of our friends come and have a good time afterward. We had wonderful cake, tea sandwiches, caviar, pâté, cheeses.

Karen: A few of Pat's kids came to the wedding and the reception. My mother's cousin from Sacramento was the only person from my family who came. My mother is extremely bigoted and homophobic. When Pat and I got together, my mother basically said that's the end of our relationship. She actually called me up one time and said, "Karen, it's time to come home now." And she's a psychiatrist!

I sent an invitation to my dad at his office so my mother wouldn't see it. After I sent an invitation to my cousin in Sacramento, I got a call from my mother for the second time in two years. She asked me who else I'd sent the invitations to. I said, "Pardon me?" And she repeated, "Who else got those invitations? Did you send any to the East Coast?" I said no; she hung up. Her family lives on the East Coast.

My father had never known anybody who had a gay or lesbian wedding, and because it was not something one did, he just blew it off. But he does take the relationship seriously. About a month after the wedding, he took us on a weekend jaunt up to Napa Valley. The length of my relationship with Pat rather than the marriage made a difference to him.

Pat: My mother and dad aren't alive. The people I invited all came, except for my oldest son. I feel fine about my support. My mother knew that I am a lesbian and didn't have any negative numbers about it. When I went to court to gain custody of my children, she was there for me. I have been more supported in my family than not, and those people that are not supportive are inconsequential to me anyway.

Karen: A friend of ours who's a jeweler made our rings. Our astrologer said we had to wear silver. I was actually kind of pissed! Getting married was something I'd been waiting for since I was six years old, and I wanted a humongous gold ring on the fourth finger of my left hand, by God, and I wanted everybody to see it! And then we had to get silver. Oh, well.

Pat: We had our astrological charts done together. Our astrologer said that December 4th at 7:23 A.M. was a good time to make the commitment to be married. So we went up to Guerneville, spent the night, got up at dawn, took a shower, washed each other and rinsed away the old, and all that good stuff, and then we got dressed and went to Jenner, where the ocean and the Russian River meet. There was no other human in sight.

Karen: I felt like we were the only two people in the world, and the sun came through the clouds, right there where we were standing. It felt very blessed.

Pat: We went through months of counseling with the minister, talking about what it meant to be in a committed relationship, how we relate to each other as individuals, who is Karen, who am I, what are we going to have to give up. It was a six-month preparation.

Karen was saying, "This is a piece of cake." I was the one thinking, Is this the right thing? This means I'm going to be with this woman the rest of my life and that's a heavy-duty commitment. I freaked out for weeks before the ceremony.

Karen: And the day of the wedding, she calmed right down. Rev. Sandmire walks in looking like what I thought God looked like when I was a little kid — tall, white hair, white robe, gold something or other around his neck — and I thought, Holy shit! All I remember was squeezing Pat's hand. She had no feeling in her hand. I don't even remember what I said! So I don't go back to my vows, because I can't recall what I said. What I go back to is the commitment.

What anniversaries do we celebrate? All of them! A gay comedian we know says that when a gay or lesbian couple is asked, "So, is your anniversary the night you met or the night you moved in together, or the night you first did it?" the answer is "Yes!"

There's so little recognition of the length of gay relationships. I think that the first year we were together before we were married was really significant. So instead of saying this is our seventh anniversary, we say this is our eighth. We have June 19th when we met, July 21st when we first dated, September 1st when I moved in, October 21st, which is Pat's birthday and when we got engaged, December 4th when we actually exchanged rings, and Cinco de Mayo, when we got married. And we're also good at Thanksgiving and Christmas.

The only time I was against marriage was when I thought you had to marry a man. When I was in school in Iowa, I heard a song one day that went, "I'll never marry, I'll be no man's wife / I expect to be single all the rest of my life." And I thought, Wow! That's a pretty song, and I like the lyrics! Very good. It never occurred to me that I could still get married. Nobody I was with before Pat ever wanted to get married. People thought it was too committed, too confining.

Pat: We'd like to see marriage legalized. It would be fantastic if we could actually go in and sign on the dotted line and say that we're going to be on each other's income tax, automatically have community property, have all the rights and benefits of married heterosexuals.

I'm really tired of people in the lesbian and gay community taking issue with the idea of a couple being married and using terms that are supposedly heterosexual. Who cares? Whether people choose to say "married" or "unionized" has very little to do with how we relate to each other. If people come up with new words that are meaningful to us, then maybe instead of "married" we can say something else. The issue is that we've decided to be together. I can't spend my time figuring out the proper word for marriage when the action is what is useful and necessary to our well-being. And it comes down to our well-being. I just want to be able to have my relationship with Karen. I don't want people messing with me.

Karen: I think the word "partner" diminishes the quality and depth of commitment, and we're not in business. I like using the terms "married" and "spouse." They allow me to function not only within our community but in society in general, and people who are not as knowledgable about our community can understand what my relationship is about. I understand the semantic controversy. But I also feel like, if you're going to criticize me for using heterosexual or patriarchal terminology, then I would like to see you make as much difference for the gay community as Pat has made in her lifetime so far. Then we'll have a discussion.

I think the domestic-partnership registration in San Francisco is the worst law that has ever been passed for gay people in this city. The fact that they got it passed without demanding some kind of tangible benefit in return is totally beyond me. It was like they were saying, We'll clean it up after we get it passed. Do it right the first time. It makes unmarried people liable for the debts of their significant other. Until there's some sort of tangible benefit attached to the significant liability, I'm not going to register. Our wills and health-care powers of attorney give us infinitely more protection under the law than this domestic-partners registration would.

Pat: It's important to me that people — gay people — realize that we need to have commitments. When people get caught up thinking that this is the heterosexual model and therefore they don't want to follow it, they don't give themselves the opportunity to grow and learn from relationships they could have.

Karen: There's so much opportunity for divisiveness, and regimentalism, and things that take the community apart. When I hear criticism, I want to say, You need to attack the enemy, which is the government and other institutions, you need to change things. People who are judgmental about what other folks are allowed to do undermine our power and our potential.

Pat: Let me tell you what happened in 1971, when I was in Los Angeles at a lesbian conference by the Daughters of Bilitis. We were going into one part of the church. In another part of the church, there was a lesbian couple, dressed in tuxedo and white gown, totally decked out in matrimonial garb. Lesbians stood on the other side of the street and booed them and made fun of them. They were awful to these people, absolutely awful. I was so amazed and shocked that lesbians would do that to other lesbians. There were these radical lesbians over here who decided that those people over there were following a patriarchal system and shouldn't do that and so they were not going to bless their relationship.

When I attended the national planning meetings in 1987 for the March on Washington, there was still controversy from people on the radical left saying, This is a terrible thing for you all to be doing, promoting marriage, which is "het," patriarchal, and on and on. I said, You can talk about all this if you want to, but we're not going to change this agenda, because there are thousands of people who want this. Over ten thousand people got married on that day.

Karen: Having had the wedding really makes a difference, having said "for better and for worse." And we have gone through some unbelievable stuff in our life together — Pat's son being killed three years ago, my mother completely rejecting me with no warning.

I changed my last name because it made me feel we were more of a family. It's just another little addition. I didn't tell Pat I was going to do it. I went to the DMV and changed it, and then I showed her my license. I filed an income-tax report under my new name. They sent me a letter and asked what I was doing. I said I got married, and they said, oh, okay.

Pat: I thought it was great. I just felt marvelous about it.

Karen: It took a while for Pat's family to open up their arms to me. You go through a period of proving yourself to anybody. They know I'm committed to them, so they give it back. I got to cut the umbilical cord on our latest grandchild. It was wonderful! Then I nearly passed out. Pat's going to cut the umbilical cord on our child. She doesn't pass out at anything.

Pat: Marriage is not all cake and ice cream. You have to work at it. Dealing with racism constantly, whether it's in the gay or the straight population, with sexism, homophobia, lesbophobia, classism within our relationship — it's difficult. Sometimes you don't like each other for a while. But with the commitment, you work through that, and we'll see what goes on. It is a commitment to grow. And you do get the cake, too. And sometimes, the pie. Karen makes one hell of an apple pie.

Editor's Note: Pat and Karen sought a black donor but found there is a serious shortage of black donors at sperm banks. They settled on a donor whose skin color best reflects a combination of their races. The baby Karen was pregnant with at the time of this interview was miscarried. Karen returned to the physician for a second donor insemination, again became pregnant on the first try, and, on July 22, 1992, gave birth to a healthy boy, Zachary David Martin Langsley Norman.

25

Todd and Jonathan Barr-Sawyer

Portsmouth, New Hampshire

On the application for the name change, they ask you the reason for wanting to change your name, and we decided to put down exactly why — that we are married to each other.

Jonathan, thirty-seven, and Todd, twenty-seven, have been together since 1987. They were married in 1990 in a Unitarian Universalist church. Both are New Hampshire natives. Jonathan is an interior designer, and Todd is an actor, singer, and dancer and an activist in the lesbian and gay civil-rights movement. They have spoken at universities and on television and have appeared on popular TV talk shows to discuss gay marriage.

❧

Jonathan: I'd never thought about having a ceremony when I was growing up through the 1970s, because I was so sick of straight society. I didn't want to do it up until the day we did it. Being older, I felt very secure with Todd, and didn't feel a need to have a wedding.

But something happened that day. It became very magical. It was the most beautiful day of my life. When I woke up that day, I felt like a very special human being, I felt very good about myself and very good about being alive. We had almost 150 guests, most of them heterosexual. No one came questioning why we were doing it. They treated us with the respect we deserve.

219

Todd and Jonathan on their wedding day

Todd: I've been through three relationships. My first lasted a long time, and I was very, very young. The second was just a fleeting moment. And then there was Jonathan.

After a couple of years into the relationship with Jonathan, I knew this was what I wanted and this was the man I've chosen to be with for my lifetime. Once I was comfortable with that concept, I wanted to celebrate it. I'm not a religious person, but I am very spiritual. I wanted to bring our family and friends together and have a big celebration, and have it be for no other reason than that two of us are proclaiming our love for each other publicly. We would never be in a typical wedding setting, so why not? Why shouldn't we have the same joy other people have when they get married? It's unbelievable to think that many couples are talked out of it.

The ceremony was held at the Unitarian Universalist church. When I phoned the church to make the arrangements, I really didn't know what to call it. (The minister gave us a certificate, so in the eyes of the church it was a marriage.) I asked if they do commitment ceremonies. They thought I was talking about a funeral! I told them I was talking about two men that were coming together to share our lives and exchange vows, and I knew they'd done that before.

We met with the minister, who asked us some questions to make sure we were really ready. He put us through the same sessions he puts a heterosexual couple through. We discussed our motives for wanting the ceremony, how long we'd been together, and how we'd come to the decision. Most gay couples he's performed weddings for have been together for about three years.

The church organist played classical music for twenty minutes while people came in and settled down. We had about 150 guests. We each had a woman stand up with us, our best friends. We wore matching tuxedos with black pants and white dinner jackets, with a teal-colored tie and cummerbund.

We walked down the side aisles, met at the front and hugged each other, then sat in the front pew. The organist played the song "Jesu, Joy of Man's Desiring" all the way through. After that, we did the personal part of the ceremony. I love to perform. So I got up and sang to Jonathan. It was the most difficult thing I've ever done in my life. The song was "Here and Now" by Luther Vandross. We had eye contact for the whole number. I was oblivious to everyone else in the whole room. It was just me and him, looking at each other, bawling, and there I was, standing up and trying to sing to him! Everyone in the church ended up crying, too.

After I sang, I sat down with him again. We took a couple of minutes to collect ourselves, then we walked up to where the minister was standing. In the book *Permanent Partners*,[1] there are some suggestions for ceremonies. We took most of the words for the minister's address from that book.

After his address, we read poetry to each other. I read a poem I'd written to Jonathan two days after I'd met him in 1987. Jonathan paints and draws, and frames things really beautifully. He had three poems mounted and framed, and he wrote a letter expressing his feelings on the back of the framed poetry. He read this letter to me, and he was sobbing when he read it. Then he read the poems. He really put a lot of thought and effort into finding the right poetry and arranging it the right way.

Jonathan: The poem Todd read me during the ceremony is beautiful. It was beautiful four years ago, and it's still beautiful. It made me feel really good that this person cares about me, that what was true four years ago is still true today.

Todd: After we finished this part, we said our vows, exchanged the rings, and then the minister made the declaration that we should "Tell the world." That was out of *Permanent Partners*, too. He looked at us and gave us a little nod, and we hugged and kissed each other. And then the hornpipe played, and we exited down the center aisle. Everyone jumped up and started shouting and applauding.

We wear our rings — simple gold bands — on our left hands, against the wishes of our gay friends, who pointed out that gay people wear their rings on the right hand. We don't; we wear it on the left hand, where we want to wear it.

Jonathan: I ended up inviting my family two weeks before the ceremony. My family lives about eighty miles from here. I have my
own life here, away from them. I didn't want to invite them or my
older friends, but Todd encouraged me to go ahead.

After I discussed it with a couple of my sisters, I felt more
comfortable with it. I sent an invitation to my parents (addressed
to "the Sawyers") and sent one to each of my six siblings and
their spouses. Five of my brothers and sisters and their spouses
came. They were frantic that they almost didn't get the opportunity to come to it. My father was the only one who didn't respond to the invitation. My mother said she would come, but
called to cancel the morning before the wedding. She was ill, but
I felt it was an excuse; I just don't think she would have canceled
out on anyone else's wedding in my family.

My first lover, who I was with for three years fifteen years ago,
flew up from Key West the day before the wedding and took care
of all the flowers. He was my father figure, my older-brother figure, that day. I felt very secure having him there.

Todd: As far as my family goes, everybody was there — my mother,
my father, nieces, nephews. My whole process of coming out was
very easy, and my family's been very accepting ever since. My
family encouraged us to do this. They helped us with preparations. My sister did the catering. She helped us make a cake in
the form of the old Federalist house that we lived in.

Jonathan: My family doesn't reject me, but they're not giving, they
really don't want to talk about it. Not even after we were on two
nationally televised shows. Todd's situation is very different.
Todd is the youngest child. He gets and gives a lot. If there's a
family gathering, we're the ones who host it. We're the ones that
have the family dinners. This was like another event we could do
where his family could come together at our instigation. Todd's
father always has a key to wherever we're living, and he just
comes in and hangs out with us.

Todd: My mother introduces Jonathan as her son-in-law, or as my
husband. "This is my son, and this is my son's spouse, Jonathan,"
or "This is my son-in-law, Jonathan." She doesn't usually get a

negative response, but if she did, she'd be able to handle herself. The way she presents it, there's no room for objection.

Jonathan: I hadn't been interested in having a ceremony originally, in part because I was afraid to stand up in front of that many people and bring that much attention to Todd and myself, to do something that controversial. I was afraid people would think it was a mockery. I was afraid of being rejected. I didn't know what was going to happen that day; I was afraid of the unknown. I guess I was a little bit homophobic. My experience of coming out was completely different from Todd's. When I discovered I was gay, I didn't have any support from my family, although they loved me.

Todd: I came out at seventeen in the beginning of my senior year. In a human-relationships class we had an assignment to write an anonymous letter to our parents, asking a question we'd never asked before. Mine was: "What would you do if your child was gay?"

That evening, parents were invited to a parent-student conference, and the papers were distributed anonymously and read aloud. When my paper was read, the parent reading it ended up in a debate with my mother: he was ready to send the kid for psychiatric help, and she was totally blowing him out of the room! So I felt it was pretty safe to give her the letter.

When I gave the letter to her after the meeting, she said she loved me, gave me a big hug, and we both started crying. She didn't even open it until we got home. Later, I found out she thought it was one of two things: I'd either gotten someone pregnant or I was gay. She's since organized a chapter of PFLAG [Parents and Friends of Lesbians and Gays] in Stratham, New Hampshire. She went out on her own and got a lot of press coverage. She and my father posed for a newspaper photo with Jonathan and I, and she got a spot on the cable channel. It infuriates her that as human beings and American citizens we don't have the same rights as others.

My father is very conservative, but, on the gay issue, he's very outspoken. He had an argument with an old friend of thirty or forty years. The man called me a pervert, and asked how my father could deal with his son being a fag and all this other stuff. Apparently my father said, "Look, if you can't accept my family, then you have no business being my friend." He's not politically active, but he's not afraid to talk about it.

We're working on our wills and powers of attorney right now. And we look forward to jointly owning property. We've talked about having children, but neither of us has any desire to raise children right now. I'd want to be more secure financially. We're not opposed to it, but we're not planning it.

We have joint checking and savings accounts; all of our money is pooled. Some months Jonathan makes more than me and some months I make more than him, and it doesn't really matter; it all goes to the same thing. We've been doing it that way since the beginning.

Though I'm very much a gay activist, we lead a quiet life. We don't go out to the bars. Like any heterosexual couple, we go out to dinner with friends, have functions we go to, take vacations together.

There's room for us to have opinions on different things; we don't have to agree on everything. Jonathan and I are total opposites, but I think it adds to the relationship. If we're having an argument, we try not to threaten each other with leaving, which is so easy to do in a gay relationship because there are no legal boundaries.

Joining our last names was Jonathan's idea, which showed me just how much sharing this experience meant to him.

Jonathan: After the ceremony, I realized it was important to me to change our name, because I felt like I had my own family, that from two other families Todd and I had created a new one. We discussed it at length and decided on the hyphenated name, which represents us each as individuals but joined as one. On the application for the name change, they ask you the reason for wanting to change your name, and we decided to put down exactly why — that we were married to each other on such and such a date. Where the form asked for consent of spouse, we signed our names. We changed our drivers' licenses, social security, credit cards — everything. It took a lot of nerve to go to the registry at superior court, and then we had to set a court date and stand before the judge. But it was wonderful walking out of that court the Barr-Sawyers.

Note

1. Betty Berzon, *Permanent Partners: Building Gay and Lesbian Relationships That Last* (New York: E. P. Dutton, 1988).

26

Pik Work and Mary Provost

Stillwater, Oklahoma

---

*We were celebrating for all gays and lesbians who've been
denied this particular joy in their lives.*

Pik, forty-three, and Mary, forty, are members of the Still-
water Friends Meeting in Oklahoma, which is affiliated with
Friends General Conference. Pik (pronounced "pick") is Choctaw
Indian. Oklahoma is her home state. Mary is a New Hampshire
native. Both describe themselves as "Quakers by convincement" as
opposed to birthright Quakers. Good friends for the last eighteen
years, they lived apart for many years, then reunited and became
involved as a couple in 1989. In the time they lived apart, Mary's
postpolio condition has largely confined her to a wheelchair. Their
marriage, in 1990, was held one year after they made their lifetime
commitment to each other. Mary and Pik's marriage was the first
same-gender marriage in the South Central Yearly Meeting (a region covering Texas, Oklahoma, Arkansas, and part of Louisiana).[1]

Mary: When a couple requests a marriage under the care of the
Meeting, they send a letter to the clerk. The clerk's role is similar
to a chairperson's; they are facilitators. The clerk reads the request to the Meeting. In our case, since it was both the first marriage under the care of the Meeting (we're relatively new) and the

227

Pik and Mary at their Quaker wedding

*Pik and Mary's wedding cake displays a
peace symbol with Pik's ancestral Choctaw
symbol for peace, a broken arrow*

first request for same-gender marriage in this Meeting, two things had to be dealt with for them to come to clearness (consensus). The first was to discover what the Meeting defined as marriage; this issue went before the whole Meeting. Was it a marriage or a ceremony of commitment? The Meeting decided that this was no less a marriage than any other. Therefore, the term "marriage" was used.

Pik: Because we were members of the Meeting, they knew us well and had anticipated it. Some had even encouraged it. A clearness committee for marriage assigned to the couple gets to know you if they don't already and finds out whether or not *you* are clear about it. The clearness committee is made up of Friends who volunteer for that role and stand by the marriage should the couple have problems. About half of our committee was also our oversight committee, which helps put the wedding together. And that's no small task to ask people to do, because with most weddings, there's a lot to do.

Mary: The clearness committee makes a recommendation about whether the Meeting should support the marriage. By approving the marriage, the Meeting is saying they take responsibility for the wellness of the marriage. (You can ask Friends within the Meeting or the Meeting as a whole to meet with you to help you reach clearness on whatever issue is bothering you.)

After the committee of clearness for marriage recommended to the Meeting as a whole that it take this marriage under its care, the Meeting had to go through clearness. In a church, the minister performs a ceremony without consent of the congregation. In the Quaker tradition, each individual must decide whether they believe, by their definition of God or the spirit, that they can sanction this marriage. If one member of the Meeting opposes the marriage, preparation goes no further until that one person reaches clearness. This is the standard decision-making process among Friends.

Pik: We're talking about a very major form of consensus here!

Clearness as a whole Meeting is done from silence, from worship. People can speak when they feel led by God or the spirit to speak. There isn't any bantering back and forth. Someone says what they feel, and then there's a pause, and then someone else says what they feel without commenting on someone else's words, then there's another pause, and so on. Hopefully, you get through this by letting everyone say how they feel about it. As people's minds change about things, they can say so. Eventually, the clerk may feel that consensus has been reached and will say what he or she feels the consensus is and ask if everyone is in agreement. If everyone is not, they'll say so then. We reached consensus within three months.

Mary: There were Friends that spoke up and affirmed the rights of all lesbians and gay men to be affirmed in the same way.

Pik: When we were in our clearness committee, they asked us questions as if our gender didn't matter. Did we have other entanglements? Was there anybody, any ex-lover, that we hadn't gotten over? What did we expect from the marriage? Did we want kids? That was probably the most surprising question we were asked.

Mary: Our marriage was a question of joy and wanting to share my joy with everyone I knew.

Pik: They told us we'd be different the next day. And we laughed! We'd been together a year and a half, we'd known each other forever. But in truth, we did feel different the next day. It's taken us a while to really be convinced that we have something we never thought we'd have a chance to have: our relationship is recognized. We stood up in front of a large group of our friends and said, We're serious about this. It's not, We're going to do this until we get tired of it.

Mary: We were married May 26th of 1990.

Pik: We stood in the house waiting for everyone to congregate. Thirty minutes before the ceremony, we were totally convinced nobody was going to come. When they did start to arrive, we were convinced they were going to figure out they didn't know what they were doing there and they would leave.

Mary: Until we entered the Meeting for worship, we were thinking that at any given point people were going to say, Excuse me, we did this for politically correct reasons and now we've changed our minds. And that speaks to our socialization, which tells us we would not be accepted. It was so deeply ingrained that we even doubted the people who love us the most. Lesbians and gay men are raised to believe this is something they will be denied. We considered it not only our marriage, but an affirmation of all lesbians and gays to have our rights and celebrate our relationships. We were celebrating for all gays and lesbians who've been denied this particular joy in their lives. And it was also a way of paying honor to our lovers past and present, alive and dead, who never had the joy of celebrating our relationship.

Pik: It's a little stunning to be a part of something this new.

Mary: The marriage took place in a worship Meeting, in the same manner as any other Meeting for worship. It was held in silence. The Choctaw tradition is that marriages be held outside, so we wanted it held outside, and we wanted it done in the manner of Friends. We had the wedding and reception at a private home by a pond under the trees.

Pik: There is a facing bench, which is just what it sounds like. I'd mentioned to a Friend that a facing bench was also very common in the Choctaw custom, that there was a bench or seat with a blanket thrown over it for the couple to sit on. (It used to be a blanket or skin; now we have chairs.) The day of the wedding, the Friend came with a very beautiful pendleton blanket he'd gotten at one of the local powwows, and he put it across the bench and then presented it to us afterward as a gift.

Mary: The worshipers were spread in a semicircle, with an aisle down the middle. The Meeting was called into silence. We entered holding hands, and walked to the facing benches. Since we had nonmembers and even nonattenders there, one individual read an introduction which explained what was going to happen and invited Friends to worship. Something similar was read afterwards, just before we left, including an invitation to speak if people felt inclined to do so, and there was some speaking after we said our vows.

Out of the silence, we stood and gave our vows. You memorize the vows and then say them exactly that way. There is no minister to prompt you. Our vows were identical:

> In the presence of God and these, our Friends, I take thee to be
> my bond mate, promising with Divine assistance to be unto thee a
> loving, faithful, and considerate bond mate until death shall sepa-
> rate us.

The marriage certificate we prepared is a three-hundred-year-old tradition among Friends. It was brought over and we signed it. Then it was read out loud by a designated person within the Meeting, and taken away. The Meeting remained in worship. Anyone in attendance could speak during that time. And then, whoever is best suited, whoever can get what we call the sense of the Meeting — when they feel it is time for worship to break, they rise and stop the Meeting. We left, and everyone present signed the certificate. From what I understand, that is the traditional manner of Friends in which a Meeting for worship for marriage is held.

Pik: The marriage certificates are very large. Ours is 18 by 24.

Mary: They contain all the particulars as to the date, time, place, name of the Meeting that took this marriage under its care, the two individuals involved, who their parents are and the specific vows. Everyone who attends the wedding signs it as witnesses. Children signed ours as well.

Pik: It's very traditional to put it on the wall in a prominent place in your home. It's amazing to get up in the morning and see this certificate with the signatures of forty people who were all there and support us in this.

Most people dressed up. We wore matching white pants, and I wore some jewelry with some of my beading work.

Mary: Pik is a silversmith, so she made our rings. We wear them on our left hand. The best way to describe our rings is to say that my hair is the color of copper, a red copper, and Pik's is salt-and-pepper gray. So she entwined silver and copper together for the rings.

Pik: After the signing of the certificate, we went up to the reception table and the party began. A tremendous wind came up. A friend of ours who's Cherokee had sent us a wedding card wishing the Great Spirit would come to us on the wind, and it did!

Mary: It was a strange coincidence, because of the two other Quaker gay commitment ceremonies, or marriages, we know of, this is the third time we've heard that a wind came up. In one case, it blew out the window of a Meeting house, blew the shutters open. In the other ceremony, there were sixty-mile-an-hour straight winds! Many Friends say that in the Bible, God is always represented as the wind.

Pik: A bit mystical, but it seems to be a common coincidence.

Mary: A couple we know who are both excellent bakers put together a six-piece cake because we had children who are allergic to milk and friends who were allergic to chocolate and others who were allergic to strawberry! They made five separate cakes, put them together, and decorated it for us.

Pik: It was a design that Mary made, which incorporated a peace symbol and a broken arrow, a traditional Indian peace symbol, because that's something that matters to both of us a lot.

Mary: We had promised we were not going to do it, but we were pressured into feeding each other the cake.

Pik: We had a mixture of all types of people. Eight or ten people were gay and some were couples. We had very few blood kin there. We have no relatives close by. It was a serious case of hard-to-get-people-there. I've got a couple of family members who would prefer to look the other way. They don't want to talk about it. Not just the marriage, but my relationship, and any of my relationships past, my way of life. I did have one sister who attended. I was amazed. My mother is living, but she's one of the look-away people.

Mary: There are five kids in my family; four out of those five are gay. And unfortunately, none of them could make it.

My family fully recognizes the relationship. The marriage makes no difference to them. But my mother and I were vastly estranged, and since we hadn't spoken in seven or eight years, I didn't feel particularly inclined to ask her to come to the wedding.

There is a national publication called *Friends Journal,* which announces marriages along with other announcements. Our Meeting sent an announcement of our wedding, and it was listed under

"Marriages." We received anniversary cards this year, even from people who've only been members or attenders for six months. When a new attender or someone new comes to the Meeting, they don't shy from the fact that this is a marriage under their care; it's not like it's under the rug, it's very open.

Pik: We celebrate our wedding anniversary. Since Mary and I have known each other so long, we'd be hard put to pick a date for our anniversary other than our marriage date.

Mary: Our marriage served as a catalyst. Since our marriage, there have been other requests for marriage under the care of the Meeting in the South Central Yearly Meeting.

Pik: I have been to a lot of weddings, but I've never seen forty wedding guests who all looked like they were going to pop their buttons off their vests they were so happy. This bunch really seemed like they felt they were a part of something.

Mary: They believe, as we do, that this commitment to each other is our will and also above our will. It is the will of the spirit, or God, or what each individual defines as God — that added a great deal. It was the additional experience of listening to that God, what we call the God within, that was particularly satisfying to this Meeting.

Pik: It's been especially nice to be regarded by straight couples the way they regard each other. This is the first time in my life, as a lesbian, I have ever felt the equality that extends to having people see me in public in an open place and cheerfully flag me down, stop and talk to me without any tendency to shy away. It's a very unique feeling.

Mary: I think our gay friends are astounded. I think they're astounded that the certificate is on the wall, and I think they're astounded at the number of people that were willing to sign it.

Our Meeting has taken the issue of durable powers of attorney under their consideration and have actually explored what they, as a Meeting, would do to help support us in the case of a medical emergency. Our clerk went to the local hospital and said he would like the staff to recognize the clerk, whether it was him or anyone else, as the minister of this Meeting. If something happened to me and Pik needed to get in, he would introduce himself as the clerk from this Meeting and say, This individual will come in at my request.

Pik: As far as wills, we haven't done as much as we need to. Finances being what they are with both of us being students right now, we haven't seen a lawyer yet for the formal will. We've handled all the rights of survivorship and other business stuff from the beginning; it didn't change at all after the marriage. The only difference is in the sense of security and commitment I've felt since the marriage. There's a security about being in the care of the Meeting that's a little hard to explain. I know that if we hit any rough spots, as couples do, and we need to talk to somebody, individually or jointly, we'll be able to. We know that there are not only people who know about our relationship, but who are pleased about our relationship and want to help how they can. And that's an extra kind of security.

Mary: It's a commitment until we die and that's the way it's going to be viewed until we die. Whether the United States recognizes it or not, this is a marriage. It doesn't matter to me whether it's legalized or not, but for financial reasons, if it was legalized, I'd do that.

Pik: If that meant going through another ceremony, that would be fine too, whatever it took.

Mary: I feel a lot more strongly about marriage since my first relationship. In my first relationship, my lover died. It was in a time when gays and lesbians were not accepted at all. When my lover was in the hospital dying, I was excluded from everything that was going on and had very little say. As I put it to the clearness committee on marriage, when she died I made a statement that never again would I deny another relationship I'm in. Not to anybody, not for any reason. That played a large part in this marriage request.

Pik: My suspicion is, were marriage legalized, a lot of people would be perfectly delighted to acknowledge it. There are people who have a hard time condoning something that isn't legal. They'd be more open about the fact that it is all right with them if it were legal.

Mary: If it were legalized, people wouldn't be allowed to ignore it.
Society would be forced to look at something they'd prefer to
keep under the rug. It would be a great joy to the gay and lesbian
community because we would no longer be ostracized. It would
be all of us together, not "us" and "them."

Pik: We rarely feel "us" and "them" anymore, which is very strange.
And I like it.

Mary: Oklahoma is very conservative. We don't go around holding
hands. We are at a very conservative college. There are incidents
of gay bashing. Being in a wheelchair, I feel particularly vulnerable.

Pik: But being physical in public is not something that people in
our generation are really into doing anyway, gay or straight. People have got to be totally tuned out to the whole idea of lesbians
to not realize we're together.

Mary: But some people may not recognize us as a couple because
one person's in a wheelchair and somebody is always with them.
Poor Pik gets the label of attendant. And people in wheelchairs
are not recognized as having a loving relationship that isn't ultra-
dependent and they're not recognized especially as having a sexual relationship. I haven't been in a wheelchair the whole time
we've known each other. Eighteen years ago, I could outrun Pik!

Pik: She's an old mountain climber.

Mary: I had polio when I was a kid, and when you get to about
thirty-five, some of us come down with postpolio. I've been in a
chair about two and a half, three years.

Pik: She had received it before I came back here after living in
another city. When we were in our younger days, we were real
little hell-raisers, to be perfectly honest. We did our share of par-
tying and running around, and our share of adventuring. That's a
nice thing to have had the opportunity to have shared with each
other.

Mary: It's nice that Pik knows the side of me that is not in a wheelchair. It makes it special for me because when times are really
bad we can laugh about the days I could run circles around her.

My being in a wheelchair was a consideration when we got back together after years of separation, always knowing where each other was but not doing anything about it. We sat down and said, Okay, do you realize this situation could get worse and that you may end up pushing a wheelchair around for the rest of your life? It was something we both had to look at. There was the guilt of her life having certain impediments. It was something they asked us in our clearness for marriage, they asked how we both felt about that issue, how we intended to handle it, could we really handle it. It was nice they even bothered to ask that question. It does make a difference in the way people accept you. And it does make a difference in our life-style, but it doesn't make a difference in the degree of love.

Pik: It doesn't make a difference to our relationship whatsoever.

Mary: I'd like to tell lesbians and gay people to hang in there. Don't give up. Don't let society dictate the level you can love on.

Pik: We both came up in a time when most people stayed in the closet, in the 1950s and 1960s, and we've seen a lot of the oppression up-close and personal. I think things are really changing. And at the same time, I'm quite sure that in this town alone there must be anywhere from ten to fifty couples running around thinking they're the only ones in the universe. So I hope we're visible.

Note

1. The traditional form of Quaker worship is based on silence without leadership from a hired minister. There is no church hierarchy; the membership is involved in a common search for truth. The discussion on same-sex marriage is taking place in Traditionalist Quaker Meetings, where members are working toward a Society-wide consensus on marriage. Because Quaker procedure is based on reaching consensus, Meetings around the country have arrived at varying decisions on recognizing sexual diversity and holding union ceremonies or celebrations of commitment "under the care of the Meeting," as it is called.

Part Four

Ceremony Officiators

27

Father Robert L. Arpin

Father Arpin is a Roman Catholic priest of the diocese in Springfield, Massachusetts. After being diagnosed in 1987 as having AIDS, he came out publicly and is still working within the church.[1] Father Arpin has performed union ceremonies primarily for gay men. They are not considered marriages, but a blessing of a commitment made between two people, a blessing of love.

❧

There is no such thing as gay marriage in the Catholic religion. With regard to what Dignity and other Christian gay groups call holy unions, I think we're dealing with some very human realities. One is that people fall in love. And in loving each other, if that love grows and matures, couples tend to want to give a gift to each other. That gift is usually a gift of self, of commitment to share life, to be supportive, to be caring, to work at intertwining their lives. Another human reality is that in any kind of relationship, people need to be supported in what they're doing. The third reality is that people like to party and like to celebrate!

In gay culture, people gather to experience each other's support in celebration, even after funerals—and we know enough about

Father Robert L. Arpin

those lately in the gay community. So, when people have something that makes them happy, they want to celebrate it. Those three elements, I think, come into play with the holy union: you have people who have found one another and who experience love, who get and give a great deal from that, and who feel they want to give more. Part of giving more is wanting to tell the world. And part of wanting to tell other people involves the give-and-take of saying to the people they tell, "Help us to love. Love is hard work. We need your support." I've helped celebrate anniversaries of gay couples who've been together for twenty-five, thirty-five years — I did one fifty-year celebration with a gay couple! And those people said the one thing that was the hardest in all of their time together was that they had very little or no support from their religious community, from society, from coworkers, from lots of people.

When I meet with a couple initially, I discuss with them the meaning of this union and make certain they are aware that in no way is this a marriage. This is a celebration of their relationship, a blessing of their love for each other, but it is not a marriage. Marriage is reserved for a man and a woman. If the couple does not want to go ahead with the ceremony with that understanding, they will have to go somewhere else for what they are seeking.

I take this whole thing very seriously and will help give inner joy to people I know by officiating at their holy union. I only officiate at ceremonies for couples I already know. I have a sense of their relationship, their love.

The people who come to me want someone they experience as one of them. I've paid my dues. And I'm someone they see in the community as trusted and real, not preaching party line, but encouraging people to find the God within.

With the couples I agree to officiate for, we meet several times before the ceremony to discuss their relationship and goals. Ceremonies take place in a variety of places, including private homes and backyards. There are often rings exchanged — rings symbolize the circle of life — they have many meanings. Nuns wear a ring as a symbol of their commitment to God; priests also wear a ring.

The ceremonies are varied, but many include the couple exchanging acknowledgment of their love for each other and vows they would like to attach to their relationship. Some ceremonies are simple and some are elaborate in terms of the number of people in attendance and the quantity of food and type of celebration following. There is usually a cake.

My role, in general in my life, is helping people pray. And that's what I do in the ceremony. In Roman Catholic theology, even at a Roman Catholic marriage, the priest is not the one to marry the couple; the couple marries each other and the priest is only a witness. The ceremony is performed by the couple for each other. For instance, a Roman Catholic priest at a marriage ceremony will never say, "With the authority vested in me, I now pronounce you husband and wife." It's not his pronouncement, it's the couple who marry one another.

In Roman Catholic theology, in a very broad theological view, marriage is one of the seven sacraments, which are signs in people's lived experience in which God touches them with grace that they may live a better life. Historically, it was a blessing of either an existing union or the church giving sanction to a civil or social agreement between a man and a woman.

Marriage, traditionally, had a lot more to do with legal rights, with children and inheritance, money and property, than it did with the couple. Marriages were very often prearranged. When the church got into the marriage business, marriages were performed not in the church but outside on the steps until as late as the twelfth century—it wasn't considered important enough to take inside.

We're in a time when there is a lot more openness in the world. If AIDS has done nothing else, it has made the world extremely aware of gay and lesbian people and issues. We're much more "out there" than we've ever been. I find—and I can speak more for the gay male community, because those are the people I work with most—that although people may not be more attracted to institutionalized religion (it has always sort of come across as the enemy for gays and lesbians), people are becoming much more spiritual. The reality of God, by any way we want to image him or her, has become much more important. And people are looking, people are searching, the community in general is much more spiritual today.

In discovering love, I think people discover that love is never just between two people, but that it's always a relationship involving at least three. And the third is the God who is made present as lovers look into each other's eyes, or touch each other's bodies, or experience the wonder of each other's souls — that somehow, they find an end product that is greater than the sum of the two. And that is part of what happens in the ceremonies — people acknowledge the presence of God in their love.

Note

1. For biographical information on Father Arpin, see the *San Francisco Examiner*'s *Image* magazine cover story, "Living in the Light" (December 10, 1989).

28

Father James Mallon

Father Mallon was ordained in Rome in 1960. He spent the next ten years in various pastoral responsibilities in the United States as novice master, in parish work, as teacher in a high school, and as chaplain to a local college. He completed his doctoral studies in Italy, then spent five years in New Zealand, where he taught at the national seminary and at the University of Otago on the South Island. He has celebrated Mass in the Philadelphia area for eight years with the local chapter of Dignity, a group of about three hundred gay and lesbian Catholics who come together to celebrate their faith. Liturgy is celebrated in the basement of an Episcopalian church.

❧

I see commitment ceremonies as a valid expression of two individuals who wish to remain in love with each other. We have no problem calling it a holy union, we would only refrain from using the word "sacrament." The reason we would not use the term "marriage" is primarily because we would not want to be aping the heterosexual approach. Just as we've given ourselves the names "gay" and "lesbian" as distinct from "homosexual," likewise we've given a

Father James Mallon

name to this particular relationship in our community. Usually the couple calls it what they will.

It isn't mandatory that someone be affiliated with Dignity for me to preside at their holy union, but if they're not in the Dignity community, we don't see why they would want us to do a ceremony, unless they're aping a heterosexual marriage. We explain that this is a commitment the Dignity community is making to the couple to help support their relationship and it doesn't make too much sense if the couple isn't part of our community.

The ceremony is orchestrated by the couple. It can either take place in the setting of a Mass or separate from a Mass. In general, there's an opening prayer by the presider, and then there are readings from Scripture. There is often a text of significance to the couple. They choose which readings they're going to do.

The vows are prepared beforehand and are usually reviewed by the presider or community. The couple meets with the priest or with a member of the community to clarify what they intend to do with this commitment. Not that we have rules and regulations about what they can and cannot do, but so they have a very clear understanding of what they're committing one another to.

It's not the traditional premarital counseling. The church has a prenuptial counseling session so that people can better understand what the church means by marriage and lifelong commitment, openness to children, and all that other stuff. We don't have any preconceived idea of what the relationship must entail, but we do think that the couples have. We're not predetermining that this is a lifelong commitment. We hope it's an unconditional commitment, and we would help them achieve that, but we don't accept that there's no such thing as divorce. The Dignity community commits itself to help the couple preserve their commitment by being available to counsel or help them, in order to give lesbian and gay couples some of the support that heterosexual couples receive.

If there's a Mass, there'll usually be a litany, or series of prayers, which the couple may choose to say or have their friends say. There is usually an exchange of rings, which are blessed by the presider, and then there is the reading of the commitment, or vows. Then, the rest of the Mass will continue as usual. If there's not a Mass, there will be the saying of the Lord's Prayer and then an exchange of peace between the couple and between them and the rest of the community.

We usually finish with a blessing. This blessing can be given by the couple to one another and to the community in the form of praise and thanks, or given by one of the community (for example, the presider) in the name of the community. If there is communion, the couple communicates one another. There is usually an exchange of rings blessed by the presider, and then the vows. It finishes with the acclaim of the community, the clapping. There's often a reception afterward. Sometimes the receptions are given by the couple, other times they're given by the community. They are sometimes very formal, and sometimes less formal.

I've done more ceremonies for women than for men. It seems that women tend to be more commitment oriented than men. But we are seeing more ceremonies overall lately, which I think is because we're more visible as a community and we have a better understanding of our rights. I don't think there are more ceremonies because couples are more interested in commitment.

I make a distinction between the hierarchy and the church. Not that they're separate, but they're not synonymous. The church, for me, is all the people of God: pope, bishops, priests, laity. I consider gay and lesbian Catholics to be as much a part of the church as the bishops.

We're not allowed to hold Mass in the Catholic church; the church has thrown us all out. They've said since Dignity is an organization that will not accept the hierarchical understanding lock, stock, and barrel, they cannot use property. Lock, stock, and barrel in this case means it's okay to be gay or lesbian, but it's not okay to live that way. Celibacy is a requirement for the clergy, and celibacy is a requirement for the people.

The hierarchical position on gays and lesbians is just one off-shoot of a very distorted vision of sexuality in general. Some of the hierarchy is working on changing it. At least a couple of bishops in the country are willing to listen, as they've shown on the abortion issue. Some at least are beginning to carry through in other areas, including sexuality. And that is tremendously hopeful and inspiring.

29

The Reverend Dee Dale

Formerly a Southern Baptist, Rev. Dale is minister of the Louisville, Kentucky, Metropolitan Community Church, part of a fellowship that consists of more than two hundred congregations representing ten countries.[1] The MCC's denominational policy fully sanctions holy unions. Counseling sessions before the union and dissolutionment procedure are denominational policy. Variation is allowed in such matters as how many hours or meetings of pre-union counseling are required, whether both members of a couple must be present if a dissolution is sought, and whether counseling is mandatory before dissolution is granted.

Rev. Dale celebrated a holy union two years into her relationship with Judy Dale, MCC district coordinator for a six-state area. They have been together for five years. Rev. Dale officiates at many holy unions, sometimes for people from surrounding southern states.

❧

People have come from as far away as Knoxville, Tennessee. Sometimes it's because their pastor couldn't do it in the time they wanted. Some particularly wanted a female. I get twice the number

Rev. Dee Dale

of women coming to me for a ceremony than men. They tend to be in their thirties or forties.

In the MCC, we have two ceremonies: the rite of blessing and the rite of holy union. We also have the rite of holy matrimony, because 20 percent of the denomination is heterosexual. I am licensed and ordained to perform any and all of those ceremonies, and I do perform heterosexual weddings.

I have refused to do rites of holy union in some situations. It's a very spiritual commitment. It's not just a celebration of the commitment they've already made to each other, it's also a commitment to God and God's service.

I don't do as many holy unions as I do the rite of blessing. That rite is good for people who may not be involved in the church, but who want to make a commitment in a marriage style. They exchange vows and rings, and at the end of that I put their hands together and perform the rite of blessing for them. Rites of blessing also help me reach the separatist community and other people in the women's community who are not always looking for God as we know it. However, they know I am a Christian minister and that the blessing I do is a rite of blessing in a Christian sense.

Ninety percent of the holy unions I do are for members of the church. I have done some for couples who are involved in a mainline denomination that would not perform this rite for them. Since I know of their commitment to each other and know that they are in an ongoing relationship in a Christian community, I don't have any problem doing that.

With a holy union, I require preceremony counseling. I also offer the counseling for those going through the rite of blessing if they want it. The counseling is four to five sessions, ranging from an hour to an hour and a half apiece. It's very similar to heterosexual wedding counseling. The only part I change is the session on legality and finances. When a heterosexual couple gets married, they don't have to worry about beneficiaries and community property, and things like that. A homosexual couple has to take legal action to protect one another so they don't lose everything when one dies. I have several lawyers and people I recommend, and I know the state laws, so I can advise the couples.

If a relationship is not working out and the couple wants a dissolution, we work with them to help with the dissolution of the relationship and maintain fellowship with both sides. Just as we came together in counseling before the holy union, I like the couple to come in and sit down with me and have it be a time of closure for them. If there's anything they need to say to each other with me present, they can do that. About 10 percent of the holy unions I've done have dissolved, which is not as bad as the divorce rate!

I've been a member of the MCC since 1978 and pastor of the Louisville MCC since 1983. I quit the Southern Baptist denomination I was with about a year and a half before I became real active for the MCC. I resigned from the Baptist church because I eventually realized that if they found out who I really am, I would be up a creek without a paddle. It was really a struggle for me, because they loved me so much and yet I always had to be on my guard that they not find out about my personal life. When you're a minister, your life is in a fishbowl. So, I chose to just go ahead and resign.

At that point in time, 1980, they would have asked me to leave if I hadn't resigned. But it's still a heated issue. The one thing that has loosened up is they've begun recognizing women in different fields. In the Southern Baptist denomination, they still don't recognize ordination of women. However, there are individual churches that make efforts to change. Baptist churches have autonomous bodies, but the various associations they belong to can choose whether or not to recognize that church if it chooses to go ahead and ordain women. Some have. My cousin was one of six Southern Baptist women ordained in the state of Texas, but after her ordination her church was no longer recognized as a member by the state Baptist association.

I have never felt exiled or not accepted by God. I felt great relief when I realized the struggle I had was just wondering how I could participate as who I am and yet not be accepted by the people I work with and in a profession I feel God is calling me to. I didn't know about MCC at that time. It wasn't until I came to Louisville (from northern Michigan) that I discovered it.

Judy and I had our holy union ceremony in 1989. It was important as a public statement of my commitment with her. But it was also important that I receive public support and that our relationship receive that support to help us. And our church does that.

We were together four or five months when we moved in together. I told Judy I didn't want to have a holy union until we'd been together a few years, since I'd just gotten out of a relationship. I told her that until I could work through things I needed to work out from my last relationship, I couldn't go through any kind of ceremony. The healing took place and I felt that same intensity, and felt secure in her love for me. I felt that she really loved me and wasn't going to walk in one day and tell me she was sorry but she didn't want to live with me anymore. I don't think I could go through that again.

We tried real hard to make the ceremony uniquely ours, and yet make it clear that not only was it proclaiming our love for one another, it was also dedicating our relationship to God's service. The music we picked was not real traditional wedding music. There were songs like "I See Jesus in You."

I wore a tux and Judy had a beautiful dress made, blue with white lace. It had some of the lace from her original wedding gown. She'd been married heterosexually before for fourteen years. This time, she says, she knew it was right.

My mother walked down the aisle with me, and a good friend of ours walked with Judy (her parents are no longer living). A best friend of more than twenty years came and stood up with us.

It was open to the whole community. We had a mix of straight and gay at our ceremony, about a fourth were straight. There were two or three nuns that I worked with, and other people I've worked with. We had about 120 people there. We celebrated communion, and then opened up communion to everyone. It was so wonderful to see our straight friends come forward and celebrate communion in our church.

We wear rings on the left hand, on our ring finger. And we were open with the jeweler when we went to buy them. We recommend jewelers that are open to us so we don't have to play games.

We're "out" in public. We don't hold hands or do things that other people would find offensive, but we also don't hesitate to ask for a single check for the two of us at restaurants. We went out for dinner not too long ago with two guys, and the waitress came up and asked how she should do the check. When we told her we wanted one check for the two of us and another for the two men, she said, "Well, isn't that unusual!" If we're in a restaurant talking about something in the community and the word "gay" or "lesbian" comes up when the waitress walks over to the table, we don't stop what we're saying. There's nothing to be embarrassed about.

We call each other "spouse." In fact, I've become so used to it now, it just comes natural. I've become real comfortable with it and want people to have to just go ahead and deal with the issue.

Judy decided she wanted to have the same name as me, so she went to probate court and had it officially changed. But nothing else really changed because of the ceremony. Everything we own is in both our names. All our money is one pot. We have wills and powers of attorney.

As a pastor, it's been real hard in the hospitals when I'm faced with who to recognize as family, and who has the final say. Any time you're dealing with persons with AIDS and other life-threatening diseases, it's very difficult.

If marriage was made legal, we'd be the first in line. I'm assuming that we would have antidiscrimination legislation in place long before we ever got the right to marry. I think marriage would just be one more step of civil rights. It's not asking for anything anybody else doesn't have.

More and more, people have begun to do the studies and have come to an understanding of being more inclusive and more open to sexual orientation. I've been learning to understand and stretch myself in my understanding of the different kinds of relationships right here in my church. Within our church right now we have a group of men that we call "the truple" — three men in relationship, each one committed to the other. At the church in Dayton, Ohio, there was a truple that was together twenty-five years. When one of them died of cancer, they added another third person after some time, and that's gone on three or four years. I've had to deal with trying to understand that. They are a very active and healthy part of our church spiritually and emotionally. I don't want to find myself being closed-minded so I can't recognize what's there. And I cannot deny the love that is there.

People are starting to realize that relationships are condoned by God in more ways than one. They are beginning to see that people are not condemned for the way that they love, but for the ways they don't love.

Note

1. The MCC was founded in Los Angeles in 1968 by Rev. Troy Perry. For the history of its founding, see Rev. Perry's autobiography, *Don't Be Afraid Anymore* (New York: St. Martin's Press, 1990). For more on the church's philosophy, see the MCC publication *Homosexuality: What the Bible Does and Does Not Say* (Los Angeles: Universal Fellowship Press, 1984), available through the MCC, 5300 Santa Monica Blvd., Suite 304, Los Angeles, CA 90029 (213) 464-5100.

30

The Reverend Jeanne MacKenzie

Rev. MacKenzie is a pastor at Westminster Presbyterian Church in Washington, D.C., a More Light (lesbian- and gay-affirming) congregation. She has been a pastor at the church for twelve years and has officiated holy unions since the early 1980s.

In 1978, the Presbyterian church passed a policy statement saying that gay and lesbian people could not be ordained, either to clergy, deacon, or elder. Some churches said they felt that "more light would be shown." In seeking more light, they passed a statement of welcome to gay people, basically, a statement that there would be no discrimination. This congregation passed an inclusiveness statement in 1983.

There are about forty More Light churches [in the early 1990s]. Some are more activist than others; all are not necessarily holy-union positive. I'd say at least half are. Forty of the three hundred clergy in our presbytery have said they would perform same-sex unions, which is a real groundswell of support. But the church as a whole is not ready to go forward.

When we started advertising in the *Washington Blade*, the gay newspaper in this area, we started receiving calls asking whether we would do same-sex unions. We call the ceremonies holy unions. Some are held in homes, some are held in the church.

The holy-union ceremony is a blessing of an already existing commitment. It doesn't begin with the ceremony. There is no formal written policy on holy unions in the More Light church.

In preparation for a holy union, I ask for three counseling sessions. We deal with the issues of communication, old baggage from families, intimacy, legal protections, budgeting. We don't discuss procedure, or even have a procedure, for dissolution of the union. I talk more about communication and clarifying expectations.

Each ceremony is very different. I don't notice any predominance in age group, and it's about equal between male and female couples. Family involvement in the holy unions is just about half-and-half. Some couples write their own service and others rely on me.

The pronouncement I make at the end reflects that we recognize and celebrate the couple as partners for life. The biggest difference to me, pastorally, between gay holy unions and marriages is that there aren't the social structures that keep people together. But it's just as well it's not legal yet because it keeps people thinking about what's different and what they want to have in a relationship instead of laying on assumptions and expectations. I think that many lesbians and gays are working to make their relationships intentionally different from marriage because marriage has so much baggage with it and so many expectations.

The Session [the ruling body of the congregation] is in charge of the use of the building. It never occurred to the Sessions of inclusive churches that the buildings shouldn't be used for same-sex unions. But they were put to the test to think about it in 1990, when there was a lot of negative publicity around a Methodist holy union we hosted.

The Dumbarton Methodist church superintendent refused the building and said the Methodist clergy could not perform a holy union. That congregation asked Westminster if they could use our building. A nonordained Methodist did that service, and we simply hosted it.

The bulletin for that union ceremony read, "Dumbarton United Methodist Community Church, in exile at Westminster." That got a lot of publicity, which started agitation in our area among the Presbyterians. The local governing body was asked to say something to us, and it said the Session had to make the decision about the building. The Session felt the building's use was all right.

I think great change is coming. Just the fact that we can talk about it is a sign of progress. There were seventeen thousand people at Gay Pride Day in Washington this past Sunday, the largest one so far in this area. Things are changing; it just takes a long time.

In our area, because we've been discussing it and people are freer to talk about it, I think some minds have changed. I think it's very healthy that we're speaking about it and people are having to make decisions about which side they stand on. It's about time.

31

Rabbi Denise L. Eger

Denise Eger is rabbi at Temple Beth Chayim Chadashim
(BCC), the lesbian and gay synagogue in Los Angeles.
Rabbi Eger has officiated lesbian and gay weddings at BCC since
she became rabbi there in 1988.

In the early years of the Metropolitan Community Church, about a
dozen Jews attended services, not as members, but to be in a safe
social space for gay people. One Wednesday night, a rap group was
held, and it happened that only the Jews showed up. They looked
around the room at each other and said, basically: "Why don't we
have our own synagogue?" That was 1972.

Temple Beth Chayim Chadashim was first called Metropolitan
Community Temple. About a year into the temple's life, they chose
a Hebrew name, Beth Chayim Chadashim, which means "house of
new life." The congregation was brought into membership in the
Reform movement in 1974. It is fully part of the parent denomination.

Rabbi Denise L. Eger

A synagogue isn't required to sanction a wedding; it's the rabbi's call. But a rabbi may have to justify it to the synagogue's board of directors due to the line of authority.

When I first became rabbi here, I noticed there were more women than men who wanted a wedding, but that's not true anymore. It's really equal. I've married couples that have been together ten years, couples that are just out of college, couples in their fifties. One couple had a reaffirmation ceremony, an interfaith couple who'd had a holy union in the MCC thirteen years earlier.

Most gay or lesbian couples who have ceremonies at BCC have been together longer than most straight couples — seven, eight, ten years. The ceremonies are really affirming what already exists.

Many people use the term "affirmation ceremony," but I use the terms "wedding" and "marriage." These terms make a lot of straight people uncomfortable. They also make some gay and lesbian people uncomfortable, because they don't want their ceremony or their relationship to imitate a heterosexual one. I believe it is a marriage — it is the bringing together of two people who love each other, who want to build a life and a family together, who want to make that public and personal commitment. That is what marriage really is about in our society.

BCC has no policy statement on same-sex marriages. My requirements for performing these ceremonies are pretty much the same as what I require of straight couples: that couples have been together for more than a year, that they have four or five meetings with me prior to their ceremony, and that there are readings in Judaism if one partner isn't Jewish.

I have refused to perform ceremonies for both gay and straight couples when I believe that they simply are not ready. Sometimes couples want to get married because they think it will solve their problems, when in fact what they need is counseling because they may be near the end of their relationship. In these cases, I suggest they wait.

I explain to all my lesbian and gay couples that there is no legal sanction in California to what I do, but they should know that our community recognizes them as a couple and that their family and friends, and certainly God, will recognize them by the statements they've made and the rites they've performed.

We also talk about ways they can document their relationship, and I refer them to *A Legal Guide for Lesbian and Gay Couples.*[1] I don't give legal advice, but I encourage them to consult an attorney and to take care of those kinds of protections and issues. And we talk about whether they need to do "prenuptial" agreements and what we would do if their relationship doesn't last.

There isn't a set procedure for termination of a marriage, but I do have some ways of handling it. I have done a number of different things for the couples who have come to me for a termination (couples who were married by the rabbi who preceded me at BCC). For those that have a *ketubah* (the Jewish wedding document), we cut it in a way that shows the end of the relationship as it was outlined and embodied in the document. In one case, one partner had the *ketubah,* the other had the wedding canopy. The partner who had the *ketubah* chose not to be present (the couples never seem to come together), so we cut the wedding canopy in half. And there are some statements I ask the couple to make, things like "you are no longer my partner, we are both free to enter into new relationships." So it's done in a way to help them reach closure. Ideally, both partners in the couple come, both should be present so there's closure for both of them.

The ceremony I use is based on a traditional Jewish wedding ceremony. I encourage couples to have a wedding canopy (a *chuppah*). I encourage them to exchange rings and vows. I ask couples (both straight and gay) to write their own vows and promises to make this aspect of the ceremony more meaningful. I encourage them to use a *ketubah,* although it is not the traditional form. The language in the *ketubah* describes the quality of the relationship and the home they are going to build together. We do the seven wedding blessings. The text of the blessings is changed a little, but it is pretty close to the original. (We'll change the gender, for example.)

We break a glass at the end of the ceremony. We use a more mystical interpretation of this tradition, that the couple is creating or affirming a relationship, and the breaking of the glass reminds them of their partnership with God and with each other.

We celebrate over the cup of wine (called *Kiддιsh*, the prayer over wine). Sometimes we read from Scripture. For men, we read David and Jonathan; for women, we read from Ruth and Naomi. (It was not a lesbian relationship, but it was definitely a woman-identified relationship in a time when women were not supposed to be together.) I like to see couples add in some liturgy, some pieces of poetry and music. We want it to be their day, not my day. At the end, I usually make a pronouncement, or affirmation.

In a traditional Jewish wedding ceremony, the father does not give away the bride. Both sets of parents escort the groom and the bride down the aisle. We often do that in gay and lesbian ceremonies.

I've seen a lot of parental involvement, at various levels of acceptance. More often than not, parents are there. Most have dealt with their own coming out around their kids over the years. Sometimes the wedding ceremony has been the catalyst for parents to finally deal healthfully with their child's gayness.

It's an interesting thing for parents. When parents find out their child is gay or lesbian, they often mourn the loss of grandchildren and fear their child will grow up alone without anyone to take care of them, there'll be no weddings, all those things. Those are all myths they get to see shattered before their eyes.

There is a definite baby boom going on. In both the male and female couples that come to me for a ceremony, there is increasing discussion about having children, adopting children, creating larger families than just the couple. Men are parenting with lesbian couples, lesbians are using gay men as sperm donors — there are all kinds of family constellations.

Couples don't have to be members of the congregation for me to perform a ceremony, but I do encourage them to join. We offer continued reinforcement around relationships. We celebrate anniversaries once a month. For example, we send all the June anniversaries a card, "*mazel tov* on your anniversary," and an invitation: the rabbi will honor you on your anniversary Friday night. And we call people up for a special anniversary blessing.

We celebrate anniversaries like that in our temple so people can see that relationships have continued reinforcement and to celebrate their success. Certainly in the lives of gays and lesbians, there are so many places where they can't celebrate who they are. So many people are not out at work. They have to omit a major part of their life through the conversational pitter-patter about what their co-workers did over the weekend with the husband or the wife, the talk about the kids.

I think the day will come when the government legalizes gay and lesbian relationships, sees them on a par with straight marriages. I think that certainly within the religious movement, this is going to be the next issue: blessing relationships and creating official ceremonies for gay and lesbian couples.

Note

1. Denis Clifford and Hayden Curry, *A Legal Guide for Lesbian and Gay Couples*, 5th ed. (Berkeley, Calif.: Nolo Press, 1988).

32

The Reverend Jim Lowder

Rev. Lowder was full-time pastor at the Dolores Street Baptist Church (DSBC) in San Francisco for nine and a half years. He is now executive director of Dolores Street Community Center, a nonprofit, multiservice organization that acts as the ministry arm of the church. The center was made a nonprofit corporation in 1988, two years after the Dolores Street Baptist Church was expelled from the denomination and lost all of its denominational funding because of its open affirmation of lesbians and gays. Among its many programs, the center now manages the church's buildings, runs three shelters for homeless people, and is developing a residence for persons who are disabled with AIDS. Dignity/ SF (a group of gay and lesbian Catholics) is one of the thirty-five religious and social-service organizations that meet regularly in the church's buildings. Rev. Lowder has officiated holy unions in the church.

☙

In November 1985, I was in the audience of a local TV talk show called "People Are Talking." The topic of the show was gay marriages in the church. I made a statement during the discussion that

Rev. Jim Lowder

Scripture has less of a sexual ethic than an ethic of relationships. I
said that I believe Scripture calls us into committed, life-giving relationships, and that it doesn't matter whether the relationship is between two women, two men, or a woman and a man.

Soon after that, I was fired from my teaching position at Golden
Gate Baptist Seminary in Mill Valley. In addition, the denominational funding that Dolores Street Baptist Church received for its
community ministries was cut off. In April of 1986, the church was
disfellowshipped from its local Southern Baptist association. In the
following months, our state convention began refusing our missions
offerings, and Golden Gate Seminary told its students that attending DSBC would jeopardize their ministry careers.

Although I made the public statement that aroused these reper-
cussions, the members of DSBC strongly supported our church's
right to be open to anyone who claimed Jesus as Lord. The few
church members who left the church during this time left more
from exhaustion over the controversy than from disagreement over
the stands the church had made.

As a matter of fact, when I came to Dolores Street as pastor in
1981, the church had already grappled with the issue of inclusiveness of gay and lesbian church members. A year before, a church
member had made a motion to fire the music minister because of
his homosexuality. After much study and soul-searching, the congregation voted to affirm his ministry. They made that decision
based not on a response to an issue, but on their relationship with
this man who had ministered to them for four years.

Memories of the church's experiences of the last decade are occasionally still painful to me. However, the outcome was not all
negative. The church came to a crossroads, turned in the direction
of inclusiveness, and survived to continue their journey of faith.
Additionally, DSBC, as well as I personally, received affirmation
and support from many Baptist clergy and lay people across the
country and from the ecumenical community in the Bay Area. Although we no longer foresee ourselves connected to the Southern
Baptist Convention (by our choice as well as theirs), we are not at
a loss for support from the larger religious community. If, in fact,

we ever did connect with a denomination, it would probably be with the more progressive American Baptist Convention.

The Southern Baptist Convention is very conservative and, since the late 1970s, has been controlled by Fundamentalists. Few Southern Baptist churches affirm openly gay men and lesbians into their congregations. There might be a few other Southern Baptist ministers who are conducting holy unions, but I don't know any personally.

The first holy union I did was in 1987. I have performed holy unions for an equal number of gay and lesbian couples. Only one or two of the couples have been church members.

In preparing for a holy union, I approach a lesbian or gay couple the same way I do heterosexual couples wanting to get married. I meet with the couple two or three times to go over some basic relationship issues. I encourage them to plan their own ceremony, even write their own vows. As in any wedding ceremony, I include the vows, a blessing and exchange of rings, and a blessing and affirmation of the couple at the end. The style of services has ranged from small, intimate and informal, to large, elaborate and formal. Parents rarely attend holy unions, but then, families of heterosexual couples rarely attend the weddings that I perform, since many San Francisco residents' parents live back East.

I've been very impressed with the degree of commitment that people seeking holy union have made to each other. Because gay marriages are not recognized by the state, and because it's been very difficult for gay people to experience affirmation in the church, people have tended to live together without seeking societal recognition of their commitment. All of the couples who have come to me have already been together for a number of years and have decided, for one reason or another, to have their relationship affirmed in the church. The reasons are usually based on the fact that the church played an important role in their individual lives prior to their becoming public with their sexual orientation.

I am coming to believe that the church should not be involved in the legal aspect of marriage. The marriage license is a state-sanctioned societal contract and is not within the province of the church. The church's role is to bless and affirm committed, life-giving relationships and to be concerned with the spiritual side of marriage. I believe the church should participate only in holy unions — for heterosexual couples, as well as for lesbian and gay couples.

33

Wiccen High Priestess
Zsuzsanna Budapest

Zsuzsanna Budapest (known by many as "Z") is an ordained minister and a high priestess. Originally from Hungary, she now lives in Oakland, California. Z is the author of *Grandmother Moon*, sequel to *Grandmother of Time*, and of *The Holy Book of Women's Mysteries*.[1] First published as *The Feminist Book of Lights and Shadows* by the Susan B. Anthony Coven No. 1 in Los Angeles two decades earlier, this work was the first women's spirituality book available in the United States and Europe. In addition to her writings, Z hosts a monthly cable television program devoted to the Goddess that is shown in the San Francisco Bay Area and in Portland, Oregon.

In the early 1970s, as part of the feminist movement, women sought to learn about and reclaim the ancient female-focused traditions that were suppressed by monotheism and Christianity. Witches (from the word *wicce*, meaning "wise one") were part of that tradition, along with high priestesses, who performed various functions, including leading trysting ceremonies, a precursor of weddings.

In ancient tradition, the hands of the two lovers or friends were bound together during the tryst ceremony to symbolize their connection: this was called "handfasting." Z prefers not to include this

Z Budapest

element in the rituals, as do many couples, who perceive the binding as having negative connotations of confinement or possession.

❧

"Tryst" means an agreement to meet, a crossroads. It also means trust. This style is created by lesbians for lesbians, but the tryst is a perfectly good ritual for anyone in love. When it comes to ceremonies and rituals, there is no such thing as a heterosexual tradition. There is Jewish tradition, and there is Christian tradition, but there is no heterosexual tradition.

I saw a need for lesbian tryst ceremonies and, with my combined spiritual and theatrical background, I set about creating one. The ceremony is simple, the purpose is complex, the participants are new to such ceremonies and move through insecurity to strength.

I've been marrying lesbian couples since the 1970s — television newscasters, actresses, lawyers — all kinds of women. I've married hundreds of lesbians in the twenty years I've been doing this. At Michigan [Womyn's Music Festival, an annual five-day event], I usually marry thirteen couples — a day. I love doing festival weddings, or "shotgun weddings," as I call them. Women are there from all over the country, from Oregon, New York, Kansas. Each is a story of a triumph, from horrendous oppression to the path of the Goddess and to this beauty.

My ceremonies are public ceremonies — we have witnesses. It's not like we run off, the three of us, into the woods for only the birds and bees to see us. There's got to be some public presence, witnesses to the public vows.

The couple must have been together a year and a day. A year and a day is as long as you need for anything important, especially a rite of passage.

I first meet with the couple to find out if they qualify, then I explain the meaning of the symbols involved. I have to teach the couples the ancient ways. The ancient ways are wiser than what we have now. I need to make sure they are willing to make a commitment beyond monogamy.

The women practice their marriage as monogamy. But the witch's wedding is for loyalty; it's beyond sexuality. We understand that the Goddess of love comes and goes. Nobody gets to control her. Mother Nature may give you the ability to have babies, but she doesn't give you the goodies that you ride on, the eternity in the eyes. So, what's left is loyalty. The agreement with the tryst is that even if you leave, you are obliged to keep in touch. You have to be there for a birthday, if you are desired to be there, you have to show up. The path of the Goddess is that you accumulate love, not get some—lose all, get some—lose all. If somebody marries me, then falls in love with somebody else, that's natural, that can happen; my marriage is not blown apart by it. But, if she never comes by, doesn't internalize me as family, then the marriage is blown apart. There is often protest: "No, no, I want this forever and ever." If that is their feeling, then I tell them they have to get a Christian minister. A pagan priestess has to deal with wisdom.

After we do that, we talk about what to wear, which is easy. The only thing I ask is that they come barefoot; this is an earth religion, so we want to feel her under our feet. Couples in the full gown-and-tuxedo weddings even come barefoot!

We talk about how they will get chalices for the altar and have them engraved with their names and the date and any sentiment they might like. The chalices represent pleasure and the Goddess of sexuality. The two chalices should be gold, silver, or ceramic. Wedding rings do not signify marriages as much as chalices do. Chalices are the true symbols of the ceremony.

The crown of flowers they put on each other's head during the ceremony represents respect, wreaths made of yellow and white roses. I have a little trouble, sometimes, talking both parties into wearing a crown. "I don't wear flowers on my head," some of them say. It just takes a little explanation—you want respect and you want it highlighted in the ceremony. Then they realize they can do it. I wear purple, the color of love, and a crown, and I'm also barefoot.

In the final part of the preceremony meeting, I explain that food is part of the ceremony; they will feed each other as symbols of psychic food — understanding. The women prepare a tray of green things, something from the roots, the stems, the leaves, and flowers and fruits (carrots, celery, cauliflower, dates, almonds, oranges). This is to invoke the Goddess of life over the tray; food is life. Then usually we wait for a bit so they can think about all this, and if they still want to go ahead, we set a date.

When a couple picks a date for the ceremony, it's sort of like choosing the karma for the life of the relationship. I usually advise couples to choose a date when the moon is new or waxing, or just before the full moon. You want a time when the energy is becoming, not already fulfilled. During a waning moon the energy is diminishing; during a waxing or new moon, the energy is growing.

The Ceremonies

"It's bad enough my daughter's a lesbian, but now it's a witch, a witch! How bad can it get?" This is the expression on the faces of many of the parents. But, if they are on good terms with their daughter, they are there because they love her. And, many times, parents and grandparents are there. For those that could not come, we light a candle.

I explain the ceremony to the relatives before it begins, so they can participate. I teach everyone how to hum to raise energy, and they've been doing that nicely. After I explain everything to the audience, they hum while the couple is led in by their best friends. They meet in front of me and then the best friends step back. To purify them, I smudge them with sage, bless their minds and their bodies for health and pleasure, bless their hearts to be open, their hands to do the Goddess's work, their feet to walk in the Goddess's path, and I bless their backs against enemies. The humming is still going on.

The couple waits barefoot outside the circle while the priestess goes from east to south, west, and north, invoking the Goddess according to ancient rites. Holding an incense burner aloft, she pauses at each quarter, saying her own invocation, or this one:

[*East*]: Hail to thee, Goddess Isis, bringer of new life and feelings, come into this circle where lovers await Your blessings! [If not lovers, say "friends."]

[*South*]: Come to this circle, fiery Goddess Heartha, Vesta, Pele! Bring Your energy to fuel this bond to be formed here today. Come bring Your excitement, joy, and ecstasy. Blessed be!

[*West*]: Hail to thee, Aphrodite! Love Goddess, Water Goddess! Come to us in this circle and bless the lovers who ask for it in Your name, come and bless this union with love!

[*North*]: Come, O beautiful Earth Goddess Demeter and Your daughter Persephone! Come and nourish us with Your love and presence. Blessed be!

Then, closing the circle, I walk to the trystees and anoint them with either a sacred oil (Rosa Lama, priestess oil, frankincense and myrrh) or blessed water.

[Anointing the forehead] I purify you from all anxiety, I purify your mind from fears; [anointing the eyes and the nose] I purify your eyes to see Her ways; [lips] your lips to speak Her names; [breast] your breast formed in strength and beauty; [genitals] your genitals I bless for strength and pleasure; [feet] your feet to walk in Her path.

Finally, I anoint the palms of the hands, saying, "I bless your hands to do the Goddess's works!"

I do this to both trystees. Now I lead them in by the hand. I hold my hands over the tray of food and [the couple] follows my example. I say:

I invoke You, Goddess of All Life, I invoke You by the foods here present, by the roots to make a strong foundation for this relationship, by the stems for standing firm and proud, by the leaves to grow and prosper together, by the flowers for joy and laughter, and by the fruits for a long and enduring time together.

Now I turn to each of the trystees in turn:

> Do you [name], take this woman [name] for your friend and lover
> for this lifetime, promise to care and love even if you love others in
> addition?

Each answers: "I do."

Then I hand them the tray of food, from which each selects
something to offer to the other. Each trystee feeds the mouth of the
other, saying: "May you never hunger!"

Then I hand them their chalices, filling them with wine, champagne, water, or other drink. Each trystee offers the other: "May
you never thirst!"

Then I hand them the wreaths, and they crown each other, saying: "Thou art Goddess!"[2]

When all that is done, it is their part to say a few things to each
other, take blessings from the audience. I put in this new feature,
this moment for the couple to say things to each other, to read
poems or explain how they met—some kind of nice, individual interaction within the couple. This is the time for the ring, although
the ring is not our symbol for bonding. We wear rings for spiritual
rather than personal reasons; the ring is a symbol of power. But
most couples exchange rings at this point.

After the rings, I invite witnesses to heap blessing upon blessing
on the couple, one by one. It's lovely to hear grandmothers call out
blessings, grandfathers . . . it's very moving. I wait until they run
out of blessings, and then I lay down the sacred myrtle broom, and,
holding hands, the trystees jump toward the east, the corner of
beginnings. [Jumping the broom is an ancient tradition that began
with jumping over a branch or tree trunk.] When they land on the
ground, they are pronounced lovers in trust. The audience applauds
wildly. Then I call on the four corners of the universe and call once
more on the Goddess of love to bless the union. And my job is
done.

Notes

1. *Grandmother Moon: Lunar Magic in Our Lives — Spells, Rituals, Goddesses, Legends, and Emotions Under the Moon* (San Francisco: Harper San Francisco, 1991); *Grandmother of Time* (San Francisco: Harper & Row, 1989); *The Holy Book of Women's Mysteries* (Berkeley, Calif.: Wingbow Press, 1989).

2. This portion of the ceremony is adapted from *The Holy Book of Women's Mysteries*, 88–89, with permission. "The Priestess" or "The two Priestesses" has been changed to "I" for the purposes of this chapter.

Resource Directory

Couples

American Civil Liberties Union (ACLU)
Lesbian and Gay Rights Project
132 West 43d St.
New York, NY 10036
(212) 944-9800, ext. 545

The ACLU offers a useful legislative-briefing series on domestic partnership and supports partners' rights and legalized same-sex marriage.

Couples National Network, Inc.
P.O. Box 26139
Tempe, AZ 85285-6139

This organization is geared toward social and informational events. It has local groups in the Los Angeles area and in Palm Springs and San Diego, Calif.; Atlanta, Ga.; Dallas and Houston, Tex.; Phoenix, Ariz.; and Auckland, New Zealand. The network publishes a newsletter and assists local groups in organizing.

Family Diversity Project EEO Seminars
P.O. Box 65756
Los Angeles, CA 90065
(213) 258-8955
(213) 258-5931

This is a clearinghouse for information on nontraditional families, domestic-partnership rights and benefits, and discrimination against unmarried individuals and couples in employment and consumer situations. The organization offers a series of publications on domestic partnership and consulting and seminars to corporations on sexual orientation and marital status discrimination in the workplace and the consumer marketplace.

"Gay in America" Series (1989)
San Francisco Examiner
Gay and Lesbian Alliance Against Defamation (GLAAD)
80 Varick St., #3E
New York, NY 10013

A sixty-four-page report featuring national poll results and articles on historical and modern issues. Reprints are $4.50, payable to GLAAD.

Lambda Legal Defense and Education Fund (LLDEF)
666 Broadway, 12th Floor
New York, NY 10012
(212) 995-8585

606 S. Olive St., #580
Los Angeles, CA 90014
(213) 629-2728

Lambda is the nation's oldest and largest legal advocate for lesbians, gay men, and people with HIV/AIDS. Since 1973 it has pursued test-case litigation and public education in a variety of areas. Its Family Relationships Project focuses on custody, visitiation, donor fertilization, domestic-partner benefits, and adoption. Lambda distributes resource manuals and publications on family and other issues, and offers free telephone consultation on weekdays between 2 P.M. and 4 P.M.

Latino/a Lesbians and Gays (LLEGO)
P.O. Box 44483
Washington, DC 20026

LLEGO is a group of organizations that serve the United States and Latin America with educational forums and networking assistance. It publishes a directory of Latino/Latina organizations around the country and in Puerto Rico and a bimonthly newsletter.

National Association of Black and White Men Together (BWMT)
584 Castro St., #140
San Francisco, CA 94114
(415) 431-1976

Men of All Colors Together (Greater Bay Area)
(415) 261-7922

Couples (and singles) meet in multiracial groups for education, cultural, political, and social activities. BWMT is primarily, but not exclusively, for men. Men of All Colors Together is a similar nationwide organization, under the umbrella of BWMT.

National Center for Lesbian Rights
1663 Mission St., 5th Floor
San Francisco, CA 94103
(415) 621-0674

This organization offers materials on parenting, foster parenting, custody and adoption, legal advice, and technical assistance for attorneys during specific weekday hours. Publications lists are available; the fee for publications is a donation to cover mailing costs.

National Coalition for Black Lesbians and Gays
P.O. Box 19248
Washington, DC 20036
(202) 389-1094

Local affiliates around the country offer a network for political and family issues. The group publishes a newsletter four times annually.

National Federation of Parents and Friends of Gays (PFOG)
8020 Eastern Ave., N.W.
Washington, DC 20012
(202) 726-3223

This nonprofit umbrella organization, composed of community-based counselors and service providers, offers educational resource materials, a speakers' bureau, and peer-counseling programs.

National Gay and Lesbian Task Force Policy Institute
Lesbian and Gay Families Project
1734 14th St., N.W.
Washington, DC 20009-4309
(202) 332-6483

The Lesbian and Gay Families Project acts as advocates for family diversity in the United States, including legal recognition and protection of gay families, domestic partnerships, and lesbian/gay parenting.

Parents and Friends of Lesbians and Gays (PFLAG)
P.O. Box 27605
Washington, DC 20038-7605
(800) 432-6459 (4FAMILY)

Through PFLAG's three hundred local chapters and information hotlines in the United States and in nine other countries, some 20,000 families and individuals work toward understanding and acceptance of gays and lesbians with the aid of support groups, literature, and outreach programs. Programs include AIDS education and advocacy, gay and lesbian youth suicide prevention, gay-rights advocacy, and public education to counter "traditional values" groups. This nonprofit organization publishes educational booklets, including "Read This Before Coming Out to Your Parents."

Selected Reading Material

Betty Berzon. *Permanent Partners: Building Gay and Lesbian Relationships That Last*. New York: E. P. Dutton, 1988.

This book draws on real-life examples to help couples improve communication and handle such conflicts as money issues and in-laws. Berzon also discusses legal matters and parenting, and offers scripts for commitment ceremonies.

John Boswell. *Christianity, Social Tolerance, and Homosexuality*. Chicago: University of Chicago Press, 1980.

A second book, tentatively titled "What God Has Joined Together: Same-Sex Unions in the Christian Tradition," is scheduled for publication in the early 1990s. A videotape of Boswell's 1988 lecture, "1,500 Years of the Church Blessing Lesbian and Gay Relationships: It's Nothing New," is available for purchase from Integrity Inc., P.O. Box 19561, Washington, DC 20036.

Denis Clifford and Hayden Curry. *A Legal Guide for Lesbian and Gay Couples*. 5th ed. Berkeley, Calif.: Nolo Press, 1988.

This guidebook features easy-to-understand information and instructions, generic forms, and important advice on many topics. It is updated every few years to ensure accuracy. Topics include preparing for medical emergencies; adoption, guardianship, and other issues related to parenting; living-together practicalities (such as renting together, owning together, writing living-together contracts, handling cash and credit); and writing your own contracts, durable powers of attorney, and wills.

Miriam Holcomb and Desma Holcomb. *Pride at Work: Organizing for Lesbian and Gay Rights*. 1990.
Lesbian and Gay Labor Network
P.O. Box 1159
Peter Stuyvesant Station
New York, NY 10009

This publication offers information on how to secure partner benefits in union settings. (The $6.00 fee includes postage and handling; $3.00 each for 10 or more copies.)

Partners Magazine for Gay and Lesbian Couples
P.O. Box 9685
Seattle, WA 98109
(206) 784-1519

The founders of *Partners Newsletter for Lesbian and Gay Couples*, Stevie Bryant and Demian, Ed.D., now publish this quarterly magazine devoted to supporting committed same-sex relationships. Back issues of *Partners Newsletter*, a sixteen-page bimonthly national resource and forum supporting committed same-sex relationships, are available dating to 1986. *Partners* identifies helpful social, political and legal organizations, publishes a list of books, tapes and films about same-sex couples and their families, and issues reports on such topics as same-sex marriage and domestic-partnership plans. Results of the *Partners* national survey of 1,266 gay and lesbian couples are available for $3.95.

Lesbian- and Gay-Affirming Religious Organizations

American Gay and Lesbian Atheists (AGLA)
P.O. Box 66711
Houston, TX 77266-6711
(713) 880-4242

Dignity USA (Gay Catholics)
1500 Massachusetts Ave., N.W., Suite 11
Washington, DC 20005
(202) 861-0017

Family Relations Committee
Friends Center
1515 Cherry St.
Philadelphia, PA 19102

This Quaker organization produces two publications: a resource guide for same-sex couples, and *In the Presence of God . . . A Quaker Marriage*, designed to help Meetings and couples prepare for marriage or commitment ceremonies. (There is a small fee; a bill is enclosed with pamphlets.)

Methodist Reconciling Congregation Program
P.O. Box 23636
Washington, DC 20026

North American Friends for Lesbian and Gay Concerns (FLGC)
P.O. Box 222
Sumneytown, PA 18084

A Quaker lesbian and gay organization, FLGC offers informational brochures and the *FLGC Guide to Groups and Gatherings*. A quarterly newsletter subscription is available. (An $8 donation is suggested, with checks payable to FLGC.)

Presbyterians for Lesbian/Gay Concerns
James Anderson
Communications Secretary
P.O. Box 38
New Brunswick, NJ 08903-0038
(908) 846-1510

Unitarian Universalist Association
Office for Lesbian and Gay Concerns
25 Beacon St.
Boston, MA 02108
(617) 742-2100, ext. 250

This organization offers a planning guide for same-gender union ceremonies that includes nine services and a sample partner contract, as well as sermons, educational videos on AIDS, and a lending library for people who do not have access to good literature about homosexuality.

Universal Fellowship of Metropolitan Community Churches (MCC)
5300 Santa Monica Blvd., Suite 304
Los Angeles, CA 90029
(213) 464-5100

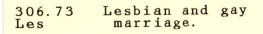

306.73   Lesbian and gay
Les   marriage.

DATE			
06/23/04			
7/14/04			
18 Feb 06			
03/21/06			
10/14/00			

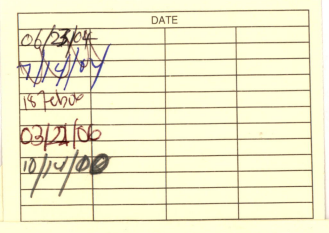